COMPARATIVE ANALYSIS

FIREARMS-CONTROL LEGISLATION AND POLICY

I. Introduction

This survey describes the different legal approaches taken by eighteen countries and the European Union (EU) with regard to ownership, possession, and other activities involving firearms.[*] The individual reports cover laws, regulations, and directives, in addition to statistical and other relevant information on gun control. The reports also address the availability or lack thereof of a constitutional right to bear arms under foreign law; the scope of firearms-related activities that are subject to licensing; conditions for the issuance of licenses, including background checks of the applicant's mental and criminal history; training, testing, and storage requirements; weapons bans; and registration procedures, including the use of a central register in some of the countries surveyed. Many reports describe legislative history and trends, which in some cases were influenced by rising crime levels or incidents of mass shootings. A bibliography of selected recent English language materials is included.

II. Mass Shootings in Foreign Countries

Incidents of mass shooting in schools and other public venues by so-called "lone wolves" are not unique to the United States. Shortly prior to the completion of this report, on January 3, 2013, a thirty-four-year-old militiaman in Daillon, Switzerland went on a shooting spree, killing three women and wounding two men with his militia weapon.

In 1987 in Hungerford, England, a gunman equipped with two lawfully owned semiautomatic rifles shot and killed sixteen people and wounded fourteen more before killing himself. In 2010 in Cumbria, northwest England, a gunman killed twelve people and wounded twenty-five using firearms he lawfully possessed.

Port Arthur, Australia, was the scene of a mass shooting in 1996, when a twenty-eight-year-old gunman armed with a semiautomatic rifle shot and killed thirty-five people and wounded eighteen others. That same year a gunman armed with two lawfully held rifles and four handguns walked into an elementary school in Dunblane, Scotland, and shot and killed sixteen four- to five-year-old children and their teacher before killing himself.

---

[*] The countries surveyed include Australia, Brazil, Canada, China, Egypt, Germany, Great Britain, Israel, Japan, Lebanon, Mexico, New Zealand, Norway, Russia, Singapore, South Africa, Spain, and Switzerland. These countries and the EU were selected based on interest in their firearms-control laws and the way these laws are implemented, the desire to cover a wide selection of continents and cultures, and the current availability of staff expertise at the Law Library of Congress.

In Germany, teenage shooters armed with semiautomatic pistols or a sawed-off percussion rifle shot schoolchildren and teachers on three different occasions in 2002, 2006, and in 2009, all ending with multiple deaths and casualties. Norway similarly witnessed a gruesome mass killing in 2011 by a man who had first bombed the government district of Oslo and then, using weapons he had lawfully acquired for hunting, shot and killed seventy-seven and wounded 242 mostly young people at a youth camp.

Incidents of mass killings are not unknown to Russians, who experienced terrorist attacks on a hospital, theater, and school in 2002 and 2004, as well as a number of more recent mass shootings in public places committed by criminals or mentally unstable people.

Mass shootings in China, where the private possession of firearms is generally banned, are rare, and the Chinese media correlates the country's strict firearms-control laws to the generally fewer crimes committed with guns and explosives in China as compared with other countries.

This report explores the different legal approaches taken by the surveyed countries regarding licensing of firearms, including requirements for proper training, safe storage, criminal and mental-health background checks, mental health, and enforcement.

III. Constitutional Right to Bear Arms

Among the countries surveyed only Mexico was found to have an express provision in its Constitution that recognizes the right of inhabitants to bear arms. This right extends to possession of arms at one's home for security and legitimate defense, with the exception of weapons that are prohibited by federal law and those reserved for the exclusive use of the Army, Navy, Air Force, and National Guard. The Mexican Constitution expressly provides that the conditions under which inhabitants may be authorized to bear arms are to be determined by federal law.

IV. Possession of Firearms by Military Personnel

Compulsory military service, which exists in several of the countries surveyed, often gives rise to special laws governing conscripts' use and possession of military weapons and ammunition. Israel and Switzerland illustrate two varied approaches to this issue. Conscription begins at age eighteen in Israel and nineteen in Switzerland, and generally ends at age forty-five in Israel and between the ages of thirty-four and fifty in Switzerland, depending on the military or militia rank of conscripts in these countries.

In Switzerland militiamen are issued personal equipment, including a personal weapon and ammunition, that they are authorized to keep in their homes even after retirement. Israel maintains a much more restrictive policy on soldiers taking military firearms on home leave and reserve service.

As a general rule, Israeli soldiers do not take their guns on home leave. Exceptions to this rule apply to soldiers who serve in combat units; serve in the West Bank or other specified areas; or obtain special authorization from high-ranking military officers, because of their officer rank or for reasons of personal safety associated with their home or service location.

Other countries surveyed similarly do not generally permit military personnel to take firearms out of their assigned duty area. In Russia, for example, military weapons are not legally permitted to leave the military compound. Military personnel cannot take weapons outside of their unit's location unless they are on a special, duty-related assignment. Others who have service weapons, including police officers, investigators, and some judges, however, may have their service firearms with them when not on duty.

V. Civilian Activities Requiring Licensing

All of the countries surveyed require licensing for various activities involving firearms and ammunition. Such activities may include selling firearms and ammunition by or through licensed dealers, as well as acquiring, possessing, owning, using, carrying, handling, trading, repairing, manufacturing, distributing, transporting, importing and exporting, training, storing, collecting, and disposing of such firearms and ammunition.

The following table lists general requirements for civilian licenses in the countries surveyed, including age limits, reasons for which firearms are allowed, the role of an applicant's criminal record and health status, mandated training or testing, and other miscellaneous requirements:

Table 1: General Requirements for Civilian Licenses

Country	Minimum Age	Recognized Reasons	Criminal History Requirements	Health Requirements	Training/Testing Requirements	Other Requirements
Australia	18	"Genuine reason" (e.g., sports, recreational shooting/hunting, collecting, or occupational requirements). Ammunition only provided to license-holders. Self-defense excluded.	"Fit and proper person" test; no convictions for violent offenses in past 5 years.	Mental/physical fitness.	Safety course.	28-day waiting period; storage requirements and inspections.
Brazil	25	Actual need for acquiring firearm; ammunition must correspond to caliber of registered gun and quantity requirements.	Submission of records indicating no prior criminal activities, police investigation, or criminal prosecution.	Evidence of psychological ability.	Evidence of technical ability.	Evidence of lawful occupancy and place of residence.
Canada	18 generally. 12–17 for minor's license (limited to non-restricted rifle or shotgun, and	For restricted firearms or prohibited handguns, must show need for use in connection with lawful profession	Criminal and domestic-violence background checks.	Mental-health background check, including addiction.	Safety tests depending on type of weapon.	Transport, storage, and display requirements.

Country	Minimum Age	Recognized Reasons	Criminal History Requirements	Health Requirements	Training/Testing Requirements	Other Requirements
	licensed adult must be responsible for firearm).	or occupation; no such requirements for ordinary shotguns and rifles, such as those used for hunting.				
China	No age specified by national law; local rules may apply (e.g., 18 according to a firearms-control rule issued by Dalian City, Shenyang Province, hereafter the Dalian Rule).	Firearms for civilian use permitted for specified "work units" in areas of sports; hunting; and wildlife protection, breeding, and research. Individual hunters and herdsmen may possess hunting rifles.	Not specified by national law; Dalian Rule requires having no criminal record and no record of having been "reeducated through labor."	Not specified by national law; Dalian Rule requires having no history of mental illness.	Special training in safe storage of firearms.	Safe storage.
Egypt	21	[no information available]	Licensing prohibited for persons convicted, sentenced, or on parole.	No mental or psychological impairment; must be physically capable of owning and using firearms.		

Country	Minimum Age	Recognized Reasons	Criminal History Requirements	Health Requirements	Training/Testing Requirements	Other Requirements
Germany	18 generally. 14–18 for supervised training or employment. 21 for marksmen, subject to exceptions.	Licenses issued to hunters, marksmen, shooting-association members, endangered persons, collectors, experts, producers and dealers, and private security firms.	No criminal record, membership in criminal or terrorist organization, or justified suspicion of potential violation.	No substance addiction, mental illness, or feeblemindedness. Psychiatric evaluation if under 25.	Knowledge of weapons technology and law; expertise in use of firearms.	Five years' residency; liability insurance coverage of up to 1 million Euros. Specified storage requirements, depending on potency of weapon.
Great Britain	18	"Good reason" to possess firearm (e.g. profession, sport or recreation, or shooting vermin). Self-defense not a good reason.	No sentence of more than three years' imprisonment or preventive detention; those receiving sentences of three months to three years cannot possess firearms or ammunition for a period of five years after date of release.	References regarding mental state, home life, and attitude toward guns; medical release form; access to firearms by unfit family members or associates may disqualify applicant.		Conditions may include specification of storage cabinets that meet British safety standards.

Country	Minimum Age	Recognized Reasons	Criminal History Requirements	Health Requirements	Training/Testing Requirements	Other Requirements
Israel	21 for citizens who served in Israel Defense Force (IDF). 27 for other citizens. 45 for permanent residents with 3 years of uninterrupted stay.	Proof of need based on place of residence or employment, occupation, or service in elite IDF reserve units.	Conviction for violent offense (including domestic violence) may result in license cancellation/ ineligibility for period defined by court.	Mental health care providers report to Ministry of Health those patients capable of endangering themselves or others; report may be forwarded to permitting authorities.	Certified appropriate training for each licensed firearm at licensed shooting ranges.	Proof of permanent residency and uninterrupted stay for period of at least three years, basic knowledge of the Hebrew language, safe storage.
Japan	18 generally. 14 for athletes. 20 for hunters.	"Specific need" (e.g., hunters; target shooters; athletes; dealers; manufacturers; exporters; collectors; and specific businesses, including lifesaving, slaughterhouses, fisheries, testing or research, and construction).	Passage of 5 years since completing sentence of imprisonment; no previous warnings or restraining orders for domestic violence.	No mental illness or other specified health problems, dementia, alcohol/drug addiction, or feeblemindedness.	Classes on firearms laws and regulations; skill test or completion of shooting classes.	Fixed abode; proof of accident insurance; not under bankruptcy restrictions.

Country	Minimum Age	Recognized Reasons	Criminal History Requirements	Health Requirements	Training/Testing Requirements	Other Requirements
Lebanon	18 generally. 16 for hunting under guardian's supervision.	Recognized reasons (e.g., hunting) tied to specific classes of weapons.	No prior sentence or conviction for heinous felonies, carrying weapons, or offenses against state security or Weapons and Ammunition Law. Foreigners cannot have been subject to revocation of residence or deportation.	No history of mental illness.		
Mexico	18	For employment/ occupation, target shooting, or hunting; or based on living circumstances or other credible factors, including self-defense in the home.	For a carrying license, no conviction for any crime committed with the use of firearms.	For a carrying license, no physical or mental impediment or drug addiction		For a carrying license, must earn living by honest means and complete any military service duty (if applicable).
New Zealand	16 for standard license. 18 for military-style semiautomatic	None required for standard license. For licenses for certain firearms, must be member of recognized	Applicant must be "fit and proper person"; no history of violence.	Two references (family and nonfamily); license may be denied where there is a history of	Safety course and written test.	Storage requirements and inspections.

Country	Minimum Age	Recognized Reasons	Criminal History Requirements	Health Requirements	Training/Testing Requirements	Other Requirements
	firearms.	pistol-shooting club; collector; employee or member of broadcasting or theatrical entity; one acquiring firearm as an heirloom or memento; or a licensed dealer. Self-defense not a valid reason.		drug/alcohol abuse or mental illness; license may be revoked if unfit person could gain access to firearm.		
Norway	21 for acquisition of revolvers, pistols, or parts. 18 for other firearms. 16–18 if weapons stored by guardian or other permit holder based on police consent.	"Reasonable grounds" for having a weapon.	Persons of "sober habits."	Sobriety and "reliability" required.	Active membership in approved shooting group or successful proficiency test for applicants 16–18 seeking to acquire rifle or shotgun.	Police endorsement required; mandatory safe storage.

Country	Minimum Age	Recognized Reasons	Criminal History Requirements	Health Requirements	Training/Testing Requirements	Other Requirements
Russian Federation	18 generally. 16 per approval of provincial legislative assemblies (usually for industrial hunting).	Self-defense, hunting, sports, receiving guns as gift/inheritance.	Criminal background check.	Physical/mental ability; no history of substance abuse.	Training and test.	Citizenship; registered permanent residence; safe storage.
Singapore	18 for target practice. 21 for self-defense.	Selected examples include membership in a registered gun club or serious threat to applicant's life with no other possible protection.	No criminal record.		Shooting proficiency test.	
South Africa	21	Collectors and museums; hunting or sport-shooting organizations or ranges; providers of training, including use of firearms in theatrical, film, or TV productions; game ranchers and hunting-business owners.	No conviction within 5 years immediately preceding the application for certain crimes related to violence, dishonesty, recklessness, or instability.	Stable mental condition; no substance abuse problem or proclivity for violence, including domestic abuse allegations or being laid off from job; competency certificate indicating applicant is "fit	Training and test on safe and efficient use of firearms, as well as applicable training and tests for specific licenses.	Fingerprinting; sportsmen must be members of accredited hunting associations.

Country	Minimum Age	Recognized Reasons	Criminal History Requirements	Health Requirements	Training/Testing Requirements	Other Requirements
		Self-defense only if it cannot be accomplished by other means.		and proper person."		
Spain	18 generally. 14–18 requires permit for hunting or sport shooting.	Hunting, target shooting, collection, self-defense, or security.	Criminal and domestic-violence background checks; certification of good behavior.	Report on the applicant's "psychophysical aptitude" conducted in designated medical facilities; physician sends final report to competent authorities of the Guardia Civil.	Theoretical and practical training and tests.	Safe storage.
Switzerland	18	For carrying license, self-defense or defense of others or property against existing dangers. Militiamen permitted to retain personal ordinance after termination of service.	For handgun-aquisitions license, no conviction for a violent crime or other specified crimes.	For handgun-acquisitions license, not suspected of being danger to self or others; not under guardianship.	Exam for theoretical and practical skills.	

Country	Minimum Age	Recognized Reasons	Criminal History Requirements	Health Requirements	Training/Testing Requirements	Other Requirements
European Union [Minimum Standards for EU Members]	18 generally; Below 18 for hunting and target shooting, subject to parental consent or guidance of licensed adult, or at approved training center.	"Good cause" as determined by individual EU Members.	Conviction for violent, intentional crime may indicate propensity for posing danger to self or society.	Must not be a danger to self or the public.	[not regulated by EU Directives]	Certain firearms subject to permit, others to declaration.

VI. Restrictions on Certain Type and Quantities of Firearms and Ammunition

All countries surveyed regulate the type and quantity of firearms and ammunition that can be acquired or possessed by license holders.

The European Union (EU) Directives, which lay down minimum standards for Member States, ban the sale and use of explosive military missiles and launchers; automatic firearms; firearms disguised as other objects; ammunition with penetrating, explosive, or incendiary projectiles; and pistol and revolver ammunition with expanding projectiles.

In complying with EU Directives and introducing additional restrictions, Germany bans both fully automatic and semiautomatic weapons that are not intended for hunting or marksmanship. It further bans pump-action shotguns with pistol grips or of a short overall length; concealed, technically advanced devices; and some multiple-shot semiautomatics in calibers less than 6.3 mm. Spain similarly bans automatic firearms; those disguised as other objects; armor-piercing, incendiary, and expanding ammunition; and "firearms designed for war use." Similar prohibitions apply in Great Britain, which bans military-style weapons and firearms disguised as other objects.

Many countries in and outside of the EU prohibit "military style" and other high capacity weapons. Australia bans certain semiautomatic and self-loading rifles or shotguns; Brazil restricts some firearms for use by armed forces, public security institutions, and qualified persons and corporations. Similar restrictions exist in Japan, which bans all "military" weapons from civilians. Canada prohibits most 32- and 25-caliber handguns and those with a barrel length of 105 mm or shorter, fully automatic weapons, converted automatics, firearms with a sawed-off barrel, and some military rifles like the AK 47. The Russian Federation bans many types of high-capacity firearms and cartridges.

Norway, Switzerland, and South Africa specifically ban fully automatic weapons; in addition, Norway bans some semiautomatic weapons and other types of firearms disguised as other objects. In addition to banning fully automatic firearms, South Africa generally prohibits transactions involving, among other things, guns, cannons, recoilless guns, mortars, light mortars or launchers manufactured to fire rockets, grenades, self-propelled grenades, bombs, and explosive devices. The list of banned weapons further includes the frame, body, or barrel of such weapons as well as any imitations or alterations. As in many other countries, the manufacture and sale of imitation guns is prohibited in China, a country that maintains strict control of the manufacturing of firearms by ensuring that designs for firearms are developed by the State Council or Ministry of Public Security.

Israel is one of many countries that strictly regulate not only the type but also the quantity of firearms and ammunition for civilian use. As a general rule, in Israel an individual who qualifies for a license may be eligible for only one firearm and fifty bullets. Possession of additional firearms may be licensed for special reasons, including when the additional firearm is an air or BB gun, when it is designed to be held as memorabilia, or when it is required for sports or for the prevention of harm to agriculture.

The survey includes two additional Middle Eastern countries—Egypt and Lebanon. Egypt, a country that recently underwent a change of leadership and is still in turmoil, has legislation that prohibits automatic assault rifles, rocket-propelled grenades (RPGs), gun silencers, and telescopic equipment used with weapons, but it appears that these laws are not currently being enforced. In Lebanon, where several armed groups operating outside any legal framework are known to exist, the law prohibits the acquisition, possession, or transport of military- or combat-style arms for civilians except in the case of disturbances or as specified by a permit from the Minister of National Defense.

In New Zealand, a total ban on military-style semiautomatic weapons was rejected in the face of opposition from user groups and the estimated cost of such a measure in terms of providing adequate compensation to current owners.

VII. National Register

Many of the countries surveyed require transactions involving firearms to be recorded. Australia, Brazil, Canada, Egypt, Germany, Israel, Singapore, Spain, and South Africa maintain national firearms registries. The EU is requiring all of its Member States to establish registries of firearms by December 2014, to which only designated authorities will have access.

Great Britain, Russia, and Switzerland currently maintain local rather than central registers of firearms.

VIII. Statistical Data on the Distribution of Firearms and Their Use in Violent Crimes

Among the countries surveyed, several appear to have experienced a reduction in the number of firearms in civilian circulation and in firearms-related crimes and deaths in recent years. Japan and Israel, for example, have steadily reduced the number of firearms licenses granted to civilians. In Israel, where 300,000 licenses were issued in the late 1980s during the first *Intifada*, the number of firearms' licenses had decreased to 170,000 by June 2012 and continues to decline.

In Australia, the number of victims of firearms-related homicides declined by half in the period between 1989–90 and 2009–10 (from 24 to 12%); Brazil experienced a reduction of 60.1% in the number of homicides between 2001 and 2007. In Canada, firearms-related homicides declined over the past thirty years and fell nearly 30% over the past four years alone. New Zealand's firearms-related deaths were also found to have decreased in the past twenty years.

In Great Britain the use of firearms in offenses decreased in 2010–11 by 13% from the previous year. However, despite the country's stringent gun laws, illegal handguns can be easily purchased and newspapers have reported that in the two years after the 1997 ban on handguns following the Dunblane massacre, the number of crimes in which handguns were carried increased by 40%.

South Africa's firearms-related crimes have reportedly dropped since enforcement of that country's stricter firearms-control law commenced in 2004. However, a direct causal connection has not yet been established because the South African Police Service stopped releasing data on the subject after 2000.

The country reports provide examples of countries with very low rates of crime involving firearms. In China, for example, where civilian gun ownership is generally prohibited, only 500 criminal offenses were reportedly committed with guns in 2011, in a country whose population numbers 1.34 billion. In Japan, where 271,100 guns were licensed in 2011, the number of gun-violence victims for the year was eight. In Spain the rate of deaths by firearms is 0.63 per 100,000 people, according to a 2010 report. Statistical data from Great Britain indicates that in 2008–2009 firearms were used in only 0.3% of all recorded crimes and were responsible for the deaths of thirty-nine people.

A direct correlation between statistical data provided in the individual country reports and specific legal requirements imposed by these countries cannot be established, given the different variables that are relevant to each country's legal, social, and cultural conditions, and the varied sources of information on which the data was based.

Prepared by Ruth Levush
Senior Foreign Law Specialist
and Project Coordinator
February 2013

AUSTRALIA

FIREARMS-CONTROL LEGISLATION AND POLICY

Summary

The sale, possession, and use of firearms are regulated by the Australian states and territories, with cross-border trade matters addressed at the federal level. In 1996, following the Port Arthur massacre, the federal government and the states and territories agreed to a uniform approach to firearms regulation, including a ban on certain semiautomatic and self-loading rifles and shotguns, standard licensing and permit criteria, storage requirements and inspections, and greater restrictions on the sale of firearms and ammunition. Firearms license applicants would be required to take a safety course and show a "genuine reason" for owning a firearm, which could not include self-defense. The reasons for refusing a license would include "reliable evidence of a mental or physical condition which would render the applicant unsuitable for owning, possessing or using a firearm." A waiting period of twenty-eight days would apply to the issuing of both firearms licenses and permits to acquire each weapon.

Alongside legislative reforms to implement the National Firearms Agreement, a national buyback program for prohibited weapons took place in 1996-1997 and resulted in more than 700,000 weapons being surrendered. Further reforms were later implemented as a result of agreements made in 2002 on firearms trafficking and handguns, as was a national buyback of newly prohibited handguns and associated parts.

A large amount of information and analysis is available regarding the number of firearms in Australia and their use in crimes or incidents resulting in death. The most recent relevant report of the Australian Institute of Criminology states that the "number of victims of firearm-perpetrated homicide (i.e. murder and manslaughter) has declined by half between 1989–90 and 2009–10 from 24 to 12 percent." Recent reports have also examined the number of illicit firearms and firearm thefts in Australia. Among the activities relating to gun control that took place in 2012 was the signing of a new intergovernmental agreement to tackle illicit firearms and firearms trafficking.

I. Background

On April 28, 1996, a twenty-eight-year-old gunman armed with a semiautomatic rifle shot and killed thirty-five people and wounded eighteen others at several locations in and around Port Arthur, a popular tourist area in Tasmania, Australia. The gunman survived and pleaded guilty to multiple homicides.[1]   He received thirty-five life sentences without the possibility of parole.[2]

Prior to this incident, gun laws in Australia could be seen as relatively lenient, and there were large variations in the regulations across the six states and two mainland territories.[3] Firearms regulation is the responsibility of individual Australian states and territories, as section 51 of the Australian Constitution does not confer lawmaking powers in relation to firearms on the federal Parliament.[4] Federal laws can be enacted regarding the import of firearms and other weapons under the overseas trade and commerce powers of the federal Parliament.[5] The Australian Constitution does not contain any explicit gun ownership rights.

In response to the Port Arthur massacre, the Australasian Police Ministers' Council (APMC) convened a special meeting on May 10, 1996, and agreed to a national plan for the regulation of firearms promoted by then Prime Minister John Howard.[6] The resolutions made at that meeting subsequently became the Nationwide Agreement on Firearms (commonly referred to as the National Firearms Agreement).[7] The proposals emerged from earlier recommendations of the National Committee on Violence, which was established in 1988 following two mass killings in Melbourne involving high-powered rifles.[8] The APMC had previously considered the need for a uniform approach to firearms regulation at meetings held between 1988 and 1995,[9]

---

[1] *See* Robert Milliken, *Tasmanian Admits Gun Massacre*, THE INDEPENDENT (Nov. 8, 1996), http://www. independent.co.uk/news/world/tasmanian-admits-gun-massacre-1351256.html.

[2] *See Gunman's Life Sentence in Tasmania Killings*, NY TIMES (Nov. 22, 1996), http://www.nytimes.com/ 1996/11/22/world/gunman-s-life-sentence-in-tasmania-killings.html.

[3] *See* JENNIFER NORBERRY ET AL., AFTER PORT ARTHUR—ISSUES OF GUN CONTROL IN AUSTRALIA (Parliamentary Library Current Issues Brief 16, 1995-96), http://www.aph.gov.au/About_Parliament/Parliamentary _Departments/Parliamentary_Library/Publications_Archive/CIB/cib9596/96cib16, under the heading "National Uniform Gun Laws?"

[4] AUSTRALIAN CONSTITUTION s 51, http://www.comlaw.gov.au/Details/C2004C00469.

[5] *Id.* s 51(i).

[6] *See* Rebecca Peters & Charles Watson, *A Breakthrough in Gun Control in Australia After the Port Arthur Massacre*, 2 INJ. PREV. 253 (1996), http://injuryprevention.bmj.com/content/2/4/253.full.pdf. For a recent discussion of the processes and impacts associated with these changes, *see* John Howard, *I Went After Guns. Obama Can Too*, NY TIMES (Jan. 16, 2013), http://www.nytimes.com/2013/01/17/opinion/australia-banned-assault-weapons-america-can-too.html?smid=fb-nytimes.

[7] *See* SAMANTHA BRICKNELL, FIREARM TRAFFICKING AND SERIOUS AND ORGANISED CRIME GANGS (Australian Institute of Criminology (AIC) Research and Public Policy Series No. 116, June 2012), http://www.aic. gov.au/publications/current%20series/rpp/100-120/rpp116.html, under the heading "Legislative Reforms."

[8] *See* NORBERRY ET AL., *supra* note 3; Duncan Chappell, *Prevention of Violent Crime: The Work of the National Committee on Violence*, *in* INTERNATIONAL TRENDS IN CRIME: EAST MEETS WEST 155 (Sandra McKillop ed., 1992), http://aic.gov.au/media_library/publications/proceedings/12/chappell.pdf.

[9] *Firearms Reform—Debated Nationally for Years*, THE AUSTRALIAN FIREARMS BUYBACK (archived website), http://pandora.nla.gov.au/nph-wb/20000426130000/http://www.gun.law.gov.au/Guns/legislation/history .htm (last visited Dec. 20, 2012).

and some state and federal laws had been changed during this period in response to shooting incidents.[10]

The 1996 National Firearms Agreement led to the considerable revision of the laws of the states and territories[11] and the implementation of a national buyback program to encourage firearms owners and dealers to surrender prohibited weapons.

After 1996 there were further shooting incidents, which led to additional action by Australian federal and state governments, including the National Handgun Agreement (2002), National Handgun Buyback Act 2003 (Cth), and National Firearms Trafficking Policy Agreement (2002).[12]

II. Relevant Legislation

The restrictions and licensing requirements relating to the purchase, possession, and use of firearms (including imitation firearms) in Australia are currently controlled by the following state and territory instruments:

- New South Wales: Firearms Act 1996, Weapons Prohibition Act 1998, and associated regulations[13]

- Victoria: Firearms Act 1996, Control of Weapons Act 1990, and associated regulations[14]

- Queensland: Weapons Act 1990 and associated regulations[15]

- Western Australia: Firearms Act 1973 and associated regulations[16]

- South Australia: Firearms Act 1977 and associated regulations[17]

---

[10] *See* Press Release, Gun Control Australia, Our Strict Gun Laws Have Saved Thousands of Australian Lives (Sept. 7, 2012), http://guncontrol.org.au/2012/09/our-strict-gun-laws-have-saved-thousands-of-australian-lives/.

[11] *See* ABIGAIL RATH & GARETH GRIFFITH, FIREARMS REGULATION: AN UPDATE (NSW Parliamentary Library Research Service Background Paper 5/99, Oct. 1999), http://143.119.255.92/prod/parlment/publications.nsf/0/121A3D471695BA8ECA256ECF000AF715/$File/FIREARMSPAPERComplete.pdf.

[12] BRICKNELL, *supra* note 7.

[13] *See generally Firearms Registry*, NSW POLICE FORCE, http://www.police.nsw.gov.au/services/firearms (last visited Dec. 21, 2012).

[14] *See generally Firearms*, VICTORIA POLICE, http://www.police.vic.gov.au/content.asp?Document_ID=34098 (last visited Dec. 21, 2012).

[15] *See generally Weapons Licensing*, QUEENSLAND POLICE, http://www.police.qld.gov.au/programs/weaponsLicensing/; *Firearms Licence*, QUEENSLAND POLICE, http://www.police.qld.gov.au/programs/weaponsLicensing/licenceApplication/licences/firearms/ (both last visited Dec. 21, 2012).

[16] *See generally Firearms*, WESTERN AUSTRALIA POLICE, http://www.police.wa.gov.au/Ourservices/PoliceLicensingServices/Firearms/tabid/1802/Default.aspx (last visited Dec. 21, 2012).

[17] *See generally Firearms & Weapons*, SOUTH AUSTRALIA POLICE, http://www.sapolice.sa.gov.au/sapol/services/firearms_weapons.jsp (last visited Dec. 21, 2012).

- Tasmania: Firearms Act 1996 and associated regulations[18]

- Northern Territory: Firearms Act and associated regulations[19]

- Australian Capital Territory: Firearms Act 1996, Prohibited Weapons Act 1996, and associated regulations[20]

A full list of current legal instruments for each state and territory are provided in an appendix to this report.

At the federal level, the importation of firearms is subject to the restrictions in Regulation 4F and Schedule 6 of the Customs (Prohibited Goods) Regulations 1956 (Cth).[21]

III. 1996 National Firearms Agreement and Buyback Program

The resolutions agreed to at the APMC meeting on May 10, 1996,[22] provided for the establishment of a uniform approach to firearms regulation that would include

- a federal ban on the importation of "all semi-automatic self-loading and pump action longarms, and all parts, including magazines, for such firearms, included in Licence Category D, and control of the importation of those firearms included in Licence Category C." The sale, resale, transfer, ownership, manufacture, and use of such firearms would also be banned by the states and territories, other than in exceptional circumstances (relating to military or law enforcement purposes and occupational categories, depending on the category of the firearm);[23]

- standard categories of firearms, including the two largely prohibited categories (C and D), which include certain semiautomatic and self-loading rifles and shotguns, and a restricted category for handguns (category H);[24]

---

[18] *See generally Firearms*, Tasmania Police, http://www.police.tas.gov.au/services-online/firearms/ (last visited Dec. 21, 2012).

[19] *See generally Firearms Licences Permits Information*, NORTHERN TERRITORY POLICE, http://www.pfes. nt.gov.au/Police/Firearms-Weapons/Firearms-licences-permits-information.aspx (last visited Dec. 21, 2012).

[20] *See generally Firearms*, ACT POLICING, http://www.police.act.gov.au/crime-and-safety/firearms.aspx (last visited Dec. 21, 2012).

[21] Customs (Prohibited Imports) Regulations 1956 (Cth), http://www.comlaw.gov.au/Details/F2012 C00724. *See generally Firearms and Weapons*, Australian Customs and Border Protection Service, http://www.customs.gov.au/site/page4372.asp (last visited Dec. 21, 2012).

[22] Australasian Police Ministers' Council (APMC), Special Firearms Meeting, Canberra, 10 May 1996: Resolutions, *available at* http://www.austlii.edu.au/au/other/apmc/, and on the Australian Firearms Buyback archived website *at* http://pandora.nla.gov.au/nph-wb/20000426130000/http://www.gun.law.gov.au/Guns/ legislation/10may_resolut.htm (both last visited Dec. 21, 2012).

[23] *Id.* res. 1.

[24] *Id.* res. 4. The full list of firearms in category C (which are prohibited except for occupational purposes) is as follows: "semi automatic rimfire rifles with a magazine capacity no greater than 10 rounds; semi automatic shotguns with a magazine capacity no greater than 5 rounds; pump action shotguns with a magazine capacity no greater than 5 rounds." The category D list (which are prohibited except for official purposes) is: "self-loading

- a requirement for a separate permit for the acquisition of every firearm, with a twenty-eight-day waiting period applying to the issuing of such permits,[25] and the establishment of a nationwide firearms registration system;[26]

- a uniform requirement for all firearms sales to be conducted only by or through licensed firearms dealers, and certain minimum principles that would underpin rules relating to the recording of firearms transactions by dealers and right of inspection by police;[27]

- restrictions on the quantity of ammunition that may be purchased in a given period and a requirement that dealers only sell ammunition for firearms for which the purchaser is licensed;[28]

- ensuring that "personal protection" would not be regarded as a "genuine reason" for owning, possessing, or using a firearm under the laws of the states and territories;[29]

- standardized classifications to define a "genuine reason" that an applicant must show for owning, possessing, or using a firearm, including reasons relating to sport shooting, recreational shooting/hunting, collecting, and occupational requirements (additional requirements of showing a genuine need for the particular type of firearm and securing related approvals would be added for firearms in categories B, C, D, and H);[30]

- in addition to the demonstration of a "genuine reason," other basic requirements would apply for the issuing of firearms licenses, specifically that the applicant must be aged eighteen years or over, be a "fit and proper person," be able to prove his or her identity, and undertake adequate safety training[31] (safety training courses would be subject to accreditation and be "comprehensive and standardised across Australia for all licence categories");[32]

- firearms licenses would be required to bear a photograph of the licensee, be endorsed with a category of firearm, include the holder's address, be issued after a waiting

---

centre fire rifles designed or adapted for military purposes or a firearm which substantially duplicates those rifles in design, function or appearance; non-military style self-loading centre fire rifles with either an integral or detachable magazine; self-loading shotguns with either an integral or detachable magazine and pump action shotguns with a capacity of more than 5 rounds; self-loading rim-fire rifles with a magazine capacity greater than 10 rounds."

[25] *Id.* res. 7.

[26] *Id.* res. 2.

[27] *Id.* res. 9.

[28] *Id.*

[29] *Id.* res. 3.

[30] *Id.*

[31] *Id.* res. 4.

[32] *Id.* res. 5.

period of not less than twenty-eight days, be issued for a period of no more than five years, and contain a reminder of safe storage responsibilities;[33]

- licenses would only be issued subject to undertakings to comply with storage requirements and following an inspection by licensing authorities of the licensee's storage facilities;[34]

- minimum standards for the refusal or cancellation of licenses, including criminal convictions for violent offenses in the past five years, unsafe storage of firearms, failure to notify of a change of address, and "reliable evidence of a mental or physical condition which would render the applicant unsuitable for owning, possessing or using a firearm";[35] and

- the establishment of uniform standards for the security and storage of firearms, including a requirement that ammunition be stored in locked containers separate from any firearms. The minimum standards for category C, D, and H firearms would include "storage in a locked, steel safe with a thickness to ensure it is not easily penetrable, bolted to the structure of a building."[36]

The above resolutions were implemented through the passage of new or amending legislation and associated regulations by the states and territories.[37] A review of the relevant legislation by the Australian Institute of Criminology (AIC) in 2008 found general compliance with the 1996 National Firearms Agreement (and the 2002 agreements regarding handguns and firearms trafficking discussed below) across the states and territories but also determined that there remained some inconsistencies between the jurisdictions.[38] Some amendments to the relevant laws were subsequently made in response to the AIC review.

In addition to requiring law changes to implement the above resolutions, the agreement provided for the establishment of a twelve-month national amnesty and compensation program, to be accompanied by a public education campaign, after which the jurisdictions would apply "severe penalties" for breaches of the firearms control laws.[39] This resolution was implemented through a national firearms buyback program, which saw the federal Parliament enacting the National Firearms Program Implementation Act 1996 (Cth).[40] The Medicare Levy Amendment

---

[33] *Id.* res. 4.

[34] *Id.*

[35] *Id.* res. 6.

[36] *Id.* res. 8.

[37] *See Successful Implementation of the Laws*, THE AUSTRALIAN FIREARMS BUYBACK (archived website), http://pandora.nla.gov.au/nph-wb/20000426130000/http://www.gun.law.gov.au/Guns/legislation/success.htm (last visited Dec. 21, 2012).

[38] *See* BRICKNELL, *supra* note 7.

[39] APMC Resolutions, *supra* note 22, res. 11.

[40] National Firearms Program Implementation Act 1996 (Cth), http://www.comlaw.gov.au/Details/C2004 C00875.

Act 1996 (Cth) was also enacted in relation to providing funding for the compensation to be paid to gun owners who handed in weapons that fell within the prohibited categories.[41]

The buyback program started in most states on October 1, 1996, and ended on September 30, 1997. More than 640,000 prohibited firearms were surrendered nationwide as part of the buyback program.[42] In addition, it was reported that about 60,000 nonprohibited firearms were voluntarily surrendered without compensation.[43] According to a telephone poll conducted in 1999 on behalf of the federal government by Gun Control Australia, there were about 3.25 million guns in Australia prior to the 1996–1997 buyback program.[44] One study on the impact of the buyback states that "[i]n terms of the absolute numbers of guns destroyed, Australia's gun buyback ranks as the largest destruction of civilian firearms in any country over the period 1991–2006."[45] The buyback was reported to have resulted in the withdrawal of one-fifth of the stock of civilian firearms in the country and substantially reduced the number of households possessing a firearm.[46]

IV. 2002 Trafficking and Handgun Agreements

In July 2002, the APMC agreed to several resolutions aimed at controlling the illegal trade in firearms in Australia. The National Firearm Trafficking Policy Agreement called for

- increased border protection;

- the introduction of nationally consistent regulation of the legal manufacture of firearms;

- the establishment of new offences or substantial penalties for matters relating to:

  - the illegal possession and supply of firearms;

  - the defacing of serial numbers;

  - conspiracy to commit interstate firearm wrongdoings; and

---

[41] Medicare Levy Amendment Act 1996 (Cth), http://www.comlaw.gov.au/Details/C2004A05036.

[42] *National Tally*, THE AUSTRALIAN FIREARMS BUYBACK (archived website), http://pandora.nla.gov.au/nph-wb/20000426130000/http://www.gun.law.gov.au/Guns/tally/tally.htm (last visited Dec. 21, 2012); AUSTRALIAN NATIONAL AUDIT OFFICE, THE GUN BUY-BACK SCHEME 6 (1997), http://www.anao.gov.au/uploads/documents/1997-98_Audit_Report_25.pdf. 6.

[43] *See* Simon Chapman & Philip Alpers, *Tight Gun Controls the Most Powerful Weapon*, THE SYDNEY MORNING HERALD (Apr. 27, 2006), http://www.smh.com.au/news/opinion/tight-gun-controls-the-most-powerful-weapon/2006/04/26/1145861416502.html.

[44] *See* Janet Phillips et al., Firearms in Australia: A Guide to Electronic Resources (Australian Parliamentary Library, Aug. 9, 2007), http://www.aph.gov.au/About_Parliament/Parliamentary_Departments/Parliamentary_Library/pubs/BN/0708/FirearmsAustralia.

[45] Andrew Leigh & Christine Neill, *Do Gun Buybacks Save Lives? Evidence from Panel Data*, 12(2) AM. LAW & ECON. REV. 510 (2010), *available at* http://andrewleigh.org/pdf/GunBuyback_Panel.pdf.

[46] *Id.* at 522.

- tighter recording and reporting provisions for dealer transactions involving firearm and major firearm parts.[47]

In addition to subsequent changes to state and territory legislation in response to the resolutions, an amendment to the federal Criminal Code Act 1995 was enacted to make it a criminal offense, "in the course of trade and commerce between any states and territories, to illegally dispose of or acquire a firearm, or to take or send a firearm from one state or territory to another, intending that the firearm will be disposed of illegally." [48]

Later in 2002, on October 21, two people were killed and five injured as a result of a shooting incident in a classroom at Monash University in Melbourne, Victoria. The gunman, who had been armed with several loaded handguns, was a licensed pistol owner and member of the Sporting Shooters Association of Australia. He was later found not guilty of the murders on the grounds of mental impairment and sentenced to spend twenty-five years in a psychiatric hospital.[49] The incident led to renewed debate about gun control laws, particularly in relation to handguns.[50]

At a meeting of the APMC in November 2002, various resolutions were agreed to, which included restricting the classes of legal handguns that can be imported or possessed for sporting purposes, changing licensing requirements for handguns, and exploring options for a buyback program for those guns deemed illegal.[51] The Council of Australian Governments (COAG) endorsed the resolutions in December 2002, and these formed the National Handgun Control Agreement.[52]

The agreed restrictions were implemented through state and territory amendment legislation[53] and through changes to the Customs (Prohibited Imports) Regulations 1956 (Cth).[54] The latter instrument was amended to

---

[47] BRICKNELL, *supra* note 7.

[48] *Id.* (referring to Crimes Legislation Amendment (People Smuggling, Firearms Trafficking and Other Measures) Act 2002 (Cth) sch 2, http://www.comlaw.gov.au/Details/C2004A01078; Criminal Code Act 1995 (Cth) pt 9.4, http://www.comlaw.gov.au/Details/C2012C00913).

[49] *See Killer Sent to Psych Hospital*, THE SYDNEY MORNING HERALD (June 17, 2004), http://www.smh.com.au/articles/2004/06/17/1087245033577.html.

[50] *See* Annabel Crabb et al., *PM Flags Tougher Gun Laws*, THE AGE (Oct. 23, 2002), http://www.theage.com.au/articles/2002/10/22/1034561495101.html; Phillip Hudson, *Government Puts 259 Guns on Banned List*, THE AGE (Nov. 8, 2002), http://www.theage.com.au/articles/2002/11/07/1036308423794.html.

[51] APMC Firearms (Handguns) Resolutions November 2002, *available at* http://www.customs.gov.au/webdata/resources/files/Mediaattachment021128.pdf.

[52] *See* Phillips et al., *supra* note 44.

[53] *See, e.g.,* NSW, Parliamentary Debates, 3 July 2003, 2733, Second Reading of Firearms Amendment (Prohibited Pistols) Bill, http://www.parliament.nsw.gov.au/prod/parlment/hansart.nsf/V3Key/LC20030703014.

[54] Customs (Prohibited Imports) Amendment Regulations 2002 (No. 4) (Cth), http://www.comlaw.gov.au/Details/F2002B00339;

prevent the importation of prohibited handguns and handgun parts with the following features by sporting shooters, or their direct sale by firearms dealers/importers to sporting shooters:

- a calibre that is greater than .38, unless the handgun is used to participate in a specially accredited sporting event in that case a calibre of up to .45 will be permitted
- a barrel length of less than 120 mm for semi-automatic handguns and less than 100 mm for revolvers and single-shot handguns, unless the handgun is a highly specialised target pistol
- a magazine/shot capacity that exceeds 10 rounds.[55]

The federal Parliament also enacted the National Handgun Buyback Act 2003, which provided for financial assistance to be granted to states in connection with the implementation of a buyback program for handguns that did not comply with the new restrictions.[56] The buyback program, which was implemented by the individual states and territories, resulted in about 70,000 handguns and more than 278,000 parts and accessories being surrendered.[57]

V. Statistical Information and Analysis

There have been multiple studies and reports over the years that provide statistics and analysis regarding various aspects of gun ownership and violence in Australia, including in relation to the impact of the 1996 reforms and buyback program. The references below to both government and academic reports or studies are not intended to be exhaustive.

A. Government Information

In 1997, following an agreement at the July 1996 APMC meeting, the AIC established a national firearms monitoring program, which includes tracking and analyzing firearm theft information.[58] The AIC also monitors homicide rates and other violent crimes,[59] including the weapons associated with these.[60] The Australian Crime Commission (ACC) provides reports and analysis on aspects of nationally significant crime, and in February 2012 it was asked to

---

[55] Phillips et al., *supra* note 44.

[56] National Handgun Buyback Act 2003, http://www.comlaw.gov.au/Details/C2004C01326. For background information *see* Australian Parliamentary Library, National Handgun Buyback Act 2003 (Bills Digest No. 155, May 22, 2003), http://parlinfo.aph.gov.au/parlInfo/download/legislation/billsdgs/7CE96/upload_binary/7CE96.pdf.

[57] Phillips et al., *supra* note 44.

[58] *See generally National Firearms Monitoring Program*, AIC, http://www.aic.gov.au/about_aic/research_programs/nmp/0002.html (last visited Dec. 21, 2012).

[59] *See generally Australian Crime: Facts and Figures*, AIC, http://www.aic.gov.au/publications/current%20series/facts/1-20.html (last visited Dec. 21, 2012).

[60] *See generally Weapons*, AIC, http://www.aic.gov.au/crime_types/violence/weapons.html (last visited Dec. 21, 2012).

undertake an intelligence assessment of the illegal firearms market.[61] Findings of some of the reports of these government entities include the following:

Firearm Numbers

- An AIC report published in 1988 stated that there were at least 3.5 million privately owned guns of all types (including registered, unregistered, licensed, and unlicensed) in Australia, with more than a quarter of Australian households possessing a gun.[62]

- In June 2012, the ACC report on illicit firearms noted that there are more than 2.75 million registered firearms in Australia held by more than 730,000 individual license holders[63] (the current population of Australia is approximately 22.8 million[64]).

- An AIC report from 2008 on the criminal use of handguns in Australia found that by June 30, 2006, 130,903 handguns had been registered in Australia (excluding South Australia), which accounted for 6% of all registered firearms at that time.[65]

- The ACC recently made a "conservative estimate" that there are more than 250,000 long-arms and 10,000 handguns in the illicit firearms market in Australia.[66] Of these, 44% were not surrendered or registered after the Port Arthur massacre and 12% were stolen or the subject of staged theft.[67]

- The AIC's 2008–09 report on firearm theft estimated that around 1,500 firearms are stolen each year, the majority being long-arms, with relatively few firearms recovered.[68]

- The 2008–09 firearm theft report also provided information on the status of compliance with firearms storage laws, finding that 60% of owners who reported a firearms theft in that year were determined to have complied with these laws. The

---

[61] Press Release, Jason Clare MP, Final Report of the National Investigation into the Illegal Firearms Market (June 29, 2012), http://www.jasonclare.com.au/media/portfolio-releases/home-affairs-and-justice-releases/949-final-report-of-the-national-investigation-into-the-illegal-firearms-market.html.

[62] AIC, FIREARMS AND VIOLENCE IN AUSTRALIA (AIC Trends & Issues in Crime and Criminal Justice No. 10, Feb. 1988), http://www.aic.gov.au/documents/A/8/4/%7BA84819A6-AC46-4A82-A049-841A3F3A9730%7Dti10.pdf.

[63] Press Release, Jason Clare MP, supra note 61.

[64] Population Clock, AUSTRALIAN BUREAU OF STATISTICS, http://www.abs.gov.au/ausstats/abs@.nsf/0/1647509ef7e25faaca2568a900154b63?opendocument (last visited Dec. 21, 2012).

[65] SAMANTHA BRICKNELL, CRIMINAL USE OF HANDGUNS IN AUSTRALIA (AIC Trends & Issues in Crime and Criminal Justice No. 361, Sept. 2008), http://aic.gov.au/publications/current%20series/tandi/361-380/tandi361.html.

[66] Illicit Firearms, AUSTRALIAN CRIME COMMISSION (ACC), http://www.crimecommission.gov.au/publications/crime-profile-series-fact-sheet/illicit-firearms (last visited Dec. 20, 2012); ACC, ILLICIT FIREARMS (Nov. 5, 2012), http://www.crimecommission.gov.au/sites/default/files/files/fact_sheets/Illicit%20Firearms%20FACT%20SHEET%20021112%20low%20res.pdf.

[67] Press Release, Jason Clare MP, supra note 61. See also BRICKNELL, supra note 7.

[68] SAMANTHA BRICKNELL, FIREARM THEFT IN AUSTRALIA 2008-09 (AIC Monitoring Report No. 16, Oct. 2011), http://www.aic.gov.au/publications/current%20series/mr/1-20/16.html.

principal location for firearm theft was private dwellings.[69]   Between 2004–05 and 2008-09, around 25% of firearm owners who reported a theft of their firearms were "found, or suspected, to be in breach of one or more firearms laws."[70]

Firearm Deaths

- The AIC's 1988 report found that one third of all reported murders in Australia were committed with firearms, with gunshot wounds being "the single most common cause of death among homicide victims" and with research showing that "guns substantially increase the probability that death, rather than injury, will be the end result of a firearm attack."[71]

- A 2003 report on firearms-related deaths between 1991 and 2001 found that

  [i]n 1991 there were 629 firearm related deaths in Australia compared to 333 in 2001. This represents a 47 per cent decrease in firearms deaths between 1991 and 2001. The incidence of both firearms suicides and firearms homicides almost halved over the 11 year period. While the number of firearms homicides has continued to decline, with 2001 recording the lowest number of firearms homicides during this period (n=47), the number of firearms suicides declined consistently from 1991 to 1998, but has since fluctuated. The number of firearm related accidents also fluctuated over the same period, from 29 firearms accidents in 1991 to 18 in 2001, but ranging between 15 and 45 over this time. While the numbers are quite small, the year 2000 recorded the highest number of firearms accidents (45 accidents) during the 11 year period.[72]

- The AIC's 2008 handgun report stated that firearms are used in an average of 20% of homicides committed each year in Australia, and that "[i]n 2005–06, firearm homicides fell to their lowest level in 13 years: 14 percent of all homicide victims. Since 1992–93, firearm homicide as a proportion of all homicides has halved, continuing a general downward trend in firearm homicide that began in the early 1980s."[73] In terms of handgun use in homicides, the report found that

  [d]uring the early to mid-1990s, handguns accounted for less than 20 percent of all firearm homicides, but over the following 10 years this percentage increased to around 50 percent. This increase immediately followed the National Firearms Agreement in 1996, and it has been proposed that restrictions in the availability and access to certain firearms, and who can own a firearm, led to greater use of

---

[69] *Id.*, under the heading "The nature of firearm theft incidents."

[70] *Id.*, under the heading "Compliance with firearm laws."

[71] Firearms and Violence in Australia, *supra* note 62.

[72] JENNY MOUZOS & CATHERINE RUSHFORTH, FIREARMS RELATED DEATHS IN AUSTRALIA, 1991-2001 (AIC Trends & Issues in Crime and Criminal Justice No. 269, Nov. 2003), http://www.aic.gov.au/publications/current%20series/tandi/261-280/tandi269/view%20paper.html.

[73] BRICKNELL, *supra* note 65. Note that the fiscal year in Australia, which is used for government reporting, budget, and tax purposes, is July 1 to June 30.

illegitimate means to acquire firearms, particularly those that are easily concealed such as handguns.[74]

- Other findings in the handgun report included that "[t]he majority of homicides, regardless of the method used to kill the victim, were 'single victim/single offender' incidents. Homicides committed by an individual using a handgun were more likely to result in multiple victims than homicides in general (11% compared with 5%), but only slightly more so when compared with all firearm homicides (9%)."[75] Furthermore, the report stated that "[t]he majority of firearms used to commit homicide in Australia since 1989–90 were held unlawfully at the time."[76]

- The most recently available AIC annual crime survey found that "[t]he proportion of homicide victims killed by offenders using firearms in 2009–10 represented a decrease of 18 percentage points from the peak of 31 percent in 1995–96 (the year in which the Port Arthur massacre occurred with the death of 35 people, which subsequently led to the introduction of stringent firearms legislation)."[77]

- A 2012 AIC report on firearm trafficking referred to a forthcoming study in stating that

  [i]n Australia, the number of victims of firearm-perpetrated homicide (ie murder and manslaughter) has declined by half between 1989–90 and 2009–10 from 24 to 12 percent. (Chan & Payne forthcoming). The predominance of handgun-perpetrated homicide, as a proportion of all firearm homicide, rose from 17 to 45 percent between 1992–93 and 2006–07 (Bricknell 2008b; Dearden & Jones 2008) but dropped again in the following three years to a little over 10 percent. For the most recent year available (2009–10), handgun homicide comprised 13 percent of all homicides that were committed with a firearm (Chan & Payne forthcoming).[78]

B. Nongovernment Studies

A range of Australian firearms statistics can also be found on the website of GunPolicy.org, a nonprofit entity hosted by the Sydney School of Public Health at The University of Sydney.[79] In January 2013, the author of that website, Associate Professor Philip Alpers, published figures relating to the impact of multiple gun buybacks and amnesties on the number of guns in Australia.[80] His research found that, due to an increasing number of guns

---

[74] *Id.* (internal reference omitted).

[75] Id.

[76] Id.

[77] AIC, AUSTRALIAN CRIME: FACTS & FIGURES: 2011 at ch 2 (Mar. 2012), http://www.aic.gov.au/publications/current%20series/facts/1-20/2011.html.

[78] BRICKNELL, *supra* note 7, under the heading "Characteristics and dynamics of firearms trafficking."

[79] *Australia – Gun Facts, Figures and the Law*, GUNPOLICY.ORG, http://www.gunpolicy.org/firearms/region/australia (last visited Dec. 21, 2012).

[80] Philip Alpers & Marcus Wilson, Australian Firearm Amnesty, Buyback and Destruction Totals: Official Tallies and Media-reported Numbers, 1987-2012 (Sydney School of Public Health, The University of Sydney, Jan. 10, 2013), http://www.gunpolicy.org/documents/doc_download/5337-alpers-australian-firearm-amnesty-buyback-

being imported into Australia, "Australians own as many guns now as they did at the time of the Port Arthur massacre, despite more than 1 million firearms being handed in and destroyed."[81] Alpers said that most of the new guns being imported are not military style semiautomatics and also that handguns are difficult to import. He also claimed that there was little evidence to suggest that illegally imported weapons are a significant issue, with the main problem being criminals obtaining legal firearms that had been lost or stolen. However, a police superintendent in New South Wales refuted this, saying that illegal imports are in fact a big challenge for police.[82]

Professor Alpers' paper for a conference on firearms policy at Johns Hopkins University held in January 2013 discussed the buybacks and cited various studies of the impact of Australia's firearms law reforms.[83]

Papers by other academic researchers relating to the impact of firearms law reforms include the following:

- J. Ozanne-Smith et al., *Firearm Related Deaths: The Impact of Regulatory Reform*, 10(5) INJ. PREV. 280 (2004). This paper examined firearms-related deaths in the state of Victoria in the context of legislative reforms in 1988 and 1996. It found that "[a]fter initial Victorian reforms, a significant downward trend was seen for numbers of all firearm related deaths between 1988 and 1995 (17.3% in Victoria compared with the rest of Australia, $p<0.0001$). A further significant decline between 1997 and 2000 followed the later reforms. After the later all-state legislation, similar strong declines occurred in the rest of Australia from 1997 (14.0% reduction compared with Victoria, $p = 0.0372$)."[84]

- S. Chapman et al., *Australia's 1996 Gun Law Reforms: Faster Falls in Firearm Deaths, Firearm Suicides, and a Decade Without Mass Shootings*, 12(6) INJ. PREV.

---

and-destruction-totals; Press Release, The University of Sydney, Australian Shooters Restock Arsenal to pre-Port Arthur Numbers (Jan. 14, 2013), http://sydney.edu.au/news/84.html?newscategoryid=1&newsstoryid=10824; Philip Alpers & Marcus Wilson.

[81] Nick Ralston, *Australia Reloads as Gun Amnesties Fail to Cut Arms*, THE SYDNEY MORNING HERALD (Jan. 14, 2013), http://www.smh.com.au/national/australia-reloads-as-gun-amnesties-fail-to-cut-arms-20130113-2cnnq.html. *See also* AAP, *Aussies Own as Many Guns as Before 1996 Port Arthur Massacre*, THE AUSTRALIAN (Jan. 14, 2013), http://www.theaustralian.com.au/news/aussies-own-as-many-guns-as-before-1996/story-e6frg6n6-1226553311691.

[82] Lisa Davies, *Illegal Guns are Not a Problem, Says Study Author – But Police Disagree*, THE SYDNEY MORNING HERALD (Jan. 15, 2013), http://www.smh.com.au/national/illegal-guns-are-not-a-problem-says-study-author--but-police-disagree-20130114-2cpt6.html.

[83] Philip Alpers, *The Big Melt: How One Democracy Changed After Scrapping a Third of its Firearms* (Conference Paper for the Summit on Reducing Gun Violence in America: Informing Policy with Evidence and Analysis, Johns Hopkins Bloomberg School of Public Health, Jan. 15, 2013), http://www.gunpolicy.org/firearms/region/cp/australia.

[84] J. Ozanne-Smith et al., *Firearm Related Deaths: The Impact of Regulatory Reform*, 10(5) INJ. PREV. 280 (2004), http://injuryprevention.bmj.com/content/10/5/280.full.

365 (2006). This paper states that "[i]n the 18 years before the gun law reforms, there were 13 mass shootings in Australia, and none in the 10.5 years afterwards." [85]

- Jeanine Baker & Samara McPhedran, *Gun Laws and Sudden Death: Did the Australian Firearms Legislation of 1996 Make a Difference?*, BR. J. CRIMINOLOGY (2006). The authors commented that the stricter gun laws introduced post-1996 in Australia did not affect firearms homicide rates and may also not have impacted gun suicide and accidental shooting death rates. They concluded that "[t]here is insufficient evidence to support the simple premise that reducing the stockpile of licitly held civilian firearms will result in a reduction in either firearm or overall sudden death rates."[86]

- Christine Neill & Andrew Leigh, *Weak Tests and Strong Conclusions: A Re-Analysis of Gun Deaths and the Australian Firearms Buyback* (Australian National University Center for Economic Policy Discussion Paper No. 555, June 2007). This paper revisits the Baker and McPhedran study above as well as examining the approaches in the Ozanne-Smith and Chapman studies. The authors state that their re-analysis of the data, either by using a longer time series or the log of the death rate, "shows a statistically significant reduction in deaths due to both firearm homicides and suicides." [87]

- Wang-Sheng Lee & Sandy Suardi, *The Australian Firearms Buyback and Its Effect on Gun Deaths* (Melbourne Institute of Applied Economic and Social Research Working Paper No. 17/08, Aug. 2008). This paper also reanalyzes data on firearms deaths that was used in previous research, using figures spanning the period from 1915 to 2004.[88] The authors used "an alternative time-series approach based on unknown structural breaks" in analyzing the data to determine the impact of the National Firearms Agreement on homicide and suicide.[89] They conclude that "[u]sing a battery of structural break tests, there is little evidence to suggest that [the NFA] had any significant effects on firearm homicides and suicides. In addition, there also does not appear to be any substitution effects – that reduced access to firearms may have led those bent on committing homicide or suicide to use

---

[85] S. Chapman et al., *Australia's 1996 Gun Law reforms: Faster Falls in Firearm Deaths, Firearm Suicides, and a Decade Without Mass Shootings*, 12(6) INJ. PREV. 365 (2006), http://injuryprevention.bmj.com/content/12/6/365.full; original article also *available at* http://tobacco.health.usyd.edu.au/assets/pdfs/Other-Research/2006InjuryPrevent.pdf.

[86] Jeanine Baker & Samara McPhedran, *Gun Laws and Sudden Death: Did the Australian Firearms Legislation of 1996 Make a Difference?*, BR. J. CRIMINOL. (2006), *available at* http://armsandthelaw.com/archives/GunLawsSudden%20DeathBJC.pdf.

[87] Christine Neill & Andrew Leigh, *Weak Tests and Strong Conclusions: A Re-Analysis of Gun Deaths and the Australian Firearms Buyback* 12 (Australian National University Centre for Economic Policy Discussion Paper No. 555, June 2007), https://digitalcollections.anu.edu.au/bitstream/1885/45285/3/DP555.pdf.

[88] Wang-Sheng Lee and Sandy Suardi, *The Australian Firearms Buyback and Its Effect on Gun Deaths*, at 6 (Melbourne Institute of Applied Economic and Social Research Working Paper No. 17/08, Aug. 2008), http://www.melbourneinstitute.com/downloads/working_paper_series/wp2008n17.pdf. This was the same data used in the Neill and Leigh study of 2007.

[89] *Id.* at 3.

alternative methods."[90]   Finally, the authors state that "[a]lthough gun buybacks appear to be a logical and sensible policy that helps to placate the public's fears, the evidence so far suggests that in the Australian context, the high expenditure incurred to fund the 1996 gun buyback has not translated into any tangible reductions in terms of firearm deaths."[91]

In a more recent study by the authors of the 2007 discussion paper listed above, the distinctions between the Australian firearm buybacks and those in other countries were noted, including differences in scale, the fact that the policy was applied nationwide and was accompanied by a ban on particular weapons, differences in geography (i.e., the lack of land borders), and the absence of firearms manufacturing in Australia.[92]   The paper examined the gun buyback and gun death data both across states and over time, and considered a number of variables and trends, in order to answer the question of "whether firearm deaths dropped proportionately more in states where relatively more firearms were bought back."[93]   The paper includes the following information and analysis:

- Nationally, firearm suicides dropped from a rate of 2.2 per 100,000 people in 1995 to 0.8 in 2006. Firearm homicides also dropped, from 0.37 per 100,000 people in 1995 to 0.15 in 2006. These figures show "drops of 65% and 59%, respectively, and among a population of 20 million individuals, represent a decline in the number of deaths by firearm suicide of about 300 and in the number of deaths by firearm homicide of about 40 per year. At the same time, the non-firearm suicide rate has fallen by 27% and the non-firearm homicide rate by 59%."[94]

- The authors found that "[t]he effect of the buyback on firearm suicides is clear. Withdrawing 3,500 guns per 100,000 individuals (approximately the rate of withdrawal due to the NFA) is estimated to reduce firearm suicides by 1.9 per 100,000. This represents a 74% decline from the 1990–95 average of 2.55, or 376 fewer deaths per year given Australia's population of around 20 million."[95]

- The authors further stated that "[t]he estimates show very consistently a marked relative decline in firearm suicides in states with higher buyback rates after 1997," while the "estimates on firearm homicides are less consistent, likely because of the greater volatility in firearm homicides."[96]   In addition, "the estimates show no

---

[90] *Id.* at 23.

[91] *Id.* at 23–24.

[92] Leigh & Neill, *supra* note 45, at 510–11 (2010). Full results of aspects of this study are also contained in Andrew Leigh & Christine Neill, *Do Gun Buybacks Save Lives? Evidence from Panel Data* (IZA [Institute for Study of Labor] Discussion Paper No. 4995, June 2010), http://ftp.iza.org/dp4995.pdf.

[93] Leigh & Neill, *supra* note 45, at 524.

[94] *Id.* at 518.

[95] *Id.* at 532–33.

[96] *Id.* at 535.

evidence that higher buyback rates were associated with any statistically significant difference in non-firearm homicide or suicide rates."[97]

- The authors concluded that "key studies based on time series data have agreed that there has been a significant fall in the number of firearm suicides in Australia since 1997" and that "[f]irearm homicides also appear to have declined substantially, though with a smaller number of deaths per year, it is more difficult to be sure that this change was related to the NFA."[98] At a minimum, they said, "there is some time series evidence against the notion that stricter gun laws have led to increases in total homicides."[99]

- The authors also concluded that "[t]here is evidence that states with relatively high firearm ownership and therefore high gun buyback rates also had relatively weak regulation prior to 1996. Then, our estimates need to be interpreted as reflecting a combination of both the removal of firearms and the relative strengthening of legislation and enforcement. We might expect to see smaller effects in the case of a buyback that was not accompanied by stricter firearm legislation."[100]

VI. Recent Discussions and Actions

Discussions about Australia's gun laws have continued in 2012, including in response to some of the above reports and findings and following various incidents involving firearms.[101]

In June 2012, federal, state, and territory governments reached an agreement on major reforms relating to combating the illicit firearms market.[102] The agreed measures include

- a federal offense of aggravated firearms trafficking across national and state borders that would carry a maximum penalty of life imprisonment;

- the national rollout of the Australian Ballistics Identification Network, currently used by the Australian Federal Police and New South Wales Police;

- the establishment of a National Firearms Register;[103]

---

[97] *Id.* at 538.

[98] *Id.* at 551.

[99] *Id.*

[100] *Id.* at 544.

[101] *See, e.g.,* Samantha Lee, *Why Do We Need Any More Semi-Automatic Pistols in Australia,* THE SYDNEY MORNING HERALD (Apr. 18, 2012), http://www.smh.com.au/opinion/society-and-culture/why-do-we-need-any-more-semiautomatic-pistols-in-australia-20120417-1x5jh.html.

[102] Press Release, Hon. Jason Clare MP, Major Agreement to Tackle the Illegal Firearms Market (June 29, 2012), http://www.ministerhomeaffairs.gov.au/Mediareleases/Pages/2012/Second%20Quarter/29-June-2012---Major-agreement-to-tackle-the-illegal-firearms-market.aspx. The agreement particularly responds to the recommendations contained in the AIC report on firearms trafficking and serious and organized crime. BRICKNELL, *supra* note 7.

[103] *See* Fran Milloy, *New Registry to Keep Track of 'Lost' Guns,* THE SYDNEY MORNING HERALD (July 4, 2012), http://www.smh.com.au/it-pro/government-it/new-registry-to-keep-track-of-lost-guns-20120704-21gn4.html.

- expansion of the ACC's firearms tracing capability;

- an assessment of vulnerabilities around the national air stream, including the international mail environment, to be jointly conducted by the ACC, Australian Federal Police, Customs, and NSW Police;

- the development of a "coordinated national operational response to crimes involving firearms including targeted enforcement of high risk groups and improving firearms technical skills capabilities."[104] This will include seeking assistance from the United States Bureau of Alcohol, Tobacco and Firearms to provide training on the latest developments in firearms and technical advice; and

- a national campaign to raise community awareness about unlicensed firearms.

The federal Minister for Home Affairs and Minister of Justice also proposed additional reforms for further consideration by the states and territories.[105] Prior to the agreement, in April 2012, the federal government established a Firearm Intelligence Targeting Team inside Customs and Border Protection to "fuse together all available intelligence from law enforcement agencies and target criminal key groups at the border."[106]

On November 28, 2012, the Crimes Legislation Amendment (Organised Crime and Other Measures) Bill 2012 was introduced in the federal Parliament.[107] This bill contains provisions arising from the first agreed measure listed above.[108]

The 1996 agreement to establish a "nationwide firearms registration system" led to the implementation of the National Firearms and Licensing Registration System. This system is currently run by CrimTrac, an entity established in 2000 to share information between the nine policing agencies. However, the current system involves "more than 30 different databases dealing with various aspects of firearms registration around the nation." *Id.* The new measures agreed in 2012 to address firearms trafficking include reducing the number of databases to three: an "Interpol-compliant National Firearms Identification Database (NFID), a 'cradle-to-the-grave' new National Firearms Registry and a national ballistic identification network capable of linking fired cartridge cases from a crime scene to the firearm used." *Id.* The new system will apparently be based on the Firearms Reference Table developed by the Royal Canadian Mounted Police, which has also been adopted by Interpol.

[104] Press Release, Hon. Jason Clare MP, *supra* note 102.

[105] *Id.*

[106] *Id. See also* Press Release, Hon. Jason Clare MP, Update on National Illicit Firearms Assessment and Establishment of Firearms Intelligence and Targeting Team (Apr. 12, 2012), http://www.ministerhomeaffairs.gov.au/Mediareleases/Pages/2012/Second%20Quarter/12-April-2012--Update-on-National-Illicit-Firearms-Assessment-and-Establishment-of-Firearms-Intelligence-and-Targeting-Team.aspx; AAP, *Government Launches New Gun Intelligence Unit*, THE AUSTRALIAN (Apr. 12, 2012), http://www.theaustralian.com.au/news/breaking-news/government-launches-new-gun-intelligence-unit/story-fn3dxity-1226325158137.

[107] *Crimes Legislation Amendment (Organised Crime and Other Measures) Bill 2012*, PARLIAMENT OF AUSTRALIA, http://www.aph.gov.au/Parliamentary_Business/Bills_Legislation/Bills_Search_Results/Result?bId=r4928. *See also* Press Release, Hon. Jason Clare MP, Tackling the Illegal Firearms Market (Nov. 23, 2012), http://www.ministerhomeaffairs.gov.au/Mediareleases/Pages/23-November-2012---Tackling-the-illegal-firearms-market.aspx.

[108] Speech, Hon. Jason Clare MP, Crimes Legislation Amendment (Organised Crime and Other Measures) Bill 2012 Second Reading Speech, Nov. 28, 2012, http://www.ministerhomeaffairs.gov.au/Speeches/Pages/2012/Fourth%20Quarter/28November-2012-CrimesLegislationAmendment%28OrganisedCrimeandOtherMeasures%29Bill2012SecondReadingSpeech.aspx.

Other activities relating to gun control laws in the states and territories in 2012 included the following:

- In New South Wales, legislation was enacted in June 2012 to place further restrictions on the sale and purchase of ammunition.[109]

- In December 2012, the New South Wales government announced that it had established a committee to provide advice on proposed new gun control legislation that would tighten restrictions in some areas.[110]

- In South Australia, the state attorney-general announced a gun amnesty campaign in June 2012, which ran from August 1 to October 31, 2012.[111] It was reported that 2,783 weapons were surrendered to authorities during the three-month period.[112]

- In Queensland, the police minister established an advisory panel in August 2012 to examine gun laws and licensing with the aim of reducing red tape for licensed firearms owners,[113] generating a strong negative response from the Queensland Police Union.[114]

- The Queensland government also introduced amending legislation in November 2012 to introduce new mandatory minimum penalties for weapons offenses "in an effort to address the unlawful use of firearms."[115] It also announced a gun amnesty for people

---

[109] *Firearms Amendment (Ammunition Control) Bill 2012*, PARLIAMENT OF NEW SOUTH WALES, http://www.parliament.nsw.gov.au/prod/parlment/nswbills.nsf/0/7D714D724CF1852DCA2579A4001B0B8C?Open &shownotes (last visited Dec. 21, 2012).

[110] AAP, *NSW Govt to Tighten Gun Control*, Herald Sun (Dec. 20, 2012), http://www.heraldsun.com.au/ news/breaking-news/nsw-gun-body-rejected-law-changes-report/story-e6frf7kf-1226540783897.

[111] *Gun Amnesty Campaign 2012*, SOUTH AUSTRALIA ATTORNEY-GENERAL'S DEPARTMENT, http://www. agd.sa.gov.au/about-agd/what-we-do/initiatives/gun-amnesty-campaign-2012 (last visited Dec. 21, 2012).

[112] *Record Haul from SA Gun Amnesty*, ABC NEWS (Nov. 1, 2012), http://www.abc.net.au/news/2012-11-01/record-haul-from-sa-gun-amnesty/4346204.

[113] Press Release, Hon. Jack Dempsey, Panel Created to Cut Weapons Red Tape (Aug. 27, 2012), http://statements.qld.gov.au/Statement/Id/80312.

[114] Rosanne Barrett, *Queensland Gun Lobby Takes Aim at Red-Tape Hold-Up*, THE AUSTRALIAN (Aug. 28, 2012), http://www.theaustralian.com.au/national-affairs/state-politics/gun-lobby-takes-aim-at-red-tape-hold-up/story -e6frgczx-1226459405120; Daniel Hurst, *'More People Will Die': Police Union Berates Gun Law Overhaul*, BRISBANE TIMES (Aug. 27, 2012), http://www.brisbanetimes.com.au/queensland/more-people-will-die-police-union-berates-gun-law-overhaul-20120827-24vdz.html.

[115] *Weapons and Other Legislation Amendment Act 2012*, QUEENSLAND POLICE, http://www.police.qld.gov.au/programs/weaponsLicensing/about/legislation/weaponsamendments2012.htm (last visited Dec. 21, 2012).

to either hand in or register their firearms.[116]   The bill was passed in December 2012.[117]

Prepared by Kelly Buchanan
Chief, Foreign, Comparative, and
International Law Division I

---

[116] *See* AAP, *Qld Government to Call Three-Month Gun Amnesty*, COURIER MAIL (Nov. 1, 2012), http://www.couriermail.com.au/news/breaking-news/qld-govt-to-call-three-month-gun-amnesty/story-e6freono-1226508282676.

[117] *Bills This Parliament*, QUEENSLAND PARLIAMENT, http://www.parliament.qld.gov.au/work-of-assembly/bills-and-legislation/current-bills-register (last visited Dec. 21, 2012).

Appendix: Current State and Territory Firearms Legislation in Australia

New South Wales

- Firearms Act 1996 (NSW)
- Firearms Regulation 2006 (NSW)
- Weapons Prohibition Act 1998 (NSW)
- Weapons Prohibition Regulation 2009 (NSW)

Victoria

- Firearms Act 1996 (Vic)
- Firearms Regulations 2008 (Vic)
- Control of Weapons Act 1990 (Vic)
- Control of Weapons Regulations 2011 (Vic)

Queensland

- Weapons Act 1990 (Qld)
- Weapons Regulations 1996 (Qld)
- Weapons Categories Regulations 1997 (Qld)

Western Australia

- Firearms Act 1973 (WA)
- Firearms Regulations 1974 (WA)

South Australia

- Firearms Act 1977 (SA)
- Firearms Regulations 2008 (SA)

Tasmania

- Firearms Act 1996 (Tas)
- Firearms Regulations 2006 (Tas)

Northern Territory

- Firearms Act (NT)
- Firearms Act Regulations (NT)

Australian Capital Territory

- Firearms Act 1996 (ACT)

- Firearms Regulation 2008 (ACT)
- Prohibited Weapons Act 1996 (ACT)
- Prohibited Weapons Regulation 1997 (ACT)

BRAZIL

FIREARMS-CONTROL LEGISLATION AND POLICY

Summary

In Brazil, the federal government has the power to legislate on issues related to firearms. The handling, trading, or possession of materials for the production of weapons without a license is criminalized. It is also a crime to expose a child or adolescent to firearms. In 2003, a more rigid federal law was enacted to regulate the registration, possession, and sale of firearms and ammunition. This law defines crimes involving firearms and fosters the disarmament of the society.

I. Legal Framework

In Brazil, the production of armaments (*material bélico*) and the arms trade are regulated by the federal government. The Penal Code criminalizes conduct involving, inter alia, the handling of materials for the production of arms devices, while the Statute of the Child and Adolescent punishes those who expose a child or adolescent to a firearm or explosive.

In an attempt to decrease crimes involving firearms, Brazil promulgated Law No. 10,826, the Disarmament Statute (*Estatuto do Desarmamento*), on December 22, 2003. This Law contains more rigid criteria for the control of firearms.

II. Constitutional Principle

Article 21(VI) of the Constitution determines that the federal government (*União*) has the power to authorize and supervise the production and trade of armaments.[1]

III. Penal Code

The Penal Code criminalizes the production, supply, acquisition, possession, or transportation, without a license, of explosive substances or devices, toxic or asphyxiating gas, or material for their production.[2] The punishment for violation of this provision consists of six months to two years of detention[3] and a fine.

---

[1] CONSTITUIÇÃO FEDERAL [C.F.], art. 21(VI), http://www.planalto.gov.br/ccivil_03/Constituicao/Constituicao.htm.

[2] *Id.* art. 253.

[3] Article 33 of the Brazilian Penal Code determines that a detention sentence must be served in a semiopen or open regime, except where there is a need for a transfer to a closed regime. CÓDIGO PENAL [C.P.], Decreto-Lei No. 2.848, de 7 de dezembro de 1940, art. 33, http://www.planalto.gov.br/ccivil_03/Decreto-Lei/Del2848compilado.htm.

IV. Child and Adolescent Statute

In 1990, Brazil enacted the Child and Adolescent Statute through Law No. 8,069 of July 13, which provides for the full protection of the child and the adolescent.[4] For the purposes of the law, a child is considered to be a person less than twelve years of age, while an adolescent is a person between twelve and eighteen years of age.[5] In some exceptional cases foreseen in the statute, it also applies to persons between the ages of eighteen and twenty-one.

In regard to firearms, the statute punishes with imprisonment[6] of three to six years anyone who sells, supplies, or hands firearms, ammunition, or explosives to a child or adolescent.[7]

For criminal purposes, the Brazilian Penal Code dictates that minors under eighteen years of age are not criminally chargeable but are subject to the rules established in special legislation.[8]

V. Disarmament Statute

Law No. 10,826 of December 22, 2003, the Disarmament Statute, regulates the registration, possession, and sale of firearms and ammunition; determines the responsibilities of the National Arms System; and defines crimes that involve the unauthorized possession, carrying, trade, and international trafficking of firearms.[9]

This Law revoked and replaced Law No. 9,437 of February 20, 1997, which had created the National Arms System (Sistema Nacional de Armas—SINARM), established the conditions for the registration and possession of firearms, and defined crimes involving firearms.

A. National Arms System

Pursuant to article 1 of Law No. 10,826, SINARM was established under the Ministry of Justice and subordinated to the Federal Police. Its jurisdiction extends over the whole country.[10]

Article 2 of Law No. 10,826 confers SINARM with the authority

(I)   to identify the characteristics and proprieties of firearms in the process of registering them;

---

[4] ESTATUTO DA CRIANÇA E DO ADOLESCENTE [E.C.A.], Lei No. 8.069 de 13 de Julho de 1990, art. 1, http://www.planalto.gov.br/ccivil_03/Leis/L8069.htm.

[5] *Id.* art. 2.

[6] A sentence of imprisonment (*reclusão*) must be served in a closed, semiopen, or open regime. *Id.* art. 33.

[7] E.C.A. art. 242.

[8] C.P. art. 27.

[9] Lei No. 10.826, de 22 de dezembro de 2003, art. 1, http://www.planalto.gov.br/ccivil_03/Leis/2003/L10.826compilado.htm.

[10] *Id.* art. 1.

(II)   to register all firearms manufactured, imported, and sold in the country;

(III)   to register all authorizations to carry firearms and renewals issued by the Federal Police;

(IV)   to register transfers of property, loss, theft, robbery, and other events likely to change the registration data, including those resulting from closure of companies involved in private security and transportation of valuables;

(V)   to identify modifications that alter the characteristics or performance of a firearm;

(VI)   to incorporate the existing police records into the SINARM register;

(VII)   to register seizures of firearms, including those involving police and court procedures;

(VIII)   to register gunsmiths operating in the country and grant licenses to perform this work;

(IX)   to register authorized producers, wholesalers, retailers, exporters, and importers of firearms, accessories, and ammunition;

(X)   to register the identification of the gun barrel, along with the characteristics of rifling impressions and microgrooves produced when a projectile is fired, according to the required marking and testing performed by the manufacturer;

(XI)   to communicate to the Secretariats of Public Security of the States and of the Federal District the records and authorizations to carry firearms in their respective territories, and to keep the records updated for consultation.

The provisions of article 2 of the Law do not apply to the firearms of the Armed and Auxiliary Forces or to firearms that are already registered with the proper authorities.[11]

B. Registration and Acquisition of a Firearm

Registration of a firearm with the responsible authority is mandatory.[12] Restricted firearms[13] must be registered with the Army Command in accordance with the regulations of the Law.[14]

To acquire a permitted firearm[15] a person must, in addition to stating the actual need for acquiring the firearm, present[16]

---

[11] *Id.* art. 2 (sole para.).

[12] *Id.* art. 3.

[13] Article 11 of Decree No. 5,123 of July 1, 2004, defines restricted firearms as those whose use is exclusively for the armed forces, public security institutions, and qualified individuals and corporations, duly authorized by the Army Command, in accordance with specific legislation. Decreto No. 5.123 de 1 de julho de 2004, https://www.planalto.gov.br/ccivil_03/_Ato2004-2006/2004/Decreto/D5123.htm.

[14] Lei No. 10,826 art. 3 (sole para.). For more information on registration of restricted firearms see article 18 of Decree No. 5,123 of July 1, 2004, https://www.planalto.gov.br/ccivil_03/_Ato2004-2006/2004/Decreto/D5123.htm.

[15] Article 10 of Decree No. 5,123 of July 1, 2004, defines a permitted firearm as one whose use is authorized for individuals as well as corporations, in accordance with the norms of the Army Command and the conditions established in Law No. 10,826 of December 22, 2003. Decreto No. 5.123 de 1 de julho de 2004, art. 10, https://www.planalto.gov.br/ccivil_03/_Ato2004-2006/2004/Decreto/D5123.htm.

(I)   evidence of suitability, through the submission of records that indicate no prior criminal activities provided by Federal, State, Military, and Electoral tribunals and that one has not been subject to police investigation or criminal prosecution, which may be provided by electronic means;

(II)   documentary evidence of lawful occupancy and place of residence;

(III)   evidence of technical capacity and psychological ability to handle firearms, attested in the manner provided for in the regulations of Law No. 10,826.[17]

After all the established requirements are met by the person interested in acquiring a firearm, SINARM will then issue a non-transferable authorization to purchase a firearm in the name of the applicant and for the weapon indicated in the application.[18] Only ammunition corresponding to the caliber of the registered gun may be acquired, and that in the quantity established in the regulations of the Law.[19] It is mandatory for the company selling the firearms to report the sale to the responsible authority and maintain a database containing all the features of the gun being sold, along with copies of the documents mentioned in article 4 of the Law.[20]

A company that sells firearms, accessories, and ammunition is legally responsible for them, and they must be registered as the company's property until they are sold.[21] The trade of firearms, accessories, and ammunition between individuals is only permitted upon authorization by SINARM.[22] The authorization referred to in article 4(§1) of the Law must be granted or denied, with the supporting reasons, within thirty business days from the date of the applicant's request.[23]

The registration certificate of a firearm, which is valid throughout the national territory, authorizes its owner to keep the firearm exclusively inside his residence or domicile, or at his workplace, as long as he is the owner of or legally responsible for the establishment or company.[24] The firearms registration certificate must be issued by the Federal Police and

---

[16] Lei No. 10,826, art. 4.

[17] For more information on evidence of technical capacity and psychological ability for handling firearms, see article 12(§3) of Decree No. 5,123 of July 1, 2004, https://www.planalto.gov.br/ccivil_03/_Ato2004-2006/2004/Decreto/D5123.htm.

[18] Lei No. 10,826, art. 4(§1).

[19] Id. art. 4(§2). Article 21(§2) of Decree No. 5,123 of July 1, 2004, determines that the amount of ammunition and number of accessories that every owner of a firearm may purchase will be determined through an administrative act (Portaria) issued by the Ministry of Defense, after consultation with the Ministry of Justice.

Administrative Act No. 1,811 issued by the Ministry of Defense on December 18, 2006, establishes the maximum annual quantity of permitted ammunition of the same caliber that a citizen can acquire in specialty stores to keep and stock as fifty units. Portaria Normativa No. 1.811, de 18 de dezembro de 2006, art. 1, https://www.defesa.gov.br/sistemas/bdlegis/dados_norma.php?numero=1811&ano=2006&serie=A.

[20] Lei No. 10,826, art. 4(§3).

[21] Id. art. 4(§4).

[22] Id. art. 4(§5).

[23] Id. art. 4(§6).

[24] Id. art. 5.

preceded by an authorization issued by SINARM.[25] A firearm registration certificate must be renewed every three years, renewal being contingent upon satisfying the requirements enumerated in sections I, II and III of article 4 of the Law.[26]

C. The Carrying of Firearms

The carrying of firearms is prohibited throughout the national territory, except in the cases provided for in specific legislation[27] and with regard to

(I)   members of the Armed Forces;

(II)   members of the bodies listed at the beginning of article 144 of the Federal Constitution;[28]

(III)   members of the municipal guard of the capitals of states and municipalities with more than 500,000 people, under the conditions established in the regulation of Law No. 10,826;

(IV)   members of the municipal guard of municipalities with more than 50,000 and less than 500,000 people, while in service;

(V)   agents of the Brazilian Intelligence Agency and agents of the Department of Homeland Security Office of the Institutional Security of the Presidency;

(VI)   members of law enforcement agencies referred to in articles 51(IV) and 52(XIII) of the Federal Constitution;

(VII)   members of the permanent staff of officers and prison guards, prison escort guards, and port guards;

(VIII) companies involved in private security and transportation of valuables as established in Law No. 10,826;

(IX)   members of legally constituted bodies of sport, whose sports demand the use of firearms, according to the regulation of Law No. 10,826, observing, as applicable, environmental laws;

(X)   career members of the Federal Internal Revenue Audit Office (Auditoria da Receita Federal do Brasil) and Audit Labor Office (Auditoria-Fiscal do Trabalho) and Tax Auditors (Auditor-Fiscal) and Tax Analysts (Analista Tributário);

(XI)   tribunals of the judiciary branch as described in article 92 of the Federal Constitution and the Public Prosecutor's Office of the Union (Ministério Público da União) and the Public Prosecutor's Office of the States (Ministério Público Estadual), for the exclusive use of its personnel that are effectively exercising security functions, in the form of regulation to be issued by the National Council

---

[25] *Id.* art. 5(§1).

[26] *Id.* art. 5(§2).

[27] *Id.* art. 6.

[28] Article 144 of the Constitution determines that public security is a duty of the State and the right and responsibility of all persons. It is exercised for the preservation of public order and the security of persons and property, through the federal police, federal highway police, federal railway police, civil police, military police, and military fire brigades. C.F. art. 144.

of Justice (Conselho Nacional de Justiça—CNJ) and the National Council of the Public Prosecutor's Office (Conselho Nacional do Ministério Público—CNMP).

The persons mentioned in items I, II, III, V, and VI of article 6 of Law No. 10,826 are entitled to carry firearms, be they privately owned or provided by their corporation or institution, even off duty, in accordance with the regulation of Law No. 10,826. The authorization is valid nationwide to those persons listed in items I, II, V, and VI of the Law.[29]

Residents in rural areas who are twenty-five years old and prove that they depend on the use of firearms to provide food subsistence for their families may be authorized by the Federal Police to carry a permitted firearm. The authorization is issued in the category of subsistence hunter for a singe-shot firearm of permitted use, with one or two barrels, a smooth bore, and a caliber equal to or lower than sixteen.[30]

A subsistence hunter who makes another use of the firearm, regardless of other criminal violations, will be charged, as appropriate, for illegal possession of a firearm or illegal shooting of a permitted firearm.[31]

In exceptional cases, upon authorization by SINARM, the Federal Police may grant a temporary and territorially limited authorization to carry a permitted firearm provided that the applicant demonstrates it is needed for the effective exercise of a professional activity involving a risk or threat to the applicant's physical integrity, meets the requirements of article 4 of Law Na. 10,826, and presents documentation proving ownership of a firearm and its registration with the appropriate authority.[32]

The authorization to carry a firearm provided for in article 6 of the Law is automatically revoked if the authorized person is detained while intoxicated or under the influence of chemical substances or hallucinogens.[33]

D. Regularization Fees

Article 11 of Law No. 10,826 lists the services that are subject to a fee, in the amounts listed in the Annex of the Law, relating to

(I)   registration of firearms;

(II)   renewal of registration certificate of a firearm;

(III)   issuance of a duplicate registration certificate of a firearm;

(IV)   issuance of a federal authorization to carry a firearm;

---

[29] Lei No. 10.826, de 22 de dezembro de 2003, art. 6(§1).

[30] *Id.* art. 6(§5).

[31] *Id.* art. 6(§6).

[32] *Id.* art. 10.

[33] *Id.* art. 10(§2).

(V)   renewal of an authorization to carry a firearm;

(VI)   issuance of a duplicate authorization to carry a firearm.[34]

E. Criminalization

For a person to own or possess permitted firearms, accessories, or ammunition in violation of the law or regulation, within his or her residence or a part adjacent to it, or at his or her workplace, when he or she is the owner or the one responsible for the company, is considered a crime and punishable with detention of one to three years and a fine.[35]

The failure of the owner or possessor of a firearm to observe the precautions necessary to prevent a person who is under eighteen years of age or mentally disabled from getting hold of the firearm is punishable with detention of one to two years and a fine.[36] The same penalties are applicable to the owner or director of a company involved in private security and transportation of valuables who fails to register a police report and notify the Federal Police of the mislaying, theft or loss of firearms, accessories, or ammunition that are under the company's custody, within the first twenty-four hours after the fact.[37]

The carrying, holding, acquiring, supplying, receiving, keeping in deposit, transporting, giving away, lending, sending, having custody of, or concealing of permitted firearms, accessories, or ammunition without authorization and in violation of a law or regulation is punishable with imprisonment of two to four years and a fine.[38] The posting of bail for such offense is not permitted, except if the firearm is registered in the name of the offending person.[39]

Whoever shoots a firearm or triggers ammunition in an inhabited place or its vicinity, in the street, or towards the street without intent to perpetrate another crime is also subject to imprisonment for two to four years and a fine.[40] The posting of bail for such offense is not permitted.[41]

The owning, carrying, holding, acquiring, supplying, receiving, keeping in deposit, transporting, giving away, lending, sending, having custody of, or concealing prohibited or restricted firearms, accessories, or ammunition, without authorization and in violation of a law or regulation, is punishable with imprisonment of three to six years and a fine.[42]

---

[34] *Id.* art. 11.

[35] *Id.* art. 12.

[36] *Id.* art. 13.

[37] *Id.* art. 13 (sole para.).

[38] *Id.* art. 14.

[39] *Id.* art. 14 (sole para.).

[40] *Id.* art. 15.

[41] *Id.* art. 15 (sole para.).

[42] *Id.* art. 16.

The same penalties are applicable to a person who

(I)   suppresses or changes the characteristic marking, number, or any identification signal of a firearm or device;

(II)   modifies the characteristics of a firearm in order to make it equivalent to a prohibited or restricted firearm for the purpose of hindering or otherwise misleading police, experts, or judges;

(III)   owns, manufactures, or uses explosive or incendiary devices, without authorization or in violation of a law or regulation;

(IV)   carries, possesses, purchases, transports, or delivers a firearm which has had its number, marking, or other identifying signal scraped, deleted, or tampered with;

(V)   sells, delivers, or supplies, even gratuitously, firearms, accessories, ammunition, or explosives to a child or adolescent; and

(VI)   produces, recharges, or recycles, without legal authorization, or tampers in any way with ammunition or explosives.[43]

The acquiring, leasing, receiving, transporting, carrying, concealing, keeping in deposit, disassembling, assembling, reassembling, tampering with, selling, displaying for sale, or otherwise using of firearms, accessories, or ammunition, for one's own benefit or the benefit of a third party, in the course of trade or industrial activity, without authorization or in violation of a law or regulation, is punishable with four to eight years of imprisonment and a fine.[44]

For the purposes of article 17 of Law No. 10,826, any form of service, manufacture, or irregular or clandestine trade, including that practiced in one's residence, is considered commercial or industrial activity.[45]

Importing, exporting, or promoting the entry or exit of firearms, accessories or ammunition into or out of the national territory, without authorization of the responsible authority, is punishable with four to eight years of imprisonment and a fine.[46]

For the crimes set forth in articles 17 and 18 of Law No. 10,826, the penalty is increased by half for prohibited or restricted firearms or accessories.[47]

For the crimes set forth in articles 14, 15, 16, 17, and 18 of the Law, the penalty is increased by half if they are committed by a member of the bodies or companies referred to in articles 6, 7, and 8 of the Law.[48]

---

[43] *Id.* art. 16 (sole para.).

[44] *Id.* art. 17.

[45] *Id.* art. 17 (sole para.).

[46] *Id.* art. 18.

[47] *Id.* art. 19.

[48] *Id.* art. 20.

Parole (*liberdade provisória*) is not granted for the crimes set forth in articles 16, 17, and 18 of the Law.[49]

F. Restricted and Permitted Firearms

Decree No. 3,665 of November 20, 2000, defines restricted and permitted firearms, ammunition, and equipment.[50]

According to article 16, the following are subject to restricted use:[51]

(I)   weapons, ammunition, equipment, and accessories that have some of the characteristics of the armaments used by the national armed forces with respect to their tactical, strategic, and technical use;

(II)   weapons, ammunition, accessories, and equipment that are not identical or similar to the armaments used by the national armed forces but have characteristics that make them suitable only for military or law-enforcement use;

(III)   short firearms, the common ammunition for which has, on exiting the barrel, an energy higher than three hundred foot-pounds or four hundred seven Joules—ammunition such as the .357 Magnum, 9 Luger, .38 Super Auto, .40 S&W, .44 SPL, .44 Magnum, .45 Colt and .45 Auto;

(IV)   long striped firearms, the common ammunition for which has, on exiting the barrel, an energy higher than one thousand foot-pounds or one thousand three hundred fifty-five Joules—ammunition such as the .22-250, .223 Remington, .243 Winchester, .270 Winchester, 7 Mauser, .30-06, .308 Winchester, 7.62 x 39, .357 Magnum, .375 Winchester and .44 Magnum;

(V)   automatic firearms of any caliber;

(VI)   smooth bore firearms with a caliber of twelve or higher and with a barrel length shorter than twenty-four inches or six hundred and ten millimeters;

(VII)   smooth bore firearms with a caliber higher than twelve, and their ammunition;

(VIII) air guns operated by compressed gas or spring action, with a caliber higher than six millimeters, which shoot projectiles of any kind;

(IX)   disguised firearms, which are characterized as devices that look like harmless objects but hide a weapon, such as a pistol-cane, revolver-pen, and the like;

(X)   a compressed air gun imitating an Fz 7.62 mm, M964, FAL;

(XI)   weapons and devices that launch chemical warfare agents or aggressive gas, and their ammunition;

(XII)   devices that are accessories of weapons and are designed to impede locating the gun, such as silencers, flash suppressors, and others, which serve to muffle the

---

[49] *Id.* art. 21.

[50] Decreto No. 3.665, de 20 de Novembro de 2000, art. 15, http://www.planalto.gov.br/ccivil_03/decreto/D3665.htm.

[51] *Id.* art. 16.

explosion or the flash of the shot, as well as devices that modify the conditions of use, such as nozzles, grenade launchers, and others;

(XIII)   ammunition or pyrotechnic devices or similar devices that can cause fires or explosions;

(XIV)   ammunition with projectiles that contain aggressive chemical elements whose effects on the person hit greatly increase the damage, such as explosive or poisonous projectiles;

(XV)   swords and rapiers used by the Armed Forces and Auxiliary Forces;

(XVI)   night vision equipment, such as goggles, periscopes, telescopes, etc.;

(XVII)   optical aiming devices with magnification equal to or greater than six times or a lens diameter that is equal to or greater than thirty-six millimeters;

(XVIII) aiming devices that use light or other means to mark the target;

(XIX)   ballistic armor for restricted ammunition;

(XX)   ballistic equipment for protection against restricted portable firearms, such as vests, shields, helmets, etc.; and

(XXI)   armored vehicles for civilian or military use.

Article 17 of Decree No. 3,665 defines permitted firearms, ammunition, and equipment as[52]

(I)   short, repeating, or semiautomatic firearms, the common ammunition for which has, on exiting the barrel, an energy of up to three hundred foot-pounds or four hundred seven Joules—ammunition such as the .22 LR, .25 Auto, .32 Auto, .32 S&W, .38 SPL and .380 Auto;

(II)   long striped, repeating, or semiautomatic firearms, the common ammunition for which has, on exiting the barrel, a maximum energy of one thousand pounds or one thousand three hundred fifty-five Joules—ammunition such as the .22 LR, .32-20, .38-40 and .44-40;

(III)   smooth bore, repeating, or semiautomatic firearms with a caliber of twelve or lower and with a barrel length equal to or greater than twenty-four inches or six hundred ten millimeters; firearms with a smaller caliber, with any barrel length; and their permitted ammunition.

(IV)   air guns operated by compressed gas or spring action, with a caliber equal to or less than six millimeters, and their permitted ammunition;

(V)   weapons whose purpose is to start sports competitions and that exclusively use cartridges containing gunpowder;

(VI)   weapons for industrial use or that use anesthetic projectiles for veterinary purposes;

(VII)   optical aiming devices with a magnification of less than six times or lens diameter less than thirty-six millimeters;

---

[52] *Id.* art. 17.

(VIII)   cartridges that are empty, or semi- or fully loaded with lead granules, known as "hunting cartridges," to be used by smooth bore firearms of permitted caliber;

(IX)   ballistic armor for permitted ammunition;

(X)   ballistic equipment for protection against permitted firearms, such as vests, shields, helmets, etc.; and

(XI)   armored passenger vehicles.

G. General Provisions

The manufacture, sale, trade, and importation of toys, replicas, and imitation firearms that could be confused for real firearms are prohibited.[53]   Exceptions to the ban apply to the acquisition of replicas and imitations intended for instruction, training, or collection by authorized users under the conditions established by the Army Command.[54]

Persons under twenty-five years of age are prohibited from acquiring firearms, except members of the entities listed in items I, II, III, V, VI, VII, and X of article 6 of Law No. 10.826.[55]

Possessors and owners of firearms acquired regularly may at any time turn them in to the Federal Police, in return for a receipt and indemnity, according to the regulations of the Law.[56]

With regard to the irregular possession of the firearms, possessors and owners of such firearms may turn them in voluntarily in return for a receipt and, assuming good faith, they will be compensated in the manner established in the regulations of the Law and absolved from punishment.[57]

A fine of R$100.000,00 (US$50,000.00) to R$300.000,00 (US$150,000.00) is imposed, according to the regulations of Law No. 10,826, on

(I)   an airline, road, rail, sea, river or lake transportation company that deliberately, by any means, makes, promotes, facilitates, or enables the transport of arms or ammunition without proper authorization or in violation of safety standards;

---

[53] Lei No. 10.826, de 22 de dezembro de 2003, art. 26.

[54] *Id.* art. 26 (sole para.).

[55] *Id.* art. 28.

[56] *Id.* art. 31. Article 70 of Decree No. 5,123 of July 1, 2004, determines that firearms, accessories, and ammunition, as mentioned in articles 31 and 32 of Law No. 10.826 of December 22, 2003, must be turned in to the Federal Police or to organs or entities accredited by the Ministry of Justice. Administrative Act (*Portaria*) No. 797, issued by the Ministry of Justice on May 5, 2011, establishes the procedures for turning in firearms, accessories, or ammunition and the indemnification provided for in articles 31 and 32 of Law No. 10,826, of December 22, 2003. Annex I of the Administrative Act defines the indemnification amounts, which range from R$100,00 (US$50.00) to R$300,00 (US$150.00), depending on the type of firearm. Portaria No. 797 de 5 de maio de 2001, POLÍCIA FEDERAL, http://www.dpf.gov.br/servicos/armas/anexos/portaria-797-2011-mj.

[57] Lei No. 10.826, de 22 de dezembro de 2003, art. 32.

(II)   a company producing firearms or in the firearms business that advertises their sale, encouraging their indiscriminate use, except in specialized publications.[58]

Promoters of indoor events with more than one thousand people must adopt, under risk of liability, the necessary measures to prevent the entry of armed persons, except in those events guaranteed by section VI of article 5 of the Federal Constitution.[59]

Companies that provide international and interstate transportation service must take the necessary measures to prevent armed passengers from boarding.[60]

H. Referendum on Firearms and Ammunition Trade

Article 35 of the Disarmament Statute prohibited the trade of firearms and ammunition throughout the national territory, except for the entities referred to in article 6 of the Law,[61] provided that this provision was approved by a popular referendum to be conducted in 2005.[62]

On October 23, 2005, a referendum on prohibiting the trade of firearms and ammunition throughout the national territory was held, and the proposal was rejected by 63.94% of the voters.[63]

VI. Disarmament Campaign

To further encourage the disarmament of the population, the government has promoted disarmament campaigns under the authority of Decree No. 5,123 of July 1, 2004, which charges the Ministry of Justice with the responsibility for establishing the procedures necessary to carry out disarmament campaigns and designates the Federal Police as the organ in charge of the regularization of firearms.[64]

To this effect, the government also maintains a website that explains the National Disarmament Campaign. According to the website,

---

[58] *Id.* art. 33.

[59] *Id.* art. 34. Article 5(VI) of the Constitution determines that everyone is equal before the law, with no distinction whatsoever, guaranteeing to Brazilians and foreigners residing in the Country the inviolability of the rights to life, liberty, equality, security, and property. Freedom of conscience and belief are also inviolable, free exercise of religious beliefs is assured, and protection of places of worship and their rites is guaranteed under the law.

[60] *Id.* art. 34 (sole para.).

[61] *Id.* art. 35.

[62] *Id.* art. 35(§1). Article 14(II) of the Constitution determines that popular sovereignty must be exercised by universal suffrage, and by direct and secret vote, with equal value for all, and, as provided by law, by referendum.

[63] *Referendo—proibição do comércio de armas de fogo e munição—23 de outubro de 2005*, TRIBUNAL SUPERIOR ELEITORAL, http://www.tse.jus.br/eleitor/glossario/termos/referendo.

[64] Decreto No. 5.123 de 1 de julho de 2004, art. 70-G, https://www.planalto.gov.br/ccivil_03/_Ato2004-2006/2004/Decreto/D5123.htm.

[t]he National Disarmament Campaign seeks to mobilize the Brazilian society to withdraw the largest possible number of firearms from circulation. The voluntary surrender of weapons by citizens is provided for in the Disarmament Statute and can be carried out at more than 2,000 collection points throughout Brazil. Beyond the collection of firearms, the campaign aims to raise awareness of the risks of having a firearm. Through the slogan "Protect Your Family. Disarm Yourself.", the campaign makes an emotional appeal, with statements based on real cases of parents who lost children in accidents or fights; ordinary situations that, with a gun, can become fatal.

Studies such as the Map of Violence, released in February 2012 by the Ministry of Justice, show a decrease in violence and a drop in homicide rates during the period of previous campaigns. Therefore, the measure has proven to be effective and fulfills the determination of the Disarmament Statute.[65]

VII. Study on the Impact of the Disarmament Statute

In March 2012, the Applied Economic Research Institute (Instituto de Pesquisa Econômica Aplicada, IPEA)[66] published a study, *Menos Armas, Menos Crimes* (*Fewer Arms, Fewer Crimes*),[67] regarding the relationship between firearms and criminality.[68]

The study begins by observing that after an increase in the occurrence of violent crimes in the United States in the second half of the 1980s, the debate regarding the role of firearms intensified. Many articles have been published asserting that more firearms results in more crime. Others argue that more firearms lead to less crime. Despite the profusion of such articles, for various reasons, including methodology, a consensus has yet to be reached on the causal effect of firearms on increased criminality.[69]

The analysis developed in the IPEA study uses information from all 645 municipalities of the state of São Paulo[70] between the years 2001 and 2007, a period in which there was a 60.1%

---

[65] *Conheça a Campanha*, CAMPANHA NACIONAL DO DESARMAMENTO, http://www.entreguesuaarma.gov.br/desarmamento/categoria/conheca-a-campanha-2012/ (last visited Jan. 30, 2013).

[66] The Institute of Applied Economic Research (IPEA) is a federal public foundation under the Secretariat of Strategic Affairs of the Presidency of the Republic. Its research activities provide technical and institutional support to government actions for the formulation and reformulation of policies and development programs. *O Ipea – Quem Somos*, IPEA, http://www.ipea.gov.br/portal/index.php?option=com_content&view=article&id=1226&Itemid=68 (last visited Jan. 30, 2013).

[67] DANIEL RICARDO DE CASTRO CERQUEIRA & JOÃO MANOEL PINHO DE MELLO, MENOS ARMAS, MENOS CRIMES (IPEA, Mar. 2012), http://www.ipea.gov.br/portal/images/stories/PDFs/TDs/td_1721.pdf.

[68] According to the IPEA, the purpose of the publication is the dissemination of results of studies directly or indirectly developed by the IPEA, which, because of its importance, provides specialized professionals with information and creates a space for debate. The opinions expressed in the publication are the sole and entire responsibility of the author(s), and do not necessarily express the views of the IPEA or the Secretariat of Strategic Affairs of the Presidency of the Republic. *Id.* at 2.

[69] *Id.* at 7.

[70] São Paulo is one of the twenty-seven states of Brazil and is located in the southern region of the southeast part of the country. It occupies an area of approximately 248,808.80 square kilometers (approximately 96,065.54 square miles), being slightly larger than the United Kingdom. São Paulo has the largest population of Brazil with

reduction in the number of homicides in these cities, making the state of São Paulo (alongside New York and Bogotá) one of the most successful international examples of cities showing a decrease in violent crime over a relatively short period of time.[71]

An opportunity to identify the desired causal effect of firearms on crime appeared when the Disarmament Statute was enacted in 2003, which substantially restricted the ability of a citizen to have access to firearms, increased the cost of acquiring and registering a firearm, and substantially increased the expected cost for an individual to travel on public roads carrying a firearm in an irregular situation.[72]

Based on the method developed in the study, two hypotheses were tested. The first was whether the availability of guns increases violent crimes, and the second, whether the availability of guns reduces crime against property. For this purpose, data from the Mortality Information System of the Ministry of Health and from the State Secretariat of Public Safety of the State of São Paulo were used. The following incidents were analyzed: intentional homicide, death by aggression, death by firearm, aggravated assault, robbery (*latrocínio*), car theft, and offenses involving illicit drugs.[73]

The data when analyzed revealed that, during the period under study, there was actually a decrease in the prevalence of firearms in the state of São Paulo.[74] The disarmament produced the significant effect of reducing lethal crimes, but had no significant impact on crimes against property. According to the study, this indirectly implies that the possibility of a potential victim being armed has no deterrent effect on the perpetration of the crime.[75] The study concluded that, apparently, with fewer guns there is less crime.[76]

VIII. Bill Amending Disarmament Statute Vetoed

On January 10, 2013, Brazilian President Dilma Roussef vetoed a bill[77] that would have amended article 6(§1) of the Disarmament Statute, which currently authorizes only certain categories of professionals, as listed in the article, to carry firearms when off duty. The bill would have extended such authorization to prison agents, prison guards, prison escort guards, and port guards.

---

more than forty million inhabitants distributed in 645 municipalities. *Conheça São Paulo*, GOVERNO DO ESTADO DE SÃO PAULO, http://www.saopaulo.sp.gov.br/conhecasp/principal_conheca (last visited Jan. 28, 2013).

[71] CASTRO CERQUEIRA & PINHO DE MELLO, *supra* note 67, at 8.

[72] *Id.*

[73] *Id.* at 9.

[74] *Id.*

[75] *Id.* at 10.

[76] *Id.*

[77] Mensagem de Veto No. 002, de 9 de Janeiro de 2013, http://www.planalto.gov.br/CCIVIL_03/_Ato2011-2014/2013/Msg/Vet/VET-002.htm.

According to the President's veto message, "expanding the authorization to carry firearms when off duty to the professionals listed in section VII of article 6 of Law No. 10,826 implies a larger number of firearms in circulation, which goes against the national policy to combat violence and against the Disarmament Statute."[78]

Prepared by Eduardo Soares
Senior Foreign Law Specialist

---

[78] *Id.*

CANADA

FIREARMS-CONTROL LEGISLATION AND POLICY

Summary

The control of firearms in Canada is predominantly governed by the *Firearms Act, the Criminal Code, and their subordinate regulations. The Criminal Code defines the main categories of firearms, which include restricted, prohibited, and non-restricted firearms. The Firearms Act regulates the possession, transport, and storage of firearms.*

Canadian law has both licensing and registration requirements for the possession and acquisition of firearms. These requirements are administered by the Royal Canadian Mounted Police (RCMP) through the Canadian Firearms Program (CFP).

Applicants are required to pass safety tests before they can be eligible for a firearms license. Applicants are also subject to background checks, which take into account criminal, mental health, addiction, and domestic violence records.

I. Overview of Firearms-Control Laws and Regulations

At the federal level in Canada, firearms are predominantly regulated by the Firearms Act[1] and Part III of the Criminal Code.[2] Apart from these federal laws, "[p]rovinces, territories or municipalities may have additional laws and regulations that apply in their jurisdiction. For example, provinces are responsible for regulating hunting."[3]

A. Categories of Firearms

The Criminal Code identifies "the various firearms, weapons and devices regulated by the Firearms Act."[4] The Code classifies firearms into three categories: restricted,[5] prohibited,[6]

---

[1] Firearms Act, S.C. 1995, c. 39, http://laws-lois.justice.gc.ca/eng/acts/F-11.6/. For a detailed timeline of Canada's firearms control laws, *see History of Firearms Control in Canada: Up to and Including the Firearms Act,* RCMP, http://www.rcmp-grc.gc.ca/cfp-pcaf/pol-leg/hist/con-eng.htm (last modified June 19, 2012).

[2] Criminal Code, R.S.C. 1985, c. C-46, pt. III, http://laws-lois.justice.gc.ca/eng/acts/C-46/.

[3] *Canadian Firearms Program: Frequently Asked Questions – General,* RCMP, http://www.rcmp-grc.gc.ca/cfp-pcaf/faq/index-eng.htm#a1 (last modified Sept. 21, 2012).

[4] *Id.*

[5] Criminal Code § 84(1) (defining "restricted firearm").

[6] *Id.* (defining "prohibited firearm").

and non-restricted.[7] Non-restricted firearms "include ordinary shotguns and rifles, such as those commonly used for hunting. But some military type rifles and shotguns are prohibited."[8] Restricted firearms include "certain handguns and some semi-automatic long guns (not all semi-automatic long guns are restricted or prohibited). Rifles that can be fired when telescoped or folded to shorter than 660 millimeters, or 26 inches, are also restricted."[9] Prohibited firearms "include most 32 and 25 caliber handguns and handguns with a barrel length of 105 mm or shorter. Fully automatic firearms, converted automatics, firearms with a sawed-off barrel, and some military rifles like the AK 47 are also prohibited."[10]

Note also that "antique firearms are not considered firearms for licensing and registration purposes."[11]

B. Licensing and Registration Requirements

1. Licensing and Permits

The Firearms Act and its supporting regulations govern the possession, transport, and storage of firearms.[12] The Act stipulates the rules for possessing and acquiring a firearm,[13] which include both licensing and registration requirements.[14] A person must have a valid firearms license to possess or acquire firearms as well as ammunition. A firearms license is issued to a license holder if he or she has "met certain public-safety criteria and is allowed to possess and use firearms."[15]

According to the RCMP website, "[i]ndividuals must be at least 18 years old to get a licence that will allow them to own or to acquire a firearm,"[16] known as a Possession and Acquisition Licence, or PAL. Applicants seeking to acquire a license for non-restricted firearms are required to pass the Canadian Firearms Safety Course (CFSC) tests.[17] If applicants are

---

[7] These are firearms that are neither restricted nor prohibited.

[8] *Firearms and Firearms Act*, THE CANADIAN BAR ASSOCIATION (CBA) BRITISH COLUMBIA BRANCH, http://www.cba.org/bc/public_media/criminal/242.aspx (last updated Nov. 2012).

[9] *Id.*

[10] *Id.*

[11] For more information, *see* CBSA, IMPORTING A FIREARM OR WEAPON INTO CANADA, http://www.cbsa-asfc.gc.ca/publications/pub/bsf5044-eng.pdf (last visited Jan. 31, 2013).

[12] Library of Parliament, Legislative Summary, *Legislative Summary of Bill C-19: An Act to Amend the Criminal Code and the Firearms Act* para. 1.2 (Nov. 11, 2011), http://www.parl.gc.ca/About/Parliament/LegislativeSummaries/bills_ls.asp?ls=c19&Parl=41&Ses=1&source=library_prb&Language=E#a3.

[13] Canadian Firearms Program: Frequently Asked Questions – General, RCMP, supra note 3.

[14] Firearms Act § 4(a).

[15] Canadian Firearms Program: Frequently Asked Questions – General, RCMP, supra note 3.

[16] Firearms Act § 7(1). *See also Highlights of Canada's Firearms Laws*, RCMP, http://www.rcmp-grc.gc.ca/cfp-pcaf/pol-leg/hl-fs-eng.htm (last modified May 14, 2008).

[17] Firearms Act § 7(1)(a). According to the RCMP website, "[t]he legislation stipulates that individuals wishing to acquire non-restricted firearms must take the CFSC [Canadian Firearms Safety Course] and pass the tests

applying for a license for restricted or prohibited firearms they must pass the Canadian Restricted Firearms Safety Course (CRFC) tests in addition to the CFSC.[18]

The PAL is the only license now available to new applicants over eighteen years old. An existing Possession-Only License,[19] or POL, can be renewed, but new ones have not been issued since 2001. According to the Canadian Bar Association (CBA), "[a] Possession-Only Licence lets you use firearms already registered to you. It also lets you borrow firearms of the same class as the ones you own."[20]

Minors aged twelve to seventeen can get a minor's license that will "allow them to possess a non-restricted rifle or shotgun, but a licensed adult must be responsible for the firearm."[21] Applicants must also complete the Canadian Firearms Safety Course and pass the test in order to get a minor's license.[22]

A PAL can be issued for a firearm of any class (non-restricted, restricted, and prohibited). However, possessing or acquiring restricted[23] or prohibited firearms is subject to very stringent requirements. The general rule is that restricted and prohibited firearms must be possessed in the holder's residence (or at a place authorized by a chief firearms officer), as recorded in the Firearms Registry.[24] According to the Act, a restricted or prohibited firearm can be transported and used under very strict and specific circumstances, including among others "for use in target practice, or a target shooting competition."[25]

Under the Firearms Act and its regulations, a person can carry a restricted firearm or prohibited handgun, whether concealed or unconcealed, only in very limited circumstances.[26] In most cases, a permit known as an Authorization to Carry (ATC) is required, such as when "an

---

OR challenge and pass the CFSC tests without taking the course." *Canadian Firearms Safety Course*, RCMP, http://www.rcmp-grc.gc.ca/cfp-pcaf/safe_sur/cour-eng.htm (last modified Aug. 27, 2012).

[18] Firearms Act § 7(1)(b). *See also Canadian Restricted Firearms Safety Course*, RCMP, http://www.rcmp-grc.gc.ca/cfp-pcaf/safe_sur/cour-res-eng.htm (last modified Feb. 5, 2004).

[19] *Applying for a New Possession Only Licence (POL)*, RCMP, http://www.rcmp-grc.gc.ca/cfp-pcaf/fs-fd/pol-pps-eng.htm (last modified Aug. 21, 2012).

[20] CBA British Columbia Branch, *supra* note 8.

[21] Firearms Act § 8. *See also Firearm Users Younger than 18*, RCMP, http://www.rcmp-grc.gc.ca/cfp-pcaf/fs-fd/minor-mineur-eng.htm (last modified Sept. 5, 2012).

[22] *Id.*

[23] *Restricted Firearms*, RCMP, http://www.rcmp-grc.gc.ca/cfp-pcaf/fs-fd/restr-eng.htm (last modified Aug. 20, 2012).

[24] Firearms Act § 17.

[25] *Id.* § 19(1).

[26] *Id.* § 20.

individual needs restricted firearms or prohibited handguns for use in connection with his or her lawful profession or occupation"[27] or to protect life.[28]

According to the RCMP, persons are allowed to possess only certain prohibited firearms "if they had one registered in their name when it became prohibited, and they have continuously held a valid registration certificate for that type of prohibited firearm from December 1, 1998, onward."[29] Moreover, a PAL "allows an individual to acquire only prohibited firearms in the same categories as the ones currently registered to them, and only if the firearms they wish to acquire were registered in Canada on December 1, 1998."[30] Restricted or prohibited firearms must also be "verified by an approved verifier if they are being transferred to a new owner and have not been previously verified."[31]

Firearms licenses are "generally valid for five years, and must be renewed before they expire."[32] It is the license holder's responsibility to apply for a license renewal.

2. Registration

Under the Firearms Act, all restricted and prohibited firearms must be registered.[33] After April 2012, pursuant to amending legislation, non-restricted firearms no longer have to be registered.[34] However, "due to a Court Order issued by the Quebec Superior Court, residents of Quebec are still required to register non-restricted firearms."[35]

All licensing and registration is managed by the Royal Canadian Mounted Police's Canadian Firearms Program (CFP).[36] The CFP manages the Canadian Firearms Registry.[37]

---

[27] Authorizations to Carry Restricted Firearms and Certain Handguns Regulations (Firearms Act), SOR/98-207, http://laws-lois.justice.gc.ca/eng/regulations/SOR-98-207/index.html.

[28] Firearms Act § 20(a).

[29] *Prohibited Firearms*, RCMP, http://www.rcmp-grc.gc.ca/cfp-pcaf/fs-fd/prohibited-prohibe-eng.htm (last modified Aug. 20, 2012).

[30] *Id.*

[31] *Selling, Giving or Trading Firearms*, RCMP, http://www.rcmp-grc.gc.ca/cfp-pcaf/fs-fd/sell-vendre-eng.htm (last modified Aug. 20, 2012).

[32] *Renewing Firearms Licenses*, RCMP, http://www.rcmp-grc.gc.ca/cfp-pcaf/fs-fd/renew-renouv-eng.htm (last modified Sept. 21, 2012).

[33] Firearms Act § 12.1.

[34] *See* CBA British Columbia Branch, *supra* note 8.

[35] *Registration of Firearms (Individuals)*, RCMP, http://www.rcmp-grc.gc.ca/cfp-pcaf/online_en-ligne/reg_enr-eng.htm. (last modified Dec. 10, 2012).

[36] *Canadian Firearms Program (CFP)*, RCMP, http://www.rcmp-grc.gc.ca/cfp-pcaf/index-eng.htm (last modified Oct. 30, 2012).

[37] Registration of Firearms (Individuals), RCMP, *supra* note 35.

C. Criminal and Psychiatric Checks

According to section 5(1) of the Firearms Act, "[a] person is not eligible to hold a licence if it is desirable, in the interests of the safety of that or any other person, that the person not possess a firearm."[38]   Therefore, "[a]n applicant for a firearm licence in Canada must pass background checks which consider criminal, mental, addiction and domestic violence records."[39] Besides criminal checks, in order to determine eligibility under the Act, authorities must consider whether within the previous five years the applicant

> has been treated for a mental illness, whether in a hospital, mental institute, psychiatric clinic or otherwise and whether or not the person was confined to such a hospital, institute or clinic, that was associated with violence or threatened or attempted violence on the part of the person against any person; or
>
> has a history of behavior that includes violence or threatened or attempted violence on the part of the person against any person.[40]

In addition to background checks, "third party character references for each gun licence applicant are required."[41]

Applicants are screened using a two-tiered process.   According to a 2010 evaluation report on Canada's Firearms Program, "[t]his process entails submitting an application requesting that the applicant provide detailed personal information; when this application is assessed by the CFP, special attention is given to those applying for a Prohibited and Restricted Firearm License."[42]   Moreover, all applicants are also "screened on an on-going basis through the provisions of 'continuous eligibility', a monitoring function that has a licensee 'flagged' for a review of their license should a matter of public safety arise after they have obtained their license."[43]

D. Storage, Transportation, and Display of Firearms

Regulations supporting the Firearms Act also stipulate specific rules "for storing, transporting and displaying firearms safely to deter loss, theft and accidents.   Provinces may have additional regulatory requirements."[44]

---

[38] Firearms Act § 5(1).

[39] *Canada — Gun Facts, Figures and the Law*, GUNPOLICY.ORG, http://www.gunpolicy.org/ firearms/region/canada (last updated Dec. 21, 2012).

[40] Firearms Act § 5(2)(b)–(c).

[41] GUNPOLICY.ORG, *supra* note 39.

[42] RCMP, RCMP CANADIAN FIREARMS PROGRAM: PROGRAM EVALUATION – FINAL APPROVED REPORT 38 (Feb. 2010), http://www.rcmp-grc.gc.ca/pubs/fire-feu-eval/eval-eng.pdf.

[43] *Id.* at 39.

[44] *Highlights of Canada's Firearms Laws*, RCMP, *supra* note 16 (discussing Storage, Display, Transportation and Handling of Firearms by Individuals Regulations (Firearms Act), SOR/98-209, http://laws-lois.justice.gc.ca/eng/regulations/SOR-98-209/index.html).

All firearms have to be unloaded when stored. Non-restricted firearms must be secured with a locking device, "such as a trigger lock or cable lock (or remove the bolt) so the firearms cannot be fired," or the firearm must be locked "in a cabinet, container or room that is difficult to break into."[45] Restricted and prohibited firearms must be secured with locking devices and be kept in a cabinet, container, or room, or must be kept "in a vault, safe or room that was built or modified specifically to store firearms safely."[46] Separate rules apply for displaying firearms in a home.[47]

Non-restricted firearms "must be unloaded during transportation."[48] Restricted and prohibited firearms must be unloaded and secured with locking devices and locked in a "sturdy, non-transparent container."[49] Moreover, bolts and or bolt carriers must be removed from automatic firearms (if removable). Also, for restricted and prohibited firearms an Authorization to Transport permit must be obtained.[50]

F. Criminal Sanctions

Both the Firearms Act and the Criminal Code contain offenses and penalties for the "illegal possession or misuse of a firearm."[51] Section 91(1) of the Criminal Code criminalizes the possession of a firearm without a license and registration certificate.[52] The Code also contains provisions on the use of firearms or imitation firearms in the commission of an offense,[53] careless use of firearms,[54] pointing of a firearm,[55] improper storage,[56] and the failure to report a lost or found firearm.[57] The Code also contains provisions for certain possession/use, trafficking, assembly, and import/export offenses.

In addition, the Firearms Act includes offenses such as contravening conditions of a license, registration certificate, or authorization;[58] making false statements to procure a license,

---

[45] *Storing, Transporting and Displaying Firearms*, RCMP, http://www.rcmp-grc.gc.ca/cfp-pcaf/fs-fd/storage-entreposage-eng.htm (last modified July 7, 2012).

[46] *Id.*

[47] *Id.*

[48] *Id.*

[49] *Id.*

[50] *Id.*

[51] *Id.*

[52] Criminal Code § 91(1).

[53] *Id.* § 85(1), (2).

[54] *Id.* § 86(1).

[55] *Id.* § 87(1).

[56] *Id.* § 86(2).

[57] *Id.* § 105(1).

[58] Firearms Act § 110.

registration certificate, or authorization;[59] and defacing or altering a license, registration certificate, or authorization.[60]

II. Impact

Numerous studies have been conducted to assess the impact of Canada's firearms legislation on firearms-related deaths. Studies have attempted to evaluate three different periods of reform, which involved Bill C-51 in 1977, Bill C-17 in 1991, and Bill C-68 in 1995.

According to a 1988 study, "the use of firearms in Canadian homicides has declined since the legislative changes in gun control and capital punishment in late 1976." However, the study found that the changes in the law had no impact on total standardized national homicide rates.[61] A 1994 report concurred that "[d]ata from Canada from 1969 to 1985 showed that the passage of a stricter firearms control law in 1977 was associated with a decrease in the use of firearms for homicide but an increase in the use of all other methods for homicide."[62] Another study on the impact of gun control legislation (Bill C-51) in Canada "suggests that controlling access to lethal means for suicide may be an effective tactic."[63]

However, according to a paper by Professor Robert Mundt,

[t]he evidence suggests that the 1977 legislation has had little perceptible impact in any of the aforementioned areas [violent crime, suicides, and accidental deaths]. One possible reason, apart from the possible conclusion that gun control has no direct effect on behaviour, is that, despite the legislation, the actual availability of firearms in the hands of Canadians has risen.[64]

A 2004 study looking at the impact of the Firearms Act on suicide found that "[a] decrease in firearm suicides was most noticeable in the under-25 age group, although it was in

---

[59] *Id.* § 105(1).

[60] *Id.* § 107.

[61] Catherine F. Sproule & Deborah J. Kennett, *The Use of Firearms in Canadian Homicides 1972–1982: The Need for Gun Control*, 30 CANADIAN J. CRIMINOLOGY 31, 34 (1988), *available at* http://heinonline.org/HOL/Page?handle=hein.journals/cjccj30&div=8&g_sent=1&collection=journals (by subscription).

[62] Antoon A. Leenaars & David Lester, *Effects of Gun Control on Homicide in Canada*, 75(1) PSYCHOL. REP. 81, summary (1994), http://www.amsciepub.com/doi/abs/10.2466/pr0.1994.75.1.81 (by subscription); *see also* Antoon A. Leenaars & David Lester, *Gender and the Impact of Gun Control on Suicide and Homicide*, 2 ARCHIVES SUICIDE RES. 223 (1996), http://www.tandfonline.com/doi/pdf/10.1080/13811119608259004.

[63] Antoon A. Leenaars et al., *The Impact of Gun Control (Bill C-51) on Suicide in Canada*, 27 DEATH STUD. 103, 120 (2003), http://www.tandfonline.com/doi/pdf/10.1080/07481180302890; *see also* Antoon A. Leenaars, *Gun-Control Legislation and the Impact on Suicide*, 28 CRISIS: J. CRISIS INTERVENTION & SUICIDE PREVENTION 50, 57, http://www.psycontent.com/content/l643741r2q063n16/ (by subscription); David Lester, *Gun Availability and the Use of Guns for Suicide and Homicide in Canada*, 91 CAN. J. PUB. HEALTH 186, 187 (May–June 2000), http://journal.cpha.ca/index.php/cjph/article/viewFile/196/196.

[64] Robert J. Mundt, *Gun Control and Rates of Firearms Violence in Canada and the United States*, 32 CANADIAN J. CRIMINOLOGY 137 (1990), *available at* http://heinonline.org/HOL/Page?handle=hein.journals/cjccj32&div=13&g_sent=1&collection=journals (by subscription).

this same age group that the general suicide rate increased the most. The reduction of firearm suicides was not accompanied by a decrease in overall suicide rates."[65] Another study found that "[t]here is no discernable impact on public safety by the firearm program"[66] instituted by the Firearms Act.

A 1998 study commissioned by the Department of Justice, which reviewed most literature available at that time, found that the impact of firearms regulations remained "somewhat inconclusive and controversial, partly because the studies have attempted to isolate the impact of the 1977 legislation, and because of the theoretical and methodological challenges, and issues of data quality and availability, inherent in this type of evaluative research."[67]

A 2004 study found "a significant decrease after passage of Bill C-17 [in 1991] in the rates of suicides and homicides involving firearms and the percentage of suicides using firearms."[68] However, more recent studies appear to present a mixed picture. A 2012 study concluded that the data "failed to demonstrate a beneficial association between [firearms] legislation and firearm homicide rates between 1974 and 2008."[69] Some criticize this study since it did not take into account suicide deaths, which account for three-quarters of gun deaths.[70]

According to 2010 data available at Statistics Canada, over the past thirty years firearm-related homicides have continued to decline.[71] Moreover, "[m]uch of the decline in firearm-related homicide since the early 1980's can be attributed to a decrease in homicides involving a rifle or shotgun."[72] According to 2011 data,

---

[65] Jean Caron, *Gun Control and Suicide: Possible Impact of Canadian Legislation to Ensure Safe Storage of Firearms*, 8 ARCHIVES SUICIDE RES. 361, 374 (2004), *available at* http://www.tandfonline.com/doi/pdf/10.1080/13811110490476752.

[66] Gary A. Mauser, *Evaluating Canada's 1995 Firearm Legislation*, 17 J. FIREARMS & PUB. POL'Y 1 (2005), *available at* http://heinonline.org/HOL/Page?handle=hein.journals/jfpp17&div=3&g_sent=1&collection=journals (by subscription); *see also* Gary A. Mauser, *Ten Myths About Firearms and Violence in Canada*, 23 J. FIREARMS & PUB. POL'Y 76 (2011), *available at* http://heinonline.org/HOL/Page?handle=hein.journals/jfpp23&div=7&g_sent=1&collection=journals (by subscription).

[67] Yvon Dandurand, Firearms, Accidental Deaths, Suicides and Violent Crime: An Updated Review of the Literature with Special Reference to the Canadian Situation (Working Document, International Centre for Criminal Law Reform and Criminal Justice Policy, 1998), http://www.justice.gc.ca/ eng/pi/rs/rep-rap/1998/wd98_4-dt98_4/wd98_4.pdf.

[68] F. Stephen Bridges, *Gun Control Law (Bill C-17), Suicide, and Homicide in Canada*, 94 PSYCHOL. REP. 819, 826 (2004), *available at* http://uwf.edu/fbridges/PR%20Gun%20Control%20Law%20Suicide%20Homicide%20Canada.pdf.

[69] Caillin Langmann, Canadian Firearms Legislation and Effects on Homicide 1974 to 2008, 27(12) J. INTERPERSONAL VIOLENCE 2303 (2012).

[70] Steve Mertl, *New Study Claims Gun-control Laws Have No Effect on Canadian Murder Rate*, DAILY BREW (blog) (Oct. 7, 2011), http://ca.news.yahoo.com/blogs/dailybrew/study-claims-gun-control-laws-no-effect-canadian-201239248.html.

[71] Tina Hotton Mahony, *Homicide in Canada, 2010*, STATISTICS CANADA, http://www.statcan.gc.ca/pub/85-002-x/2011001/article/11561-eng.htm (last modified Oct. 26, 2011).

[72] *Id.*

[t]here were 158 homicides committed with a firearm in 2011, 13 fewer than the previous year. The 2011 rate of 0.46 firearm homicides per 100,000 population was the lowest in almost 50 years. The recent decline in the rate of firearm homicides is mainly due to a drop in the rate of homicides committed with a handgun, which has fallen nearly 30% over the past four years. However, handguns still accounted for about two-thirds of all firearms used to commit homicide in 2011.[73]

III. Distribution of Firearms

According to the *2007 Small Arms Survey*,[74] Canada was then ranked thirteenth in the world out of 178 countries surveyed in civilian gun ownership, with a ratio of 23.8 firearms per 100 people.[75] At that time, the estimated total number of guns held by civilians in Canada was 9,950,000.[76]

According to data of the RCMP, as of September 2012 Canadians held 1,927,693 valid licenses for firearms,[77] which equates to 5,758 licenses per 100,000 population.[78] In 2011, the RCMP reported that there were 7,861,902 firearms registered to individuals and businesses.[79]

Prepared by Tariq Ahmad
Legal Research Analyst

---

[73] *Homicide in Canada, 2011*, STATISTICS CANADA, http://www.statcan.gc.ca/pub/85-002-x/2012001/article/11738-eng.htm.

[74] *See* Annex 4, Aaron Karp, *Completing the Count: Civilian Firearms, in* SMALL ARMS SURVEY 2007: GUNS AND THE CITY 67 (Cambridge Univ. Press., Aug. 27, 2012), http://www.smallarmssurvey.org/file admin/docs/A-Yearbook/2007/en/Small-Arms-Survey-2007-Chapter-02-annexe-4-EN.pdf; *see also* Palash R. Gosh, *Connecticut Shooting: How Canada Views America's School Massacre and Gun Culture*, INT'L BUS. TIMES (U.S. ED.) (Dec. 19, 2012), http://www.ibtimes.com/connecticut-shooting-how-canada-views-americas-school-massacre-gun-culture-949300.

[75] *Id.*

[76] *Id.*; *see also* GUNPOLICY.ORG, *supra* note 39.

[77] *Facts and Figures (July – September 2012) Canadian Firearms Program*, RCMP, http://www.rcmp-grc.gc.ca/cfp-pcaf/facts-faits/index-eng.htm.

[78] *Id.*

[79] ROYAL CANADIAN MOUNTED POLICE, COMMISSIONER OF FIREARMS REPORT – 2011 (2012), http://www.rcmp-grc.gc.ca/cfp-pcaf/rep-rap/2011-comm-rpt/index-eng.htm.

CHINA

FIREARMS-CONTROL LEGISLATION AND POLICY

Summary

Firearms have been tightly controlled in China ever since the establishment of the People's Republic of China. Currently, the primary statute in regulating firearms is the Firearms-Control Law, which took effect on October 1, 1996. Criminal offenses relating to firearms control are governed by the Criminal Law.

The Firearms-Control Law generally prohibits any private possession of firearms in China with extremely limited exceptions. Aside from firearms for military use, the Law categorizes firearms as those for official use and those for civilian use. Firearms for official use are strictly confined to the police, procuratorial personnel working on investigations, and customs personnel. In addition, guards and escort personnel working for important state defense enterprises, financial institutions, storehouses, and scientific research institutions may carry firearms if the firearms are necessary for the performance of their duties. Firearms for civilian use are permitted for specified "work units" in three areas: sports; hunting; and wildlife protection, breeding, and research. Individual hunters in hunting areas and herdsmen in pastoral areas may possess hunting rifles, which cannot be removed from those areas.

The Criminal Law provides harsh penalties for gun-control violations. Illegal possession of firearms is punishable by police supervision, criminal detention, or fixed-term imprisonment for up to seven years. Illegally manufacturing, trading, transporting, mailing, or storing five military guns, five gunpowder-propelled nonmilitary guns, ten other nonmilitary guns, fifty military bullets, five hundred nonmilitary bullets, three hand grenades, or any explosive devices that can cause serious damage is punishable by fixed-term imprisonment of not less than ten years, life imprisonment, or death. The same punishments may be imposed for theft or robbery of firearms, and using firearms to commit robbery.*

---

* A previous version of this report was prepared by Tao-tai Hsia and Constance A. Johnson of the Law Library staff in May 1997.

I. Introduction

A. History of Firearms Control in the People's Republic of China

Firearms are very tightly controlled in China. Firearms control has been in place for most of the history of the People's Republic of China (PRC). Only about twenty months after the formal establishment of the PRC, the Provisional Measures on Firearms Control were published on June 27, 1951 (Provisional Measures).[1] Many of the articles in the Provisional Measures were designed to identify and gain control of the large number of firearms that were within the territory of China at the time as a result of the long period of civil war that ended with the Chinese Communist Party's victory in 1949. For example, there was a provision authorizing public security organs (police) at all levels to take an inventory of all the firearms in the area, and permits could then be issued to those authorized to have firearms.[2]

Under the Provisional Measures, aside from military personnel, government officials of a certain rank who needed firearms for their duties and who obtained approval from higher-level supervisors could receive authorization to carry guns. Faculty and students in nonmilitary schools and personnel in publicly owned factories, stores, enterprises, and mass organizations could carry guns if doing so was necessary for the performance of their duties, as long as they obtained approval from certain high-level government organs.[3] Privately operated enterprises were allowed to keep the guns they already had if they reported the guns for registration with the public security organs, were approved, and were issued licenses.[4] The "firearms" regulated in the Provisional Measures were rifles, carbines, pistols, and all other kinds of long or short guns, with the exception of hunting rifles.[5]

In 1981, the 1951 Provisional Measures were replaced by the Measures on Firearms Control (Measures).[6] The new Measures expressly brought hunting rifles and sport-shooting guns under regulation.[7] Hunters and hunting units were generally allowed to possess hunting rifles under the Measures. Other citizens over eighteen years of age could possess up to two hunting

---

[1] Qiangzhi Guanli Zanxing Banfa [Provisional Measures on Firearms Control] (approved for publication by Zhengwu Yuan, June 27, 1951), GONGAN FAGUI HUIBIAN [COLLECTION OF PUBLIC SECURITY LAWS AND REGULATIONS] 228–31 (1980).

[7] Id. art. 15.

[3] Id. arts. 7 & 8.

[4] Id. art. 10.

[5] Id. art. 1.

[6] Zhonghua Renmin Gongheguo Qiangzhi Guanli Banfa [The PRC Measures on Firearm Control] (approved by the State Council, Jan. 5, 1981, put into effect by the Ministry of Public Security, Apr. 25, 1981), ZHONGHUA RENMIN GONGHEGUO GONGAN FAGUI XUANBIAN [SELECTED COLLECTION OF PUBLIC SECURITY LAWS AND REGULATIONS IN THE PEOPLE'S REPUBLIC OF CHINA] 97–102 (1982).

[7] Id. art. 2.

rifles.[8] Furthermore, the Measures added articles specifically to regulate the firearms brought into and out of the country by foreigners.[9]

On July 5, 1996, the Law of the People's Republic of China on Firearms Control (Firearms-Control Law) was adopted by the Standing Committee of the National People's Congress (NPC) to replace the 1981 Measures.[10]

B. Legislative Framework

The Firearms-Control Law, which took effect on October 1, 1996, is the primary statute for regulating firearms.[11] The Law authorizes the central government agencies, in particular the Minister of Public Security (MPS), to issue detailed rules regulating specific aspects of firearms control. For example, the MPS and the General Administration of Sport jointly issued the Measures for the Administration of Guns for Competitive Sport Shooting in 2010, which took effect on January 1, 2011.[12] Agencies authorized to use guns also issue their own gun rules, such as the Rules of the People's Procuratorate on Gun Administration, issued in 1998 by the Supreme People's Procuratorate.[13]

Supplementing the provisions provided by the Firearms-Control Law are articles in the Criminal Law governing firearms control.[14] The Law on Penalties for Administration of Public Security also contains a provision establishing penalties for minor offenses related to illegally carrying guns and ammunition.[15]

II. Possession of Firearms

The approach of the Firearms-Control Law is to prohibit any private possession of firearms in China except under extremely restricted conditions. Compared with its predecessor, the range of

---

[8] *Id.* art. 6.

[9] *Id.* arts. 24–29.

[10] Firearms-Control Law, Chinese text *in* ZHONGHUA RENMIN GONGHEGUO GUOWUYUAN GONGBAO [GAZETTE OF THE STATE COUNCIL OF THE PEOPLE'S REPUBLIC OF CHINA] 805–14 (Aug. 1, 1996), English translation *available at* Westlaw China (by subscription).

[11] *Id.*

[12] Sheji Jingji Tiyu Yundong Qiangzhi Guanli Banfa [Measures for the Administration of Guns for Competitive Shooting Sports] (Sept. 20, 2010), MPS website, http://www.mps.gov.cn/n16/n1282/n3493/n3778/n4288/2526414.html.

[13] Renmin Jianchayuan Qiangzhi Guanli Guiding [People's Procuratorate (SPP) Rules on Administration of Guns] (issued July 9, 1998), SPP website, http://www.spp.gov.cn/site2006/2006-02-22/00026-76.html.

[14] Zhonghua Renmin Gongheguo Xingfa [PRC Criminal Law] (promulgated by the NPC, July 1, 1979, revised Mar. 14, 1997, effective Oct. 1, 1997, last amended Feb. 25, 2011), XINBIAN ZHONGHUA RENMIN GONGHEGUO CHANGYONG FALU FAGUI QUANSHU [NEW COMPLETE FREQUENTLY-USED LAWS AND REGULATIONS OF THE PEOPLE'S REPUBLIC OF CHINA] 6-1 to 6-46 (2012), English translation *available at* LUO WEI, AMENDED AND ANNOTATED CRIMINAL CODE OF CHINA (2012).

[15] Zhi'an Guanli Chufa Fa [Law on Penalties for Administration of Public Security] (adopted by the NPC Standing Committee, Aug. 28, 2005), art. 32, 2005 THE LAWS OF THE PEOPLE'S REPUBLIC OF CHINA 55, 63.

groups and individuals permitted to possess guns is significantly narrowed. The 1981 provision allowing citizens over eighteen years of age to possess two hunting rifles was abolished; instead, the new Law permits only hunters and herdsmen to possess hunting rifles in areas delineated by provincial governments, subject to approval, and such guns cannot be brought out of these hunting or pastoral areas.[16]

A. Definition

"Firearms" under the Firearms-Control Law is defined to mean "various guns that are propelled by gunpowder or pressurized air, and that use tube-like equipment to shoot metal balls or other materials that are powerful enough to injure or kill people or render them unconscious."[17] The manufacture, distribution, and transport of the main parts or components of guns and of ammunition are also subject to this Law.[18]

Firearms are divided into three categories according to the purposes of their use: (1) military firearms,[19] (2) firearms for official use, and (3) firearms for civilian use.[20] Military firearms (those used by the army and the armed police) are separately regulated by the State Council and the Central Military Commission.[21]

B. Firearms for Official Use

Firearms for official use are confined to police attached to public security organs, state security organs, prisons, reeducation camps, the courts, and the procuratorates, as well as to procuratorial personnel working on investigations and customs personnel. Guards and escort personnel working for important state defense enterprises, financial institutions, storehouses, and scientific research institutions may also be issued firearms for official use, providing that the firearms are necessary to the performance of their duties and the MPS gives its approval.[22] In 1998, the MPS published the Measures for Equipment of Firearms for Official Use, a set of concrete rules that govern its policies "according to the principle of strict control."[23] Even for the firearms for official use, the process is not automatic; a firearms-possession permit from the MPS or its provincial-level counterparts must be obtained.[24]

---

[16] Firearms-Control Law arts. 6, 10, 12.

[17] *Id.* art. 46.

[18] *Id.* art. 48.

[19] Article 2(2) of the Law states, "[w]here other regulations are formulated by the State Council and the Central Military Commission regarding control of guns with which the Chinese People's Liberation Army, the Chinese People's Armed Police Forces, and the Militia are armed, those regulations shall apply." *Id.* art. 2(2).

[20] *Id.* ch. 2.

[21] *Id.* art. 2(2).

[22] *Id.* art. 5.

[23] Gongwu Yongqiang Peibei Banfa [Measures on Equipment for Guns for Official Use] (republished by the MPS, Aug. 28, 2002, Gong An Bu Gong Zhi [2002] No. 128), Chinese Government Public Information Online (Shandong Station), http://govinfo.nlc.gov.cn/sdsfz/xxgk/sdsgat/201209/P020120914242146736728.doc.

[24] Firearms-Control Law art. 7.

C. Firearms for Civilian Use

There are three categories of "work units" in which civilian use of firearms is permitted:

- "sports units" that are specifically engaged in shooting sports and for-profit shooting ranges, which are set up with the approval of the provincial government authorities;

- hunting grounds, which are set up with the approval of the provincial government authorities; and

- wildlife protection, breeding, and research institutions, if firearms are necessary in their operations.[25]

The types of firearms permitted are specific to their functions, be they sport-shooting guns, hunting rifles, or anesthetizing guns.[26]

Individual hunters in hunting areas and herdsmen in pastoral areas may apply to county-level public-security organs in the area for permission to carry hunting rifles. To do so, they must present their hunting licenses, where applicable, and identification cards.[27]

The MPS is authorized by the Law to develop detailed rules for all civilian firearms use, to be issued with the approval of the State Council.[28] In addition, there is a specific prohibition in the Law against removing firearms from shooting ranges or hunting rifles from designated hunting or pastoral areas.[29]

As with the possession of firearms for official use, permits for the possession of firearms for civilian use must be obtained from public security organs at specified levels.[30]

D. Day-to-Day Management of Firearms

Anyone permitted to have firearms has the legal responsibility to ensure they are stored and used safely, and must undergo special training in this regard.[31] One must have a permit to carry firearms, and firearms may not be carried in areas where they are not permitted. Moreover, should they be lost or stolen, the authorities must be notified immediately.[32]

---

[25] *Id.* art. 6.

[26] *Id.*

[27] *Id.* art. 10.

[28] *Id.* art. 6.

[29] *Id.* art. 12.

[30] *Id.* arts. 7–11.

[31] *Id.* arts. 23–24.

[32] *Id.* art. 25.

Those weapons that do not meet technical standards must be disposed of by the police. Public security officials at the provincial level have the responsibility to destroy such firearms. As an additional safety measure, the Law authorizes the authorities to conduct inspections to determine that the proper permits have been obtained, that firearms are being used properly, and that they are in good condition.[33]

III. Manufacture and Distribution of Firearms

The state has established a licensing system for the manufacture and distribution of firearms. According to the Firearms-Control Law, no one, whether an individual or an enterprise, may manufacture or distribute firearms without a license. Firearms for official use as defined by the Law must be manufactured at enterprises designated by the state to do so, while those for civilian use may be made by enterprises nominated by the relevant department of the State Council and approved by the MPS. The manufacturing license and distribution license are valid for a period of three years and may be renewed through an application process.[34] The state imposes quotas on the number of guns to be made and distributed for civilian use, and the Law outlines the system for establishing the quotas.[35] Facilities that manufacture or distribute firearms are required to follow strict security measures and to submit to regular inspections and record checks by the authorities; in some cases, police personnel may be stationed at manufacturing plants.[36]

Guns must be made to strict technological standards, and enterprises may not change their design functions or structures. The name of the manufacturer, the model code, and the serial number must be printed on each gun.[37] Designs for firearms are developed by the State Council and the MPS.[38] Imitation guns are prohibited by law from being manufactured or sold.[39]

IV. Local Transportation of Firearms

No one may transport firearms in China without approval. Anyone needing to transport firearms must obtain a transportation permit from the public security organs by reporting the types and numbers of the firearms to be transported, together with information on the means of transportation to be used and the routes to be followed. The transportation permit is issued by the public security organs where the recipient of the firearms is located: at the municipal level for intraprovincial transportation, or the provincial level for interprovincial transportation.[40]

---

[33] *Id.* arts. 27–29.

[34] *Id.* arts. 13–15.

[35] *Id.* arts. 16–17, 19.

[36] *Id.* arts. 18(2), 20.

[37] *Id.* art. 18.

[38] *Id.* art. 21.

[39] *Id.* art. 22.

[40] *Id.* art. 30.

The manner in which guns are handled in transportation is also regulated by the Firearms-Control Law. Secure, enclosed facilities are to be used, and special personnel are to be assigned as escorts. Local police are to be notified if any overnight stops are made. Guns and ammunition are to be transported separately, and mailing of firearms is strictly prohibited.[41]

V. Transporting Firearms into and out of China

Like its predecessor, the 1996 Firearms-Control Law also contains provisions on transporting firearms into and out of China. No one may cross the border with firearms without approval from the MPS, with limited exceptions for foreign diplomatic personnel and sports delegations bringing guns in or out of the country for shooting sports.[42] When firearms are brought into the country, they must be registered, with approval documents, at the border checkpoint. At that time, customs officers will issue a clearance and an application must be made for a permit to carry the firearms within the country. Once the final destination within China is reached, possession permits must be applied for from the local police. When firearms are taken out of the country, approval documents are to be presented at the departure border checkpoint, where a clearance will be issued.[43]

The Law contains special provisions for foreign diplomatic personnel. Permission must be obtained in advance from the Ministry of Foreign Affairs for diplomats to bring firearms into the country. The firearms must be kept within the institution that the personnel represent, and notice should be given to the Ministry when the firearms are removed from China.[44] When firearms are carried into the country in a foreign vehicle for transit through China, this must be reported at the border and the vehicle sealed until it leaves the country.[45] Foreign sports delegations that come to participate in shooting events, and Chinese athletes going abroad for the same purpose, must obtain approval from the General Administration of Sport to carry their sports guns.[46]

VI. Offenses and Penalties

A. The Firearms-Control Law

The Firearms-Control Law, like the 1981 Measures, does not detail punishments for major gun-related offenses; instead, it links offenses with specific Criminal Law provisions. The Law assigns punishments for minor firearms offenses as follows:

- Enterprises that are licensed to do business making and selling firearms can have their licenses suspended or revoked if they exceed their authorization as to types or

---

[41] *Id.* arts. 31–32.

[42] *Id.* arts. 33 & 36.

[43] *Id.* art. 37.

[44] *Id.* art. 34.

[45] *Id.* art. 38.

[46] *Id.* art. 35.

quantities of weapons, deal in incorrectly labeled weapons, or market items internally that are meant for export.[47]

- Those who transport firearms without properly following the regulations for security and safety can be punished with criminal detention for up to fifteen days if the case is not serious enough to constitute a crime under the Criminal Law.[48]

- Anyone who leases or lends firearms in violation of the Law can be detained by public security organs for a period of up to fifteen days or fined up to 5,000 yuan (about US$803) if the case is not serious enough to constitute a crime under the Criminal Law.[49]

- Those who disregard stipulated technical standards in manufacturing firearms, carry them to places where they are not permitted, fail to report thefts of firearms promptly, fail to surrender improperly made firearms, or make or sell counterfeit firearms, aside from possible criminal indictments, may be warned, fined, or detained for up to fifteen days. Counterfeit firearms are to be confiscated, a fine of up to 5,000 yuan may be imposed, and in serious cases business licenses may be revoked.[50]

- Police who improperly allocate guns, illegally issue permits to carry guns, keep confiscated items for themselves, or otherwise fail to carry out duties regarding firearms in a way that causes adverse consequences will be investigated to determine criminal responsibility and can be subjected to disciplinary punishment, even if they are not held liable under the Criminal Law.[51]

B. The Criminal Law

Cases of serious firearms-control offenses are punishable under the Criminal Law, which provides harsh penalties for gun-related offenses. Detailed rules on the application of these Criminal Law provisions are provided by the Supreme People's Court (SPC) through judicial interpretations. The most recent version of the interpretation (SPC Interpretation) was published in 2009 and took effect on January 1, 2010.[52]

1. Crimes Endangering Public Security

Most gun-related offenses are regulated by Criminal Law articles under the chapter "Crimes Endangering Public Security." Article 125 of the Criminal Law provides that those who

---

[47] *Id.* art. 40.

[48] *Id.* art. 42.

[49] *Id.* art. 43.

[50] *Id.* art. 44.

[51] *Id.* art. 45.

[52] Zuigao Renmin Fayuan Guanyu Shenli Feifa Zhizao, Maimai, Yunshu Qiangzhi, Danyao, Baozhawu deng Xingshi Anjian Juti Yingyong Falv Ruogan Wenti de Jieshi [The SPC Interpretation on Certain Issues Regarding the Specific Application of Laws in the Trial of Criminal Cases Involving the Illegal Manufacture, Trading, and Transportation of Guns, Ammunition, and Explosives] (issued Nov. 16, 2009, effective Jan. 1, 2010), SPC website, http://www.court.gov.cn/qwfb/sfjs/201002/t20100210_1069.htm.

illegally manufacture, trade, transport, mail, or store any guns, ammunition or explosives be sentenced to fixed-term imprisonment of not less than three years but not more than ten years; if the circumstances are serious, the offender is sentenced to fixed-term imprisonment of not less than ten years, life imprisonment, or death. According to the SPC Interpretation, illegally manufacturing, trading, transporting, mailing, or storing five military guns, five gunpowder-driven nonmilitary guns, ten other nonmilitary guns, fifty military bullets, three hand grenades, and explosive devices that can cause serious damage may be deemed "serious circumstances" under article 125 of Criminal Law, which are punishable with death.[53] When it is a work unit or enterprise that is guilty of the offense, that entity is fined and responsible management personnel may be subject to the same punishments as an individual convicted of the crime.[54]

Enterprises legally designated or permitted to manufacture or distribute firearms that do not follow firearms-control regulations are subjected to fines, and their leaders may be punished with up to five years of imprisonment. If the circumstances are serious, their punishment is from five to ten years; in "especially serious" cases, the sentence is ten years or more, or life imprisonment.[55] The Criminal Law outlines the actions that in general trigger these penalties. These actions include exceeding the limits of quantity or variety the enterprise is permitted to make or sell, for the purpose of illegal sales; manufacturing unmarked, redundantly marked, or falsely marked firearms, also for the purpose of illegal sales; and illegally selling firearms, which includes selling arms within China that were made for export.[56] According to the SPC Interpretation, illegally manufacturing more than twenty guns, selling more than ten guns, or "other flagrant circumstances such as those causing serious consequences" may constitute "serious circumstances"; illegally manufacturing more than fifty guns, selling more than thirty guns, and "other flagrant circumstances such as those causing serious consequences" may be deemed "especially serious" and are punishable with life imprisonment.[57]

According to article 127 of the Criminal Law, the stealing or forcible seizure of firearms, ammunition, or explosives is punishable, depending on the seriousness of the case, with three to ten years of imprisonment, ten or more years, life imprisonment, or even the death penalty. Moreover, robbery of any guns, ammunition, or explosives, or stealing or forcibly seizing such articles from state organs, members of the armed forces, the police, or the people's militia is punishable by fixed-term imprisonment of not less than ten years, life imprisonment, or death.[58]

Anyone illegally possessing, concealing, lending, or leasing firearms, ammunition, or explosives is subject to police surveillance, criminal detention, or imprisonment for up to seven years, depending again on the seriousness of the case.[59] "Illegal possession" means persons not authorized to be equipped with guns and ammunition possessing these articles in violation of the

---

[53] *Id.* arts. 1–2.

[54] Criminal Law art. 125(3).

[55] *Id.* art. 126.

[56] *Id.*

[57] SPC Interpretation art. 3.

[58] Criminal Law art. 127.

[59] *Id.* art. 128.

gun-control laws, while "illegal concealing" refers to those authorized to be equipped with guns and ammunition keeping the articles in private beyond the period of authorization and refusing to hand them over.[60]

Those who have legal charge of firearms but lose them and do not report the loss promptly may be punished with up to three years of imprisonment or criminal detention.[61] Those who endanger public security by illegally carrying firearms, ammunition, or explosives into public places or onto public transportation may be punished, when circumstances are serious, with up to three years of imprisonment, criminal detention, or public surveillance if the circumstances are serious.[62]

2. Armed Robbery

Under ordinary circumstances, robbery is punishable by fixed-term imprisonment of three to ten years with a fine. However, under certain circumstances, the penalties may be increased to fixed-term imprisonment of more than ten years, life imprisonment, or death, with a fine or confiscation of property. Using firearms to commit robbery is one such circumstance.[63]

C. Law on Penalties for Administration of Public Security

The Law on Penalties for Administration of Public Security contains one provision on minor offenses related to illegally carrying firearms. A person who illegally carries firearms and ammunition, or crossbows and daggers, may be detained for not more that five days and may, in addition, be fined not more than 500 yuan; if the circumstances are relatively minor, he is given a warning or fined not more than 200 yuan. A person who illegally carries firearms and ammunition, or crossbows and daggers, to a public place or aboard public transportation may be detained for not less than five days but not more than ten days and may, in addition, be fined not more than 500 yuan.[64]

VII. Concluding Remarks

On the morning of December 14, 2012, the same day as the Sandy Hook Elementary School shooting in the US, a man in central China's Henan Province walked into an elementary school and began attacking children with a knife. Twenty-three of the children were injured, according to the report of the official Xinhua News Agency, but none seriously. The man had allegedly obtained the weapon when he burst into an elderly woman's house near the elementary

---

[60] SPC Interpretation art. 8.

[61] Criminal Law art. 129.

[62] *Id.* art 130. The last set of punishments also applies to those carrying controlled types of knives and materials of a combustible, radioactive, poisonous, or corrosive nature.

[63] *Id.* art. 263.

[64] Zhi'an Guanli Chufa Fa [Law on Penalties for Administration of Public Security] (adopted by the NPC Standing Committee, Aug. 28, 2005) art. 32, 2005 THE LAWS OF THE PEOPLE'S REPUBLIC OF CHINA 55, 63.

school earlier that morning, hit her, and then stabbed her with the kitchen knife he picked up in the house.[65]

One American commentator used this incident in China to highlight the difference between the US and China's approaches to firearms control, writing, "[t]hat's the difference between a knife and a gun."[66] The domestic media in China likewise acclaims China's "strictest firearms-control policy," asserting there are significantly fewer crimes committed with guns and explosives in China than in many other countries. There were only five hundred criminal offenses committed with guns and two hundred explosions reported nationwide in 2011, according to Xinhua,[67] in a nation with a population of about 1.34 billion.

Nevertheless, the country still faces the challenges of the illegal possession, manufacture, and trade of firearms, as well as armed offenses. From time to time the MPS has launched campaigns to fight firearms-control offenses.[68] According to the most recent statistics released by the MPS, the police uncovered about 670 secret sites for the illegal manufacture and distribution of guns in the campaign launched in 2012. After investigating around 14,000 cases involving the illegal possession, manufacture, and trade of guns and explosives, the police apprehended 20,000 suspects belonging to 360 criminal organizations; 160,000 guns and 2,780 tons of explosives were seized during the campaign.[69]

Prepared by Laney Zhang
Senior Foreign Law Specialist

---

[65] *China School Attach Suspect Arrested*, XINHUANET (Dec. 17, 2012), http://news.xinhuanet.com/english/china/2012-12/17/c_132045807.htm.

[66] James Fallows, American Exceptionalism: The Shootings Will Go On, THE ATLANTIC (Dec. 14, 2012).

[67] Gong'an Jiguan Yanda Sheqiang Shebao Fanzui, Chiqiang Baozha Fanzui An Tongbi Xianzhu Xiajiang [Public Security Organs Strongly Cracking Down on Crimes Involving Guns and Explosives, Such Crimes Significantly Decreased Compared with Previous Years], XINHUANET (Oct. 18, 2012), http://news.xinhuanet.com/legal/2012-10/18/c_123841645.htm.

[68] *Id.*

[69] *China Uncovers 670 Gun-related Crime Dens*, XINHUANET (Jan. 16, 2013), http://news.xinhuanet.com/english/china/2013-01/16/c_124235386.htm.

EGYPT

FIREARMS-CONTROL LEGISLATION AND POLICY

Summary

    The principle legislation relating to firearms control in Egypt is Law No. 394 of 1954. The Law prohibits the acquisition or possession without a permit of smooth-barrel guns, pistols, and shotguns. It also sets forth exemptions from the need to obtain a permit to acquire or own a firearm for specified categories of persons, and forbids the licensing of firearms in some cases. Furthermore, Law No. 394 prohibits the manufacture, import, trade, and repair of weapons, firearms, and their ammunition without a license. In 2012, article 26 of the Law was amended to enhance the penalties for acquiring and possessing unlicensed firearms and ammunition. In the same year a presidential decree created a temporary amnesty program for individuals in possession of firearms without a permit.

    There is apparently a lack of enforcement of Law No. 394 due to the deterioration of the security situation after what is known as the "January 25th Revolution." One of the key factors leading to the spread of unlicensed weapons in the black market is the rise of smuggled firearms.

    In an effort to combat the proliferation of unlicensed firearms, the Egyptian authorities have adopted an array of initiatives and programs. Those initiatives are aimed at confiscating unlicensed guns and guns stolen guns from police stations, arresting the smugglers and dealers of illegal firearms, and encouraging individuals possessing unlicensed weapons to surrender those weapons.[*]

I. Firearms Licensing Requirements and Restrictions on Use

The principle legislation on firearms control in Egypt is Law No. 394 of 1954.[1] The Law prohibits the acquisition or possession without a permit of smooth-barrel guns, pistols, and shotguns.[2]

The issuance, withdrawal, and revocation of licenses for firearms permitted under Law No. 394 are the prerogative of the Minister of the Interior. The chiefs of security in the provinces act on the Minister's behalf in licensing firearms, while local police chiefs issue permits to possess

---

[*] A previous version of this report was prepared by George N. Sfeir of the Law Library staff in August 1997.

[1] Law No. 394 of 1954, AL JARIDAH AL RASMIYAH [OFFICIAL GAZETTE] No. 53 *bis* of July 8, 1954.

[2] *Id.* art. 1, sched. 2, sched. 3 pt. 1, & sched. 3 pt. 2, respectively.

"white weapons," such as bayonets, daggers, lances, switchblades, and pointed canes. The chiefs of security also have the authority to decide which types of firearms will be licensed and the duration of the license.

Normally, permits are issued for three-year periods and are renewable for three-year periods. Tourists, however, are issued temporary permits to carry firearms for six-month periods.[3] All permits are personal; Law No. 394 prohibits the transfer of weapons and firearms to persons who are not licensed to acquire or own weapons and firearms.[4]

Applications for permits must be accompanied by a police record and include the photograph and signature of the applicant. The permit itself contains the name, age, profession, nationality, and residence of the licensee; a description of the firearm and the purpose for which it is licensed; the date of issue and expiry of the permit; and any conditions imposed on the use of the firearm. A licensee may occasionally be required to resubmit information and records previously provided with the application for a permit and to notify the authorities of a change of address. When a licensee loses or relinquishes his firearm by sale or other form of transfer to another licensee or gun merchant, he is required to inform the authorities and hand them his permit for endorsement. The new owner must present the firearm to the authorities for identification purposes.[5]

Law No. 394 prohibits the carrying of weapons and firearms in public places, particularly those where liquor is served; gambling casinos; and where conferences, meetings, and festivals are held.[6]

II. Exempt Persons

Law No. 394 of 1954 sets forth exemptions from the need to obtain a permit to acquire or own a firearm for specified categories of persons; however, these individuals are required to notify the police within one month of the acquisition of a firearm. The first category of individuals includes

- present and former cabinet ministers;
- active military officers and certain senior government officials, appointed by presidential decree;
- former military officers and government officials of the rank of major general and director general;
- present and former regional governors and directors;

---

[3] *Id.* arts. 2–4.

[4] *Id.* art. 3.

[5] *Id.* art. 4.

[6] *Id.* art. 11.

- members of the diplomatic and consular corps, both Egyptian and foreign, on condition of reciprocity for Egyptian diplomats;

- certain officials of the Intelligence Service;[7] and

- present and former members of the People's Assembly (lower chamber) and Shura Council (upper chamber), who must also provide their local police station with information concerning the number and description of the firearms they own.[8]

The second category of persons exempt from the provisions of Law No. 394 concerning the acquisition and ownership of firearms are village chiefs and rural estate elders, with one firearm permitted per person, as well as members of the armed forces and police as far as government-issued firearms and weapons are concerned.[9]

III. Restricted Persons

Law No. 165 of 1981, which amended Law No. 394 of 1954, forbids the licensing of firearms for persons who

- have not reached twenty-one years of age;

- have been convicted of a felony or sentenced for a criminal act or for the illicit use of a firearm, are under parole supervision, or have been convicted of trading in explosives or drugs, among others; or

- suffer from a mental or psychological malady, are vagrants, or are physically incapable of owning and using firearms (i.e., have poor eyesight or other physical weaknesses that would impair the safe and secure use of a firearm).[10]

IV. Prohibited Weapons and Equipment

Specified categories of firearms and related equipment, such as automatic assault rifles, rocket-propelled grenades (RPGs), gun silencers, and telescopic equipment used with weapons are prohibited.[11]

V. Regulation of Manufacturers and Dealers

Law No. 394 of 1954 prohibits the manufacture, import, trade, and repair of weapons, firearms, and their ammunition without a license.[12] Moreover, the Law imposes restrictions on the location and conditions related to establishments manufacturing or trading and repairing firearms.

---

[7] *Id.* art. 5.

[8] Law No. 162 of 2003, 50 AL JARIDAH AL RASMIYAH 2003, Dec. 12, 2003, p. 2.

[9] Law No. 394 of 1954, art. 5.

[10] Law No. 165 of 1981, 42 AL JARIDAH AL RASMIYAH 1981, Dec. 12, 1981, pp. 4–8.

[11] Law No. 394 of 1954, art. 1.

[12] *Id.* art. 12.

For instance, article 15 stipulates that individuals engaged in the sale or repair of firearms must meet certain qualifications. Article 13 prohibits any trade in or repair of firearms in rural areas. Article 18 bans the sale and repair of firearms and ammunition in one location. Article 20 establishes limits on the number of such establishments in each district and province of the country. Article 24 restricts the transfer of firearms and ammunition from one place to another without a permit.

VI. Offenses and Penalties

In 2012, Law No. 6 of 2012 amended article 26 of Law No. 394 of 1954. This article was amended to enhance the penalties for possessing and acquiring unlicensed firearms and ammunition. It punishes individuals that acquire or possess without a permit those firearms described in Schedule 2 of the Law, such as shotguns, with a prison term and a fine that may not exceed EGP5,000 (approximately US$782). The punishment increases to a fine not exceeding EGP15,000 (about US$2,347) and a term of hard labor if the firearms in question are among the weapons described in part 1 of Schedule 3, such as pistols of all kinds and guns with rifled barrels. The amended article also enhances the punishment for acquiring or possessing the firearms described in part 2 of Schedule 3, such as machine guns, automatic assault rifles, and explosives, to include life imprisonment with hard labor and a fine not exceeding EGP20,000 (about US$3,129).

Similarly, under the amended article 26, the acquisition and possession, without a permit, of ammunition for all types of weapons mentioned in Schedules 2 and 3 is punishable by a prison term and a fine not exceeding EGP5,000 (about US$782). If the accused has a previous criminal record, the punishment must be life imprisonment and a fine that may not exceed EGP20,000 (about US$3,129).

Likewise, the amendment penalizes individuals committing the crime of acquiring or possessing in public places non-permitted weapons (and related ammunition) or explosives with hard labor or life imprisonment with hard labor, and a fine that may not exceed EGP20,000 (about US$3,129). The term "public places" includes modes of public transportation and places of worship. If an individual intended to use those weapons or ammunition in any act against public order and security or to undermine the system of government, the constitution, national unity and social harmony, he must be punished by the death penalty.[13]

Under article 28 of Law No. 394, the penalty for the manufacture, import, sale, and repair of firearms listed under Schedule 2 of the Law without a license is imprisonment and a fine of between EGP500 and EGP1,000. The punishment is imprisonment with an enhanced penalty of hard labor for the crime of manufacturing, importing, selling, and repairing firearms listed in Schedule 3, part 1 of the Law. In the case of firearms listed in Schedule 3, part 2, the punishment is life imprisonment with hard labor.[14]

---

[13] Law No. 6 of 2012, 2 AL JARIDAH AL RASMIYAH 2012, Jan. 12, 2012, pp. 5–8.

[14] Law No. 394 of 1954, art. 28.

VII. Amnesty

Presidential Decree 90-2012 of 2012 amended article 31(a) of Law No. 394 by creating an amnesty for individuals who acquire or possess firearms without a permit. Under this Decree, individuals who surrender their illegal weapons to the police will not be charged. Amended article 31(a) provides that individuals possessing or acquiring firearms or ammunition mentioned under Schedules 2 and 3 of the Law without a permit will have amnesty. There will be no charges or convictions if those individuals surrendered the unlicensed weapons and ammunition to the Directorate of Police or police station within 180 days from the enforcement date of Decree 90-2012 (October 14, 2012). Individuals who stole firearms and hid them are also exempt if they return the stolen firearms during the 180-day grace period.[15]

VIII. Enforcement and Current Practices

A. The Scope of the Problem

Apparently, Law No. 394 is not being enforced at present due to the deterioration of the security situation in Egypt following the "January 25th Revolution"[16]— the popular uprising that began on that date in 2011, which led to the downfall of the regime of former President Hosni Mubarak. Ordinary citizens rushed to purchase all types of firearms, such as shotguns, homemade rifles, pistols, and automatic weapons, in the face of the security vacuum created in the months after the January Revolution.[17] Reflecting the lack of enforcement, an illegal arms manufacturer recently acknowledged his trade in an interview with *The Egyptian Gazette* and stated that, unlike before, he is not afraid of being raided by the police.[18]

In spite of the enhanced sanctions against individuals possessing or acquiring firearms illegally, the trade of unlicensed firearms has increased at an alarming rate. Illegal firearms circulating in the markets are smuggled, made at home, or stolen from the police.[19] The high demand for unlicensed firearms, despite their illegality, has caused their prices to double and triple in some cases. For instance, the price of a smuggled AK47 has reached EGP60,000 (about US$9,000) in some cases, compared to the previous cost of EGP15,000 to EGP20,000 (about US$2,347–$3,129). Locally-made shotguns that take 16mm and 12mm cartridges, which

---

[15] Presidential Decree 90-2012, 41 AL JARIDAH AL RASMIYAH 2012, Oct. 14, 2012, p. 3.

[16] Mohammed Elmeshad, *Smuggled, Stolen and Homemade, Guns Flood Egypt's Streets*, EGYPT INDEPENDENT (June 26, 2011), http://www.egyptindependent.com/news/smuggled-stolen-and-homemade-guns-flood-egypt%E2%80%99s-streets.

[17] *Id.*

[18] Mohssen Arishie, *Panicking Egyptians Snap up Homemade Guns*, THE EGYPTIAN GAZETTE (May 30, 2012), http://213.158.162.45/~egyptian/index.php?action=news&id=18688&title=Panicking%20Egyptians%20snap%20up%20home-made%20guns.

[19] According to news reports, more than 11,000 firearms were stolen from police stations and prisons when they were stormed by gangs and thugs on January 28, 2011. *Minister of Interior: New Regulation to Deal with Unlicensed Firearms*, AL AHRAM NEWSPAPER (Jan. 7, 2012), http://digital.ahram.org.eg/articles.aspx?Serial=759289&eid=145 (in Arabic).

previously sold for EGP300–500 (US$46–$76) now cost EGP1,000 to 2,000 (US$153–$307).[20] Stolen police pistols are priced from EGP200–300 (US$30–$46). Finally, the price of a new, locally-made 9mm handgun, known as a "Hilwan," reached EGP16,000 (about US$2,457), compared to EGP4,000 (US$616) previously.[21]

Shotguns and homemade rifles are used on the streets on a daily basis against law enforcement personnel and private citizens. For example, street vendors used homemade rifles to shoot at the police in one of the main squares of Cairo in October 2012. This shooting incident led to the injury of two policemen and the death of one street vendor.[22] In another incident in December 2012 where firearms were used among private citizens, shotguns caused the death of ten people during clashes between the supporters and opponents of current Egyptian President Mohammed Morsi.[23]

According to news reports, the number of unlicensed weapons in Sinai increased by 50% after January 25, 2011. Unlicensed firearms are commonly used by tribesmen and tribal chiefs in Sinai to protect their land and families.[24] Illegal firearms are also used in Sinai by a group of individuals calling themselves "Global Jihad." In recent months, those jihadists carried out multiple terrorist attacks against Egyptian police and army personnel operating in the region.[25]

B. Routes of Smuggled Firearms

One of the principle factors leading to the spread of unlicensed weapons in the black market is the rise of smuggled firearms. There are two main routes for smuggling firearms into Egypt: Libya (the western border) and Sudan (the southern border).

Media outlets have reported that there was a significant surge in the number of smuggled weapons from Libya after the overthrow of Muammar al Gahdafi's regime. Smuggled weapons not only include light firearms, such as automatic and sniper rifles, but also heavy weaponry. These types of weapons include heavy projectiles, rocket-propelled grenades, Grad rockets, and anti-aircraft ammunition.[26]

---

[20] Elmeshad, *supra* note 16.

[21] Dena Rashad, *Sticking to One's Guns?*, AL AHRAM WEEKLY (June 15, 2011), http://weekly.ahram.org.eg/2011/1051/eg72.htm.

[22] *Police Shoot Street Vendor Dead*, AL MASRY AL YOUM (Oct. 15, 2012), http://www.egyptindependent.com/news/police-shoot-street-vendor-dead.

[23] *Report: Live Ammo, Bird Shot Killed Protestors at Presidential Palace*, EGYPT INDEPENDENT (Dec. 21, 2012), http://www.egyptindependent.com/news/report-live-ammo-bird-shot-killed-protesters-presidential-palace.

[24] *Interior Minister: Sinai Citizens Have Role in Protecting Egypt's Borders*, EGYPT INDEPENDENT (Aug. 10, 2012), http://www.egyptindependent.com/news/interior-minister-sinai-citizens-have-role-protecting-egypt-s-borders.

[25] Mohamed Fadel Fahmy, *Egypt's President Condemns Deadly*, CNN (Aug. 8, 2012), http://www.cnn.com/2012/08/06/world/africa/egypt-violence/index.html.

[26] *Police Find Prohibited Firearms, Ammunition Northeast of Cairo*, EGYPT INDEPENDENT (Apr. 06, 2012), http://www.egyptindependent.com/news/rpg-and-ammunition-found-fayed-news-2.

Similarly, firearms dealers took advantage of the armed conflict in Darfur and Chad by smuggling illegal weapons to Egypt. According to news reports, firearms and ammunition are smuggled from Sudan and Chad through southern Egypt. Bedouin tribes cross the desert from Chad to Sudan with all types of weapons left over from tribal warfare. They then bring the weapons across the Egyptian border. Once these weapons arrive in southern Egypt, they are shipped to Cairo to be sold.[27]

C. Programs and Initiatives Addressing Unlicensed Guns

In an effort to combat the use of unlicensed firearms, the Egyptian authorities have adopted an array of initiatives and programs. Those initiatives are aimed at confiscating unlicensed guns and guns stolen from police stations, arresting smugglers and dealers of illegal firearms, and encouraging individuals possessing and acquiring unlicensed weapons to surrender those weapons.

In recent months, the Ministry of Interior (in charge of homeland security) stepped up its campaign against dealers of unlicensed firearms. For example, the Minister of Interior reportedly declared in August 2012 that police forces were able to confiscate 20,000 unlicensed weapons in Sinai in the previous months.[28] As of January 2012, the Ministry of Interior announced that it was able to locate and confiscate 5,415 pieces of firearms that were stolen from police stations, according to news reports. Law enforcement personnel also succeeded in confiscating 11,768 unlicensed firearms from private citizens.[29]

Members of the police force worked closely with the army to intercept shipments of smuggled, illegal weapons and to arrest smugglers. For example, border guards and police forces in the western border areas created various security checkpoints on the highways and patrolled the desert areas located closest to the borders. In a recent incident, security officials were able to confiscate 108 Grad rockets (ground-to-ground missiles) and 400,000 rounds of anti-aircraft ammunition.[30]

The Egyptian government has adopted various amnesty programs to encourage citizens to surrender their unlicensed firearms. In September 2012, Egyptian President Mohammed Morsi announced in media outlets the amnesty program mentioned above that was created by the amendment of article 31(a) of Law 394 of 1954.[31] In June 2011, the Minister of Interior announced that the Ministry would offer financial awards to individuals who surrendered their unlicensed weapons. He also promised that the Ministry would facilitate administrative procedures related to the issuance of licenses for weapons.[32] Likewise, in an effort to curb the use of

---

[27] Elmeshad, *supra* note 16.

[28] EGYPT INDEPENDENT, *supra* note 24.

[29] AL AHRAM NEWSPAPER, *supra* note 19.

[30] *Authorities Intercept Weapons Smuggling from Libya*, EGYPT INDEPENDENT (Nov. 21, 2012), http://www.egyptindependent.com/news/authorities-intercept-weapons-smuggling-libya.

[31] Magdy Samaan, *Egyptians Will Not Hand Over Weapons to Morsi*, THE ATLANTIC COUNCIL (Sept. 21, 2012), http://www.acus.org/files/Samaan%209.21.pdf (in Arabic), *and* http://www.acus.org/?q=print/71739 (in English).

[32] *Interior Ministry Declares Firearms Amnesty Until End of June*, EGYPT INDEPENDENT (June 22, 2011),

unlicensed firearms, in August 2011, the Minister of Interior issued a decision that exempts those who surrender their unlicensed and stolen police weapons from legal accountability and grants them licenses to carry firearms for the purpose of self-defense.[33]

Prepared by George Sadek
Senior Legal Information Analyst

---

http://www.egyptindependent.com/news/interior-ministry-declares-firearms-amnesty-until-end-june.

[33] Yousry el Badry, *Interior Ministry to Grant Arms Licenses to Those Who Hand in Stolen Weapons*, EGYPT INDEPENDENT (Aug. 13, 2011), http://www.egyptindependent.com/news/interior-ministry-grant-arms-licenses-those-who-hand-stolen-weapons.

GERMANY

FIREARMS-CONTROL LEGISLATION AND POLICY

Summary

The German system of gun control is among the most stringent in Europe. It restricts the acquisition, possession, and carrying of firearms to those with a creditable need for a weapon. It bans fully automatic weapons and severely restricts the acquisition of other types of weapons. Compulsory liability insurance is required for anyone who is licensed to carry firearms.

In recent years, German gun-control law underwent several reforms that made it even more stringent. A new Weapons Act became effective in 2003 after a school shooting in the city of Erfurt in which a student killed sixteen persons. The new Act restricted the use of large caliber weapons by young people and strengthened requirements for the safe storage of firearms.

Another reform was enacted in 2009 in response to the massacre at Winnenden, in which an eighteen-year-old killed fifteen people in the course of a school shooting. This latest reform led to the creation of a federal gun register and to intense governmental monitoring of gun owners' compliance with requirements for the safe storage of firearms. Pursuant to the reformed legislation, the authorities may at any time request access to the premises of any registered gun owner to monitor whether proper safe-storage procedures are being observed.

I. Development of German Gun-Control Law

A constitutional right to bear arms is not part of the German legal tradition.[1] Instead, the development of German gun-control law mirrored the turbulent history of Germany. The concepts of the current licensing system date back to the Firearms and Ammunition Act of 1928;[2] which was enacted at a time when armed militias roamed the land and firearms from World War I were still in private hands. The Hitler regime demilitarized the enemies of National Socialism with the help of several restrictive and discriminatory decrees.[3] When this was accomplished, a more lenient Weapons Act was enacted in 1938.[4] It exempted party hacks from licensing requirements and aimed at improving the combat skills of the population.

---

[1] K. OSWALD, DAS NEUE WAFFENRECHT 9 (Melsungen, 1980).

[2] Gesetz über Schusswaffen und Munition, Apr. 12, 1928, REICHSGESETZBLATT (RGBL.) I, p. 143.

[3] Gesetz gegen den Waffenmissbrauch, Mar. 28, 1931, RGBl. I, at 77; Vierte Verordnung des Reichspräsidenten, Dec. 8, 1931, RGBL. I, p. 742.

[4] Waffengesetz, Mar. 18, 1938, RGBL. I, p. 265.

After World War II, scattered laws of the occupying powers were in effect in different parts of West Germany together with fragments of the Weapons Act of 1938 until a constitutional change in legislative powers in 1972[5] paved the way for federal legislation on gun control. The first federal Weapons Act was enacted in 1972, and reformed and repromulgated in 1976.[6] Its primary goal was to restrict the availability of firearms in order to prevent crime.[7]

A new, even more stringent Weapons Act became effective in 2003.[8] Between 2003 and 2008 it was amended several times for the purpose of facilitating a more effective use of gun registers by law enforcement. The amendments also restricted the rights of heirs to own inherited guns and allowed the authorities of the states to enact special restrictions for especially endangered urban areas.[9]

In 2009, the Weapons Act was amended[10] in response to a school shooting at Winnenden in which a seventeen-year-old gunned down fifteen persons in his former school (see Section II (B) below for statistics on school shootings). The 2009 reform made it more difficult for individuals to own multiple firearms, increased some qualifying-age requirements for juveniles at shooting ranges, and allowed the authorities to monitor the safe storage of weapons in private homes more effectively.[11]

The 2009 reform also called for the creation of a National Weapons Register, which was scheduled to commence operations by January 1, 2013, one year earlier than required by the European Union (EU) Firearms Directive.[12] Compliance with the remainder of the Directive had already been accomplished with the enactment of the 2009 reform, which far exceeds European requirements.[13]

---

[5] Gesetz zur Änderung des Grundgesetzes [31st Act Amending the Constitution], July 28, 1972, BUNDESGESETZBLATT [BGBL.] [official law gazette of the Federal Republic of Germany] I, p. 1305.

[6] Waffengesetz [Weapons Act], reenacted Mar. 8, 1976, BGBL. I, p. 432.

[7] 80 Verhandlungen des Deutschen Bundestages 11434 (1972).

[8] Waffengesetz [WaffG] [Weapons Act], Oct. 11, 2002, BGBL I at 3970, as amended, up-to-date version *available at* http://www.gesetze-im-internet.de/waffg_2002/index.html.

[9] GUNTHER GADE & EDGAR STOPPER, WAFFENGESETZ KOMMENTAR 8–11 (2011).

[10] Viertes Gesetz zur Änderung des Sprengstoffgesetzes, BGBL. I, p. 2088.

[11] GADE & STOPPER, *supra* note 9, at 10.

[12] Council Directive 91/477/EEC of 18 June 1991 on the control of the acquisition and possession of weapons, 1991 O.J. (L 256) 51, as amended, consolidated version at http://eur-lex.europa.eu/LexUriServ/Lex UriServ.do?uri=CONSLEG:1991L0477:20080728:EN:PDF.

[13] GADE & STOPPER, *supra* note 9, at 10.

II. Statistics

A. Incidence of Gun-Related Crime

For 2010, the Federal Criminal Police Office reported a total of 3,216 homicides. Of these, 147 were perpetrated by gunshot, and in another 13 cases the victim was threatened with a gun.[14] For 2009, the Office reports 3,269 homicides, 179 of which were committed by gunshot, with a gun being used as a threat in another 14 reported cases.[15] The German population is approximately 81.7 million.[16]

B. School Shootings

Germany has suffered several school shootings in the last decade, the most egregious of which occurred in 2002, 2006, and 2009. In 2002, a nineteen-year-old, who had been expelled from his high school in Erfurt, entered the school armed with a semiautomatic pistol, shot and killed sixteen persons, most of them teachers, and then shot himself.[17] In 2006, an eighteen-year-old entered his former school and shot and wounded five persons before killing himself. He was armed with a sawed-off percussion rifle and a sawed-off bolt-action rifle.[18] The incident led to increased statutory restrictions of the online distribution of violent computer games to juveniles.[19]

In 2009, in the massacre at Winnenden, a seventeen-year-old entered his old school armed with a semiautomatic pistol and started a shooting spree, which he continued while fleeing from the police, killing a total of fifteen persons and himself and wounding many more.[20] The shooter had obtained the gun from his father's bedroom, where it had been kept unlocked. The father was convicted of negligent homicide for the failure to lock up the gun, yet on appeal the Federal Court of Justice reversed the decision because of procedural errors. A new trial against the father is pending. It appears that prior to the massacre, the alleged perpetrator had been

---

[14] Polizeiliche Kriminalstatistik 2010, at Grundtabelle 010000, https://www.bka.de/nn_196810/Shared Docs/Downloads/DE/Publikationen/PolizeilicheKriminalstatistik/pksJahrbuecher/pks2010__6steller.html?__nnn=true.

[15] POLIZEILICHE KRIMINALSTATISTIK 2009, at Grundtabelle 00000, https://www.bka.de/nn_196810/Shared Docs/Downloads/DE/Publikationen/PolizeilicheKriminalstatistik/pksJahrbuecher/pks2009__6steller.html?__nnn=true.

[16] STATISTISCHES JAHRBUCH 2011, Ch. 2.1 Bevölkerung, https://www.destatis.de/DE/Publikationen/StatistischesJahrbuch/GesellschaftundStaat/Bevoelkerung.pdf?__blob=publicationFile.

[17] Thüringer Justizministerium, Medieninformation 22/2004, Bericht der Gutenberg-Kommission zu den Vorgängen am Erfurter Gutenberg-Gymnasium, http://www.thueringen.de/de/home_page/presse/12251/uindex.html (last visited Jan. 17, 2013).

[18] *Aufgesetzter Kopfschuss*, TAZ.DE (DIE TAGESZEITUNG) 2 (Nov. 2006).

[19] DEUTSCHER BUNDESTAG DRUCKSACHE 16/8546; Murad Erdemir, *Killerspiele und gewaltbeherrschte Medien im Fokus des Gesetzgebers*, KOMMUNIKATION UND RECHT 223 (2008). Erstes Gesetz zur Änderung des Jugendschutzgesetzes, June 24, 2008, BGBL. I, p. 1075.

[20] BADEN-WÜRTTEMBERG, EXPERTENKREIS AMOK 7, http://www.stiftung-gegen-gewalt-an-schulen.de/media/BERICHTExpertenkreisAmok.pdf.

undergoing psychiatric counseling. The father is thus suing the psychiatric clinic, holding the clinic liable for failing to inform him of the dangerous condition of his son, who allegedly had uttered death threats to the psychiatric personnel and about which the father had not been told.[21]

C. Gun Ownership.

According to the first computations of the newly created National Weapons Register, close to 5.5 million firearms are privately owned in Germany and the total number of gun owners is approximately 1.4 million individuals.[22] The percentage of households in which guns are owned varies among the German states. Gun ownership is lower in the states located in former East Germany and in the city states of Berlin, Hamburg, and Bremen. In these, the percentage ranges from 3.2 to 5.7 of all households. In the formerly West German states, the percentage ranges from 6.2% to 12.3%.[23]

III. Current Gun-Control Law

A. Overview

Germany has one of the most stringent gun control laws in the world.[24] The current Weapons Act deals with guns suitable for private ownership. It contains a highly differentiated regime for licensing the acquisition, possession, and carrying of permitted weapons that restricts, according to criteria of need, the number and types of guns that can be owned or purchased, and has specific age restrictions for different types of weapons. The Act bans automatic firearms, regulates the production of and trade in weapons, and has reporting requirements that allow the tracing of every legally owned firearm, including those acquired through inheritance. Moreover, the Act contains stringent and enforceable requirements for the safe storage of guns. The Act is implemented by the administrative authorities of the states, except for the newly created National Weapons Register, which is a federal agency.

B. Licensing

A license is required for any dealings with a firearm, and various types of licenses can be granted depending on the need of an applicant. The most common ones are the license to acquire and possess a weapon (weapons-possession license, *Waffenbesitzkarte*), and the license to carry a weapon (weapons-carrying license, *Waffenschein*).[25] Certain general requirements apply to the

---

[21] *Amoklauf von Winnenden, Vater des Täters will psychiatrische Klinik verklagen*, SPIEGELONLINE, http://www.spiegel.de/panorama/justiz/winnenden-vater-von-tim-k-will-psychiatrische-klinik-verklagen-a-875234.html (last visited Jan. 17, 2013).

[22] *Nationales Waffenregister*, BUNDESVERWALTUNGSAMT (Jan. 2, 2013), http://www.bva.bund.de/cln_228/nn_2156988/DE/Aufgaben/Abt__III/NWR/Aktuelles/NWR__Inbetriebnahme.html (last visited Feb. 11, 2013).

[23] *Anzahl der registrierten Schusswaffen im Privatbeseitz*, STATISTA, http://de.statista.com/statistik/daten/studie/177598/umfrage/privater-legaler-waffenbesitz-nach-bundeslaendern/ (last visited Jan. 17, 2013).

[24] GADE & STOPPER, *supra* note 9, at 10.

[25] WaffG § 10.

granting of all licenses, and specific additional requirements apply to different types of licenses. In particular, there are special rules for hunters[26] and marksmen.[27]

Licenses must generally be reviewed by the authorities after three years, even if they have been granted for an indefinite time. The authorities may also review licenses at shorter intervals, particularly if there appears to be a reason for scrutiny. Moreover, licenses can be tailor-made to the specific situation of the applicant by adding special restrictions,[28] such as limits as to time and place and special safe-storage requirements.[29]

The general requirements for obtaining any type of weapons license are

- a minimum age of eighteen years;
- the proven reliability of the applicant;
- knowledge of weapons technology and law, and expertise in the use of a firearm;
- five years of residency in Germany; and
- a need for the weapon.[30]

Under the reliability criteria, certain criminal records disqualify an applicant, as does membership in a criminal or terrorist organization or the justified suspicion of the authorities that the applicant would abuse the license or not live up to its requirements.[31] Additional disqualifying circumstances are the lack of legal capacity; personal disabilities, such as addiction to alcohol or drugs; mental illness or feeblemindedness; and any other indications that the applicant might not live up to the licensing requirements. The authorities must verify the criteria through the search of criminal records, police databases, and any other information that they deem relevant.

A need for a weapon, and therefore a license, is recognized for hunters, marksmen, members of traditional shooting associations, endangered persons, collectors, experts, producers and dealers, and private security firms. For these groups, the public interest in safety and order will be balanced with the interest of the potential gun owner. If licenses are sought for other purposes, the public safety interests may well prohibit their being granted, given the fact that one purpose of German gun control law is to hold down the number of guns under private ownership.[32]

---

[26] *Id.* § 13.

[27] *Id.* § 14.

[28] *Id.* § 9.

[29] GADE & STOPPER, *supra* note 9, at 80.

[30] WaffG § 4.

[31] *Id.* § 5.

[32] ANDRÉ BUSCHE, WAFFENBESITZKARTE UND WAFFENSCHEIN 14 (4th ed. 2009).

A weapons-possession license authorizes the acquisition of a specified number of weapons. The license will generally be valid for acquisition purposes for one year and will be granted indefinitely for the purpose of possessing the weapon. The number of weapons to be permitted depends on the needs of the applicant. For hunters, permits will grant an indefinite number of long arms but only two short arms,[33] whereas members of traditional shooting associations are restricted to three repeating long arms.[34]

Marksmen are generally allowed to own three semiautomatic long arms and two short arms. For each acquisition of a firearm, however, marksmen must apply separately for a license that permits acquisitions for up to one year.[35] If the marksmen have requirements for additional firearms for their practice or for competitive sport, these must be documented by the shooting club.[36]

The criteria for granting a weapons-carrying license are very restrictive. They usually require proof that the applicant is seriously endangered and that the danger could be alleviated through the carrying of a weapon.[37] Some exceptions are made for hunters and for the personnel of private security firms.[38] Holders of a weapons-carrying license must carry liability insurance with coverage of up to 1 million euros.[39]

C. Age Requirements

The general age requirement for a weapons license is eighteen years.[40] A higher age limit of twenty-one years, however, exists for a weapons-possession license for marksmen. This higher age limit was introduced after the Winnenden school shooting,[41] but makes exceptions for properly certified shooting clubs that use weapons of a lower potency. An eighteen-year-old participant in such a club may obtain a license for a suitable firearm.[42] On the other hand, marksmen below the age of twenty-five who apply for their first weapons-possession license must undergo a psychiatric evaluation.[43]

---

[33] WaffG § 13(2).

[34] BUSCHE, *supra* note 32, at 31.

[35] ANDRÉ BUSCHE, WAFFENRECHT 76 (6th ed. 2010).

[36] WaffG § 14; *see also* Ferdinand Bauer & Wolfgang Fleck, *Die wichtigsten Neuregelungen im Waffengesetz 2009*, GEWERBEARCHIV 16 (2010).

[37] BUSCHE, *supra* note 32, at 38.

[38] WaffG § 28.

[39] WaffG § 4 (1) no. 5.

[40] WaffG § 4.

[41] GADE & STOPPER, *supra* note 9, at 135.

[42] *Id.*

[43] BUSCHE, *supra* note 32, at 32.

In general, the Weapons Act prohibits the handling and use of weapons by persons below the age of eighteen.[44] Exceptions to this principle exist for young people who are using a firearm in a training program or employment relationship under proper supervision,[45] or at shooting ranges. Prior to the 2009 reform, fourteen-year-olds were permitted to shoot with high-caliber guns at shooting ranges. The reform raised this age limit to eighteen.[46] However, young people between the ages of fourteen and eighteen may still be trained in marksmanship with less potent firearms under properly accredited supervision.[47]

D. Prohibited and Restricted Firearms

Germany categorizes firearms as either weapons of war or weapons suitable for civilian use. War weapons are listed in the War Weapons Act and cannot be circulated among the population.[48] Weapons that are potentially suitable for civilian use are governed by the Weapons Act and its prohibitions and restrictions.

The Weapons Act bans fully automated firearms.[49] It also bans semiautomatic firearms that are not intended for hunting or sport shooting; pump-action shotguns with pistol grips or of a short overall length; firearms that are concealed in other objects; firearms that can be disassembled into unusually small parts; lasers, lights, projectors, and night-vision devices that can be mounted on the firearm to throw light on the target; and certain multiple-shot short arms in calibers under 6.3 millimeters, where the projectiles are not propelled solely by the priming charge.[50]

Pump-action shotguns with pistol grips were banned in 2008 in response to the Erfurt massacre of 2002.[51] The above-described multiple-shot short arms were banned at the same time because shots fired with these weapons are able to penetrate bulletproof vests.[52]

Firearms that are not banned are still subject to various restrictions on the basis of licensing provisions and intended use. Thus, for persons who require a firearm for self-defense, the authorities may, based on their judgment, issue a license for only a particular type of firearm.[53] For marksmen, many restrictions ensue from the limits placed on the number of firearms that can be owned.

---

[44] WaffG § 2(1).

[45] WaffG § 3.

[46] BADEN-WÜRTTEMBERG, *supra* note 20, at 44.

[47] WaffG § 27(1) no. 2.

[48] Kriegswaffengesetz, repromulgated Nov. 22, 1990, BGBL. I at 2506, as amended.

[49] WaffG, Anlage 1 (zu § 1(4)) no. 62.

[50] BUSCHE, *supra* note 35, at 39.

[51] *Id.* at 65.

[52] GADE & STOPPER, *supra* note 9, at 10.

[53] *Id.* at 84.

E. Safe Storage of Firearms

Licensed gun owners are responsible for keeping their weapons under lock and key, and the law provides detailed specifications on the quality of the storage containers; these vary according to the potency of the weapons.[54] Owners must inform the authorities of the safe-storage measures taken as well as allow the authorities to enter their dwellings for the purpose of monitoring compliance with safe-storage regulations.[55]

It appears that such access must be granted without a search warrant, and, even though the German Constitution protects the privacy of the home, access cannot be refused if there is a threat of imminent danger.[56] Random inspections, however, must be expected at any time and without any probable cause or suspicion. This increased right of the authorities to conduct inspections was enacted in 2009 in response to the Winnenden school shooting, and much has been said about the interpretation of this right.

It appears that the authorities may only inspect for compliance with weapons-storage regulations but not conduct any other searches.[57] If the weapon is outside of its container and the owner claims to have been cleaning the weapon, the authorities will have to evaluate this claim.[58] It also appears that a homeowner has the right to refuse entry to the authorities if he or she has a good reason. A homeowner who frequently refuses entry, however, may be violating the statutory duty to cooperate with the authorities on the safe storage of weapons,[59] which may lead to revocation of the license. The far-reaching inspection rights of the authorities aim to ensure that gun owners will have an incentive to keep their guns locked up.[60]

Special safe-storage rules are also in effect for inherited firearms. An heir who is not licensed to possess firearms must prevent the use of the inherited firearm by installing a blocking device. If the heir is licensed, he or she must register the gun within one month of acquisition by inheritance. An unlicensed heir has one month to apply for a weapons-possession license,[61] which will be granted or denied in accordance with the generally prevailing licensing criteria.[62]

---

[54] WaffG § 36(1) & (2).

[55] *Id.* § 36(3).

[56] *Id.*

[57] Bauer & Fleck, *supra* note 36, at 16.

[58] Id.

[59] WaffG § 36(3).

[60] GADE & STOPPER, *supra* note 9, at 306.

[61] WaffG § 20.

[62] GADE & STOPPER, *supra* note 9, at 177.

F. Registration

The provisions on the registration of firearms ensure that every legally owned gun is registered with the authority that granted the weapons license. The acquirer of a firearm must register it within two weeks of acquisition,[63] and the authorities must keep records that allow for the tracing of a firearm's ownership from the time of its manufacture.[64] Moreover, the weapons authorities must communicate ownership records to the local Registers of Domicile,[65] (who record the domicile of every inhabitant of Germany[66]), while the Registers of Domicile are to inform the weapons authorities of every change in residency or the death of a gun owner.[67] This information is helpful for keeping track of inherited guns and enforcing recording and licensing requirements.

The efficiency of the registration system has been greatly enhanced with the newly created National Weapons Register commencing its operation in January 2013.[68] Now the approximately 550 weapons authorities provide data on firearms registration to the National Register. All weapons registers, be they local or national, provide their information to other German authorities to the extent reconcilable with German privacy legislation.[69]

Prepared by Edith Palmer, Chief,
Foreign, Comparative, and
International Law Division II

---

[63] WaffG § 10(1a).

[64] *Id.* § 44a.

[65] WaffG § 44.

[66] Melderechtsrahmengesetz [Framework Act on Domicile Registry], repromulgated Apr. 19, 2002, BGBL. I, p. 1342, as amended.

[67] *Id.* § 2(2) no. 6.

[68] WaffG § 43a; Nationales Waffenregistergesetz, June 25, 2012, BGBL. I at 1366; NATIONALES WAFFENREGISTER, http://www.bva.bund.de/cln_228/nn_2156988/DE/Aufgaben/Abt__III/NWR/node.html?__nnn=true (last visited Feb. 11, 2013).

[69] *Id.* § 43.

GREAT BRITAIN

FIREARMS-CONTROL LEGISLATION AND POLICY

Summary

Great Britain has some of the most stringent gun control laws in the world. The main law is from the late 1960s, but it was amended to restrict gun ownership further in the latter part of the twentieth century in response to massacres that involved lawfully licensed weapons. Handguns are prohibited weapons and require special permission. Firearms and shotguns require a certificate from the police for ownership and a number of criteria must be met, including that the applicant has good reason to possess the requested weapon. Good reason does not include self-defense or a simple wish to possess the weapon. The secure storage of weapons is also a factor when licenses are granted.

I. Introduction

Great Britain has the reputation of having some of the tightest gun control laws in the world.[1] Only police officers, members of the armed forces, or individuals with written permission from the Home Secretary may lawfully own a handgun.[2] This stringent legislation may, in part, account for Britain's relatively low statistics for the use of firearms in crime—in 2008–2009 firearms were used in only 0.3% of all recorded crimes and were responsible for the deaths of thirty-nine people.[3] This report covers the law relating to the lawful ownership of firearms and offenses for unlawful possession.

Firearms laws governing the country have generally been enacted in a reactive manner in response to massacres and overwhelming public support that backed the introduction of prohibitions on firearms. The laws cover a number of weapons, including handguns, shotguns, imitation firearms, deactivated firearms, and air weapons. This report focuses on the requirements to lawfully own a shotgun, firearm, or a prohibited weapon for residents of Britain.

---

[1] Ian Burrell, Legitimate Firearm Users Think that Tougher Restrictions Miss the Target, THE INDEPENDENT (London), Jan. 15, 2001, at 3.

[2] Firearms Act 1968, c. 27 § 5, http://www.legislation.gov.uk/ukpga/1968/27/section/5; *see also* Burrell, *supra* note 1.

[3] Home Office Statistical Bulletin, Homicides, Firearm Offences and Intimate Violence 2008/09, http://webarchive.nationalarchives.gov.uk/20110218135832/http://rds.homeoffice.gov.uk/rds/pdfs10/hosb0110.pdf.

II. History of Firearms Law

A. Early Regulation

Early acts regulating the ownership of firearms were fairly limited. The Gun Licenses Act 1870 and the Pistols Act 1903 served primarily as Acts to generate revenue and required owners to hold a license from the post office. The system was described as generally ineffective.[4] In 1920, the Firearms Act[5] was passed, to stop firearms from being used by criminals and "other evilly disposed or irresponsible persons."[6] While one aim of the restriction was to curb violent crime, it was believed that other reasons included concerns over uprisings in Russia spilling over into Britain, particularly with the end of World War I and the return of thousands of troops trained in the use of firearms and an increase in the number of such weapons in circulation.[7] This Act set out the basis for the licensing system of firearms that is still in operation today, providing the chief officer of police in the district the applicant lives with the authority to issue licenses. When enacting this legislation, the right to bear arms by citizens was considered; however, "this was countered by the argument that such redress was adequately obtainable through the ballot box and by access to Parliament and the courts."[8] Further controls were introduced in 1937 to allow conditions to be attached to certificates and to place more stringent restrictions on particularly dangerous weapons such as machine guns.[9]

The laws were consolidated and amended in 1968 with the enactment of the Firearms Act, which is the legislation still used today.

B. Modern Developments in Firearms Legislation

The development of major changes in modern day firearms legislation in Britain has generally been preceded by tragedy and a change in public attitude and opinion towards the ownership of firearms.

---

[4] Peter H. Burton, *Firearms Licensing – Time for Reform*, 145 New L.J. 882 (June 16, 1995). There is no further page number given, I believe that 882 may be it, NLJ articles are fairly short. Maybe (accessed via Lexis).

[5] Firearms Act 1920, 10 & 11 Geo. 5, c. 43, www.legislation.gov.uk/ukpga/1920/43/pdfs/ukpga_19200043_en.pdf.

[6] Burton, *supra* note 4.

[7] *Id.*

[8] Law Library of Congress, United Kingdom: Firearms Legislation (1997) at 6 (on file with author).

[9] Firearms Act 1937, 1 Edw. 8 & 1 Geo. 6, c. 12, https://www.legislation.gov.uk/ukpga/1937/12/pdfs/ukpga_19370012_en.pdf.

1. The Hungerford Massacre and the Firearms (Amendment) Act 1988

In 1987 Michael Ryan shot and killed sixteen people, including his mother, and wounded fourteen more before killing himself in what became known as the Hungerford massacre.[10] Ryan used two high-velocity semiautomatic rifles, a US M1 carbine, and an assault rifle that he lawfully owned to perpetrate the massacre.[11] The Firearms (Amendment) Act 1988[12] was passed as a direct result of this incident. The 1988 Act banned the ownership of high-powered self-loading rifles and burst-firing weapons, and imposed stricter standards for issuing ownership certification for pump-action shotguns with a magazine of more than two bullets. When enacting this legislation, the government considered that the tightened controls were justified as it had to safeguard the public at large, but at the same time "protect the interests of the legitimate shooting community."[13]

The legislation did not result in the complete cessation of shootings—just a year after the law was enacted Robert Sartin, who suffered from schizophrenia, killed one person with a shotgun and wounded sixteen more.[14] However, the Hungerford massacre that preceded the legislation saw a changed attitude to guns by the police, and tighter checks before certificates were issued.[15]

2. Dunblane and the Firearms (Amendment) Act 1997

Close to ten years after Hungerford, in 1996, another massacre occurred at an elementary school in Dunblane, Scotland. This incident bears strong similarities to the Sandy Hook shootings in the US.[16] Thomas Hamilton walked into a primary (elementary) school in Dunblane, Scotland, and shot and killed sixteen small children, aged four to five, and their teacher in the school gym before killing himself. Hamilton lawfully held the two rifles and four handguns that he used for the massacre, and had lawfully held firearms for almost twenty years prior to this incident.[17]

The Firearms (Amendment) Act 1997[18] was passed in response to overwhelming public opinion that firearms should be banned from use by the civilian population. The law did not

---

[10] Michael McCarthy, *Echoes of the Day Horror was Visited on Hungerford; The Parallels with Michael Ryan's Rampage in 1987 Are Striking*, INDEPENDENT (London), June 3, 2010, at 4; Hugh Muir, *Gun Panic Sets In . . . but Is It Justified*, THE GUARDIAN (London) Oct. 11, 2003, at 11.

[11] McCarthy, *supra*, note 10, at 4.

[12] Firearms (Amendment) Act 1988, c. 45, http://www.legislation.gov.uk/ukpga/1988/45/contents.

[13] Firearms Act 1968: Proposals for Reform ¶ 4, *cited in* THE HON LORD CULLEN, THE PUBLIC INQUIRY INTO THE SHOOTINGS AT DUNBLANE PRIMARY SCHOOL ON 13 MARCH 1996, Cm. 3386 1995-6, ¶ 9.111, *available at* http://www.ssaa.org.au/research/1996/1996-10-16_public-inquiry-dunblane-lord-cullen.pdf.

[14] Nicholas Timmins, *Are We Hostages to Gun Culture*, THE INDEPENDENT (London), Mar. 14, 1996, at 13.

[15] *Id.*

[16] Burrell, *supra* note 1, at 3.

[17] Sarah Boseley & Michael White, *Who Licensed Him to Kill*, GUARDIAN (London), Mar. 15, 1996, at 1.

[18] Firearms (Amendment) Act 1997, c. 5, http://www.legislation.gov.uk/ukpga/1997/5/contents.

introduce a complete ban on firearms, but served to essentially prohibit the private ownership of handguns in Britain.[19]

3. Cumbria

In 2010 Derrick Bird killed twelve people and wounded twenty-five in Cumbria, a county in northwest England.[20] He lawfully possessed the firearms used in the shootings.[21] Parallels were drawn between the Hungerford massacre in 1987 and the Cumbria massacre in 2010. The number of fatalities were higher by four people in the Hungerford massacre, where sixteen were killed, compared with twelve in the Cumbria massacre, but the number of casualties were significantly higher in the Cumbria massacre—twenty-five wounded compared to fifteen. The difference in these figures was, in part, attributed to the weapons used to perpetrate the crimes.[22] Unlike previous mass shootings, this did not lead to a major change in firearms legislation.

4. Public Inquiry After Dunblane

A public inquiry was held after the Dunblane massacre to investigate the circumstances that led to the shootings, consider the issues that arose from the shootings, and make recommendations.[23] Lord Cullen led the inquiry and made a series of recommendations that firearms laws be tightened, but rejected calls for an outright ban on the possession and use of guns.[24]

The inquiry considered whether the availability of weapons under the Firearms Act and incidences of crime involving firearms were inherently connected. Lord Cullen determined that the banning of handguns for target shooting or shooting clubs could not be justified. Instead, he recommended that self-loading pistols and revolvers held for target shooting be restricted by disabling them while not in use.[25]

The House of Commons Home Affairs Committee had also narrowly recommended against an outright ban on handguns.[26] The Committee considered that banning the lawful ownership of

---

[19] Burrell, *supra* note 1.

[20] Martin Wainwright, *Derrick Bird Inquest Returns Verdict of Unlawful Killings and Suicide*, GUARDIAN (London), Mar. 25, 2011, http://www.guardian.co.uk/uk/2011/mar/25/derrick-bird-inquest-unlawful-suicide.

[21] James Meikle & Helen Carter, *Cumbria Shootings: Government Warns Against Rash Changes to Gun Laws*, GUARDIAN (London), June 3, 2010, http://www.guardian.co.uk/uk/2010/jun/03/cumbria-shootings-theresa-may-gun-laws-review.

[22] McCarthy, *supra* note 10, at 4.

[23] THE HON LORD CULLEN, *supra* note 13, Terms of Reference at 2.

[24] *Id.* ¶ 1.7.

[25] *Id.* ¶ 9.112.

[26] House of Commons, Home Affairs Committee, Possession of Handguns H.C. 393 (1995–96).

handguns would be redundant if unlawful handguns remained easy to obtain and that "a prohibition could only result in a minimal improvement in public safety."[27]

The government response to the Cullen Report was the introduction of the Firearms (Amendment Act) 1997, which went considerably further than the recommendations put forth by both the inquiry and the House of Commons Committee. Overwhelming public opinion backing the ban of handguns appears to have led both the government and the opposition party to agree on the ban.[28] The Home Secretary announced in the House of Commons his disagreement with the findings of Lord Cullen's report:

> I propose to go considerably further than Lord Cullen has suggested in two respects. First, we shall ban all handguns from people's homes. I do not agree with Lord Cullen that it would be safe to allow single-shot handguns to remain in the home. I believe that they should be subject to the same controls as those imposed on multi-shot handguns.
>
> Secondly, we shall outlaw high-calibre handguns of the kind used by Thomas Hamilton. Low-calibre handguns—.22 rimfire handguns—will have to be used and kept in licensed clubs. We believe that a distinction needs to be made between high-calibre handguns, which are principally made for police and military use, and .22 rimfire handguns, which are largely intended for target shooting.[29]

Other ideas voiced after the Dunblane massacre included a system requiring holders of firearms and shotguns to obtain an annual certificate of fitness to hold a firearm from their doctor each year. The gun lobby objected to this, citing the cost, and the British Medical Association also opposed the move, claiming that it would be impossible for doctors to provide such "sanity certificates." [30] While past mental illness, alcoholism, and drug addiction is taken into account when issuing firearms or shot gun certificates, the British Medical Association has stated that

> it is virtually impossible for a doctor to make a judgement about someone's fitness to hold a gun . . . . And given the number of certificates issued annually—each is renewable every three years—it would be frankly impossible for psychiatrists to provide a full psychiatric examination of everyone holding a certificate, and there would be no guarantee even then that you would spot the people at risk [31]

Doctors were also concerned over their potential liability if they provided a clean bill of health for a certificate and the holder later went on a rampage.

C. Compensation

---

[27] Law Library of Congress, *supra* note 8, at 3, *citing* House of Commons, Home Affairs Committee, Possession of Handguns, H.C. 393 (1995–96).

[28] *Id.*

[29] 282 PARL. DEB., H.C. (6th ser.) 832–33 (1996), http://www.publications.parliament.uk/pa/cm199596/cmhansrd/vo961016/debtext/61016-26.htm.

[30] Timmins, *supra* note 14, at 13.

[31] *Id.*

After the ban on handguns, the government established a £150 million (approximately US$200 million) program to compensate handgun owners for firearms that they handed in to police stations during an amnesty period that ran from July 1997 through February 1998. Handgun owners were able to opt for one of three levels of compensation:

(1) A flat rate for individual items;

(2) Payment at a rate published for individual items;

(3) Payment provided in accordance with an independent valuation. This typically occurred where a firearm had been adapted and its value increased beyond the listed price.[32]

This compensation program was criticized by some who considered that companies were not typically compensated for any losses they faced or incurred as a result of legislative changes.[33]

The amnesty and buyback program led to the surrender of 162,000 weapons and 700 tons of ammunition.[34]

III. Firearms Laws

The Firearms Act 1968 is the primary piece of legislation that controls the use and possession of firearms. It has been amended many times and provides for over fifty firearms-related offenses that aim to control and restrict firearms use.[35] The Act is described as a "regulatory regime that is coercively enforced by way of criminal offences and penal sanctions."[36] Different categories of weapons are provided for by the Act, including firearms, prohibited weapons, shot guns, air weapons, and imitation firearms.

A. Definition of Firearm

Section 57(1) of the Firearms Act 1968 defines "firearm" as

> . . . a lethal barreled weapon of any description from which any shot, bullet or other missile can be discharged and includes –
> (a) any prohibited weapon, whether it is such a lethal weapon as aforesaid or not; and
> (b) any component part of such a lethal or prohibited weapon; and
> (c) any accessory to any such weapon designed or adapted to diminish the noise or flash caused by firing the weapon.[37]

---

[32] Right to Compensation Under Firearms (Amendment) Act 1997, THE LAWYER, May 12, 1998, at 11.

[33] *Id.*

[34] Burrell, *supra* note 1, at 3.

[35] Firearms Act 1968, c. 27 sched., http://www.legislation.gov.uk/ukpga/1968/27/schedule/6.

[36] BLACKSTONE'S CRIMINAL PRACTICE 2011 (Peter Murphy et al. eds., 2011).

[37] Firearms Act 1968, s. 57(1).

While the definition of firearm refers to lethal barreled weapons, it is not further defined by statute. When considering if an item is a lethal barreled weapon the court established a test "that a weapon is lethal if it is capable of causing injury from which death might result, regardless of the maker's intention."[38] Thus the question of whether an item is a lethal barreled weapon is a question of fact. The Court of Appeal has ruled that the judge should consider whether the item is capable of being used as a firearm and the jury should then determine whether it is a lethal weapon.[39]

B. Prohibited Weapons

There are a number of firearms that are prohibited in Britain. It is an offense to possess, purchase, acquire, manufacture, sell, or transfer these prohibited weapons without the written authority of the Defence Council or Scottish Ministers.[40] The Defence Council or Scottish Ministers can attach any conditions that they believe are necessary to any authority permitting ownership to ensure that a prohibited weapon or ammunition is secured and will not endanger public safety or the peace.[41]

Prohibited weapons include military style weapons, firearms disguised as other objects, and

> a) any firearm which is so designed or adapted that two or more missiles can be successively discharged without repeated pressure on the trigger;
> (ab) any self-loading or pump-action rifled gun other than one which is chambered for .22 rim-fire cartridges;
> (aba) any firearm which either has a barrel less than 30 centimetres in length or is less than 60 centimetres in length overall, other than an air weapon, . . . a muzzle-loading gun or a firearm designed as signalling apparatus;
> (ac) any self-loading or pump-action smooth-bore gun which is not an air weapon or chambered for .22 rim-fire cartridges and either has a barrel less than 24 inches in length or . . . is less than 40 inches in length overall;
> (ad) any smooth-bore revolver gun other than one which is chambered for 9mm. rim-fire cartridges or a muzzle-loading gun;
> (ae) any rocket launcher, or any mortar, for projecting a stabilised missile, other than a launcher or mortar designed for line-throwing or pyrotechnic purposes or as signalling apparatus;
> (af) any air rifle, air gun or air pistol which uses, or is designed or adapted for use with, a self-contained gas cartridge system;
> (b) any weapon of whatever description designed or adapted for the discharge of any noxious liquid, gas or other thing; and

---

[38] BLACKSTONE'S CRIMINAL PRACTICE, *supra* note 36 ¶ 12.6 (referring to Read v. Donovan [1947] KB 326).

[39] *Id.* (referring to Singh [1989] Crim. L.R. 724).

[40] Firearm Act 1968, § 5, http://www.legislation.gov.uk/ukpga/1968/27/section/5.

[41] *Id.*

(c) any cartridge with a bullet designed to explode on or immediately before impact, any ammunition containing or designed or adapted to contain any such noxious thing as is mentioned in paragraph (b) above and, if capable of being used with a firearm of any description, any grenade, bomb (or other like missile), or rocket or shell designed to explode as aforesaid.[42]

---

[42] *Id.*

C. Lawful Ownership and Use: Certification

The Firearms Act 1968 makes it unlawful to possess, purchase, or acquire a firearm, shotgun, or ammunition that is not prohibited in Britain without a certificate,[43] although this regulation is subject to certain exemptions.[44] For the purposes of licensing, shotguns are distinguished from firearms, which are defined above. Individuals who wish to obtain a certificate to possess a firearm or shotgun must apply to the chief officer of the police in the area in which they reside and show that they have a "good reason" to possess each weapon. The term "good reason" is "one of the most substantial and complex areas of discretion that chief officers may exercise in licensing firearms."[45] The reasons for ownership must be genuine and substantial, and the police are expected to make reasonable inquiries to determine the reason. These include verifying the species present on land for those wishing to shoot animals to ensure that the firearm for which the certificate is sought is suitable for the purpose.[46] Where target shooting is the reason, the police must verify that the applicant is a member of a club.[47]

The desire to own a particular weapon or the claimed need for self-defense are not deemed to be sufficiently good reasons to obtain a firearms certificate.[48] Firearms inquiry officers may visit the applicant to determine whether their good reason is bona fide.[49] It is an offense to either knowingly or recklessly make a false statement to obtain, either personally or for another person, a firearm or shotgun certificate.[50]

Until recently, individuals under eighteen years of age could legally purchase or hire firearms, shotguns, and ammunition in Great Britain. A Directive from the European Union altered this: the age that firearms may be purchased has been harmonized within the European Union to eighteen years of age.[51]

---

[43] *Id.* §§ 1–2.

[44] *Id.* §§ 7–15.

[45] Home Office, *Firearms Law Guidance to the Police*, 2002, ¶ 13.2, http://www.homeoffice. gov.uk/publications/police/firearms/HO-Firearms-Guidance.pdf?view=Binary.

[46] *Id.* at 77. A table shows the types of firearms considered suitable for shooting animals.

[47] *Id.* ¶ 13.4.

[48] Firearms Act 1968, c. 27 § 30A, http://www.legislation.gov.uk/ukpga/1968/27/section/30A.

[49] *FAQs*, METROPOLITAN POLICE, http://content.met.police.uk/Site/firearmslicensingfaqs (last visited Jan. 21, 2013).

[50] Firearms Act 1968, c. 27 § 28A, http://www.legislation.gov.uk/ukpga/1968/27/section/28.

[51] Firearms Acts (Amendment) Regulations 2010, SI 2010/1759, http://www.legislation.gov.uk/ uksi/2010/1759/made.

1. Shotgun Certificate

Applications for a shotgun[52] certificate must include

- a completed application form as provided for by the Firearms Rules;[53]

- four passport-sized photographs, one signed by a referee (reference) that it is a true likeness of the applicant;[54] and

- a signed statement by a referee that the information contained in the application is correct and that they know of no reason that the person should not be allowed to possess a shotgun.

The person providing the signed statement must "(a) be resident in Great Britain, (b) have known the applicant personally for at least two years, and (c) be a member of Parliament, justice of the peace, minister of religion, doctor, lawyer, established civil servant, bank officer or person of similar standing."[55]

Shotgun certificates may be granted by the chief officer of police if he is satisfied that the applicant's possession of a shotgun will not pose a danger to public safety or the peace. Certificates will not be granted if the chief officer of police

(a) has reason to believe that the applicant is prohibited by this Act from possessing a shot gun; or

(b) is satisfied that the applicant does not have a good reason for possessing, purchasing or acquiring one.[56]

The term "good reason" for possession of shotguns includes reasons connected with the certificate holder's profession, sport or recreation, or shooting vermin.[57] The requirement for "good reason" to possess a shotgun was introduced after the Hungerford massacre and concerns that weapons were being purchased for self-defense.[58]

---

[52] Shotgun is defined in section 1(3) of the Firearms Act 1968, c. 27 as "(a) . . . a smooth-bore gun (not being an air gun) which – (i) has a barrel not less than 24 inches in length and does not have any barrel with a bore exceeding 2 inches in diameter; (ii) either has no magazine or has a non-detachable magazine incapable of holding more than two cartridges; and (iii) is not a revolver gun[.]"

[53] The Firearms Rules 1998, SI 1998/1941, ¶ 5(1) & sched. 2, http://www.legislation.gov.uk/uksi/1998/1941/schedule/2/made.

[54] *Id.* ¶ 7(1).

[55] *Id.* ¶ 6(2).

[56] Firearms Act 1968, c. 27 § 28(1A), http://www.legislation.gov.uk/ukpga/1968/27/section/28.

[57] Firearms Act 1968 § 28(1B), http://www.legislation.gov.uk/ukpga/1968/27/section/28.

[58] LAW LIBRARY OF CONGRESS, *supra* note 8, at 11 (citing Home Office, *Firearms Act 1968 Proposals for Reform,* Cmnd. 6, No. 261 (1987), ¶ 25).

2. Firearm Certificate

Applications for a firearm certificate must include

- a completed application form as provided for by the Firearms Rules;[59]

- the names and addresses of two people acting as referees, who must be residents of Great Britain, of good character, and have personally known the applicant for at least two years;[60] and

- four passport-sized photographs, one signed by the applicant and one signed by a referee.

The referees are used to "provide confidential character statements in which they are expected to answer in detail about the applicant's mental state, home life and attitude towards guns."[61]

The chief officer of police may grant a firearm certificate if he is satisfied that the applicant is not prohibited by the Firearms Act from possessing a firearm; is fit to be entrusted with a firearm; has good reason for possessing, purchasing, or acquiring the firearm or ammunition; and that the applicant's possession of the firearm does not pose a danger to public safety or the peace.[62]

3. Medical Requirements for Firearm and Shotgun Certificates

The application forms for both firearm and shotgun certificates require information such as the medical history of the applicant, including a release that allows the police to obtain the applicant's medical history from his/her doctor. The police typically check with the doctor if there is "evidence of alcoholism, drug abuse or signs of personality disorder. Social services can also be asked for reasons to turn down an applicant."[63]

Guidance on the implementation of the firearms law states that the authority to obtain the applicant's medical history is not routinely used, but rather used

> . . . in cases where there are genuine doubts or concerns about the applicant's medical history that may have a bearing on the applicant's suitability to possess firearms. The authority should be used only where the doubts or concerns about the applicant's medical history appear to require more detailed information to enable the final assessment of the application to be conducted. Such doubts or concerns might be prompted by the

---

[59] The Firearms Rules 1998, SI 1998/1941, sched. 1, http://www.legislation.gov.uk/uksi/1998/1941/schedule/1/made.

[60] *Id.* ¶ 4(3).

[61] Dominic Casciani, *Gun Control and Ownership Laws in the UK*, BBC, Nov. 2, 2010, http://www.bbc.co.uk/news/10220974.

[62] Firearms Act 1968, c. 27 § 27, http://www.legislation.gov.uk/ukpga/1968/27/section/27.

[63] Casciani, *supra* note 61.

applicant's answers to the medical questions on the application, or they may arise from other information available to the police.[64]

The ability of the police to check the applicant's medical history is not time limited to the initial application period for the certificate. The police may, at any time during the life of the certificate, check with the applicant's doctor if concerns over the applicant's fitness to possess firearms arise.[65]

4. Conditions of Ownership of Firearms

A firearm certificate details the type and number of weapons that it covers, including identification numbers and quantities of ammunition the holder may purchase or acquire and possess at one time.[66] Conditions under which the firearm may be used may be attached to any certificate granted. In certain cases, conditions are imposed by statute—for example, rifles or muzzle-loading pistols covered by a certificate can only be used for target shooting, and the holder of the certificate must be a member of an approved rifle or muzzle-loading pistol club.[67]

Conditions of the certificate for both firearms and shotguns include keeping the weapon and ammunition secured in a safe place when not in use to prevent access by an unauthorized person, and promptly reporting any loss or theft to the police. There are very specific levels of security that must be met to prove the secure storage of firearms, including cabinets that meet specific British safety standards.[68]

When considering whether firearms are kept safely, the police must take into account whether any unauthorized access to the firearms may occur, including by family members and associates who pose a danger to public safety.[69] "Unauthorized access" has been broadly interpreted to include situations where individuals other than the holder of the certificate have access to the keys for the secure storage where the firearms are kept.[70]

An example of how strictly the secure storage requirements for weapons are interpreted was highlighted in 2000 when Arthur Farrer, a former partner at Farrer & Co., the Queen's lawyers, informed his eighty-one-year-old mother where he kept the keys to his gun cupboard. The police revoked Farrer's license, a decision that was later upheld by the Court of Appeal, despite the police indicating that Farrer's mother never handled the guns or otherwise expressed any interest in them.[71]

---

[64] Home Office, *supra* note 45, ¶ 10.20.

[65] *Id.* ¶ 10.24.

[66] Firearms Act 1968, c. 27 § 27, http://www.legislation.gov.uk/ukpga/1968/27/section/27.

[67] Firearms (Amendment) Act 1997, c. 5 § 44(1), www.legislation.gov.uk/ukpga/1997/5/contents.

[68] Home Office, *supra* note 45, ch. 19.

[69] *Id.* ¶ 12.9.

[70] *Id.*

[71] *Id.* ¶ 19.7, Regina v. Chelmsford Crown Court, Ex parte Farrer, [2000] 1 WLR 1468; *It's Been a Bad Week Fore*, THE LAWYER, Mar. 13, 2000, at 64.

5. Duration and Revocation of Certificates

Once granted, a firearm certificate is typically valid for a five-year period.[72]   However, firearm certificates may be revoked if the person is

- A danger to public safety or to the peace;
- Of intemperate habits;
- Of unsound mind;
- Unfit to be entrusted with such a firearm;
- A prohibited person under the Firearms Act; or
- No longer has 'good reason' for possession.[73]

Each case is judged on its own merits and circumstances.   The police have provided guidance on how the above terms should be interpreted.   Criteria that justify the revocation of a certificate for "intemperate habits" include evidence of alcohol or drug abuse; aggressive or antisocial behavior, such as domestic disputes; or hostility towards a group of people. Consideration is also given to

> disturbing or unusual behaviour of a kind which gives rise to well-founded fears about the future misuse of firearms. A pattern of abuse should generally be regarded more seriously than a single incident, although isolated incidents should not be disregarded in the assessment of the person concerned and their fitness to possess a firearm.[74]

When determining whether a person is unfit to possess a firearm, the police consider whether the person is a prohibited person under the Firearms Act, whether they have any convictions or cautions, or whether they have any other known involvement in criminal offenses.[75]   Cases where a refusal to grant a certificate, or the revocation of a certificate, have been upheld include where the holder had drunk-driving convictions and where a spouse of the holder had two prior drug convictions but continued to associate with drug users.[76]

Refusing to grant, or revoking, a license on the grounds that the applicant or holder is of "unsound mind" is a sensitive area. Guidance to the police notes the difficulties of providing a definition of the term that covers every eventuality, and points out that it is "impractical for a psychiatric assessment to be conducted on an applicant's suitability to possess firearms."[77] Instead, the police are required to consider any "signs of depression, suicidal tendencies, long-standing or intermittent periods of either emotional instability or unpredictable behaviour. Chief officers should also be alert to any of these signs exhibited by existing certificate holders."[78]

---

[72] Firearms Act 1968, c. 27, § 28A, http://www.legislation.gov.uk/ukpga/1968/27/section/28A.

[73] *Id.* §§ 27–28; *see also* Home Office, *supra* note 45.

[74] Home Office, *supra* note 45, ¶ 12.8.

[75] *Id.* ¶ 12.3.

[76] *Id.* (citing Dabek v. Chief Constable of Devon and Cornwall, 155 J.B. Rep. 55 (1990)).

[77] *Id.* ¶ 12.9.

[78] *Id.*

Periods of detention under the Mental Health Act are considered; however, the guidance specifically notes that there should be "no correlation between periods of imprisonment and periods of detention under the Mental Health Act."[79]   In cases where there have been past instances of mental health issues such as depression, the police must

> remember[] that simply because a person has received treatment in the past for certain illnesses or conditions, such as depression or stress, it does not automatically follow that they are unfit to possess a firearm. It is simply one of the factors to be considered with all other evidence relating to the applicant's character and history. In such cases, account should be taken of the latest medical opinion.[80]

Shotgun certificates may be revoked by the chief officer of police if he is satisfied that the holder is prohibited by the Act from possessing a shotgun, or if the individual poses a danger to public safety or the peace through his or her possession of the shotgun.[81]

Individuals convicted of an offense under the Firearms Act, or a crime where a term of imprisonment is imposed, may be ordered by the court to forfeit or dispose of any firearm or ammunition held, and cancel any firearm or shotgun certificate held by the individual.[82]

6. Appealing the Denial of a Certificate

The refusal of the police to grant a firearm or shotgun certificate is appealable to the Crown Court (or the Sheriff in Scotland).[83]   In these cases, the court is exercising an administrative function; therefore the normal rules of evidence do not apply in these cases.[84] One commentator has noted that, in practice, decisions by the police to refuse a certificate can in some cases be arbitrary and be made for reasons such as "the nature of a person's lifestyle or associates, to (which is rare) criminal activity."[85]   Frustrations have been voiced regarding the appeals process both by the police, who consider that in certain instances their decisions are overturned without full consideration,[86] and by the applicants for certificates, who consider that the process, which is expensive and therefore in many instances inaccessible, is against their favor due to the evidentiary rules.[87]

---

[79] *Id.*

[80] *Id.*

[81] Firearms Act 1968, c. 27, § 30C, http://www.legislation.gov.uk/ukpga/1968/27/section/30C.

[82] *Id.* § 52, http://www.legislation.gov.uk/ukpga/1968/27/section/52.

[83] *Id.* § 44, http://www.legislation.gov.uk/ukpga/1968/27/section/44.

[84] Kavanagh v. Chief Constable of Cornwall [1974] Q.B. 624 (C.A.). *See also* Burton, *supra* note 4.

[85] *Id.*

[86] Duncan Campbell, *Gun Laws: Police and Clubs Call for Calm Amid Firearms Outcry*, GUARDIAN (London), Mar. 15, 1996, at 2.

[87] *Id.*

7. Statistics on Certificates Granted

While the legislation that authorizes possession of firearms is relatively stringent, certificates are still granted. For the period 2008-2009, 138,728 certificates for firearms and 574,946 certificates for shotguns were in effect. In March 2012, almost 142,000 firearm certificates were in effect and over 560,000 shotgun certificates.[88] The refusal rate of certificates for these weapons is low, at 1 and 2%, respectively. In 2008-2009, 1,300 certificates were revoked.[89]

The Metropolitan Police has stated that firearms certificates in its area are granted predominantly for "single shot rifles of any caliber, self-loading .22RF rifles (and corresponding ammunition) and muzzle loading pistols."[90]

8. Prohibited Individuals

Individuals absolutely prohibited from obtaining a firearm or shotgun certificate include those who have been sentenced to any form of custody or preventive detention for three years or more.[91] Those with sentences for more than three months but less than three years cannot possess firearms or ammunition for a period of five years after the date of release.[92]

9. Exemptions from Certification

There are a number of exemptions for holding firearm and shotgun certificates. These include, *inter alia*, exemptions for

- holders of temporary permits, which are typically granted to allow an executor to dispose of a weapon that belongs to the estate he or she is administering;

- authorized firearms dealers who handle weapons for which they do not personally hold a certificate;

- people licensed to slaughter animals, who may possess a slaughtering instrument and ammunition in the slaughterhouse where they are employed;

- auctioneers, carriers, or warehousemen possessing firearms in the ordinary course of business;

- people possessing firearms during and for theatrical, film, and television production, performances; or rehearsals or theatrical productions;

---

[88] Home Office, *Firearm and Shotgun Certificates in England and Wales 2011/12*, http://www.homeoffice. gov.uk/publications/science-research-statistics/research-statistics/police-research/hosb1012/hosb1012?view=Binary.

[89] Casciani, *supra* note 61.

[90] *Firearms Applications*, METROPOLITAN POLICE, http://content.met.police.uk/Site/firearms licensingfirearmsapplications (last visited Jan. 21, 2013).

[91] Firearms Act 1968, c. 27, § 21, http://www.legislation.gov.uk/ukpga/1968/27/section/21.

[92] *Id.*

- people holding firearms at athletic meetings for the purpose of starting a race or for other sporting purposes;

- people using air weapons or miniature rifles that do not exceed .23-inch caliber at a miniature rifle range, or shotguns at an approved time and place for shooting artificial targets;[93]

- firearms on board a ship as part of its equipment;

- people who borrow the shotgun of an occupier of private premises[94] for use on that private premises only.[95]

D. Clubs and Firearms

As noted above, shooting clubs may be used by people who do not hold a firearm or shotgun certificate. There are stringent conditions that must be met for a club to be approved. Approval is from the Home Secretary for clubs in England and Wales, and from the Secretary of State for clubs in Scotland. Once approved as a club under the Act, any members may possess firearms or ammunition without a certificate "when engaged as a member of the club in connection with target shooting."[96]

Authorities must ensure that clubs meet the following extensive criteria prior to approval:

- the club is a genuine target shooting club with at least 10 members at all times and a written constitution;

- the principal officers of the club are responsible people who can be entrusted with the proper administration of the club;

- members are of good character;

- the club must appoint a member to act as a liaison officer with the police, and the chief officer of police must have confidence that this person is providing the police with such information as they require to ensure that the activities of the club and its members are conducted properly and safely and give no cause for concern;

- the club maintains a register of the attendance of all members together with details for each visit of the firearms which they used . . . ;

- the club will inform the police of any holder of a firearm certificate who has ceased to be a member for whatever reason;

---

[93] Firearms (Amendment) Act 1988, c. 45 § 15(1), http://www.legislation.gov.uk/ukpga/1988/45/contents.

[94] The term "occupier" is not defined in the Act. Guidance to the police recommends that, until judicially defined otherwise, the term be interpreted in accordance with section 27 of the Wildlife and Countryside Act 1981. Section 27 states "that 'occupier' in relation to any land, other than the foreshore, includes any person having any right of hunting, shooting, fishing or taking game or fish." Home Office, *supra* note 45, ¶ 6.14.

[95] Firearms Act 1968, c. 27 §§ 8–15, http://www.legislation.gov.uk/ukpga/1968/27/part/I/crossheading/special-exemptions-from-sections-1-to-5.

[96] Firearms (Amendment) Act 1988, c. 45 § 15(1), http://www.legislation.gov.uk/ukpga/1988/45/contents.

- the club will inform the police if any member who holds a firearm certificate has not shot with the club for a period of 12 months;

- the club will inform the police of any application for membership, giving the applicant's name and address, and of the outcome of any application;

- members, prospective members and guests must sign a declaration that they are not prohibited from possessing a firearm or ammunition by virtue of section 21 of the Firearms Act 1968 (which applies to persons who have served a term of imprisonment);

- the club has regular use of ranges with safety certificates for the categories of firearm in respect of which approval is being sought or given, as the case may be;

- the security arrangements for the storage of club firearms and ammunition are satisfactory;

- the club does not run a day or temporary membership scheme;

- the club does not have more than 12 guest days a year. Guest members must be either members of a recognised outside organisation or people who are known personally to at least one full member of the club;

- guests must be supervised on a one-to-one basis at all times when handling firearms and ammunition by either a full club member or someone who is a coach with a qualification recognised by the UK or national Sports Council. The club secretary must notify each guest day to the police firearms licensing department of the area in which the guest day is to take place at least 48 hours in advance;

- anyone who applies for membership must be sponsored by at least one full club member;

- before becoming a full member, individuals must have a probationary period of at least three months during which time they must attend and shoot regularly. The probationary member must be given a course in the safe handling and use of firearms on a one-to-one basis by someone who is either a full member of the club or who is a coach with a qualification recognised by the Great Britain Target Shooting Federation and governing bodies;

- until a probationary member has satisfactorily completed a course in the safe handling and use of firearms, he/she must be supervised at all times when in possession of firearms or ammunition by either the range officer, or a full member of the club, or someone who is a coach with a qualification recognised by the Great Britain Target Shooting Federation and/or governing bodies;

- there is nothing else that would make the club unsuitable for approval.[97]

IV. Minimum Sentencing Laws

Strict penalties and mandatory minimum sentencing further enhance the laws regulating gun ownership in Britain. A number of firearms offenses carry mandatory minimum prison

---

[97] Home Office, *Approval of Rifle and Muzzle-loading Pistol Clubs* (Apr. 2012), http://www.homeoffice. gov.uk/publications/police/firearms/approval-rifle-pistol-clubs.

sentences, which is the minimum term provided for by the offense unless there are exceptional circumstances that justify deviating from this.[98]   One result of this law is that anyone found unlawfully possessing a firearm faces a five-year mandatory minimum jail sentence.

The government has raised concerns that mandatory minimum sentencing is applied inconsistently, attributed in part to differing interpretations of the term "exceptional circumstances."[99]   In an attempt to clarify this, the Court of Appeal held that circumstances are "exceptional" if the imposition of the minimum term would result in an arbitrary and disproportionate sentence.[100]

V. Effectiveness of the Legislation

In 2010/11 fifty-two victims of homicide were killed by firearms. This figure includes the twelve victims of the Cumbrian shootings. Of the total recorded offenses for this period, 11,227 involved firearms. The use of firearms in offenses has been slowly falling for the past seven years, and by 2010/11 had decreased by 13% from the previous year. Handguns were used for 3,105 offenses in 2010/11, down almost 17% from 2009/10. There was a slight increase in the number of offenses that involved shotguns; however, these still remain fairly low and range between 580–640 offenses per year.[101]

The following table lists Home Office statistics for firearms used during offenses, for parliamentary years 2000/01 through 2010/11:[102]

Weapon Used*	2000/1	2001/2	2002/3	2003/4	2004/5	2005/6
Shotgun	73	111	107	104	135	154
Hand gun	400	648	640	590	780	1024
Other firearms	909	1,120	1,432	1,673	2,989	2,644
All firearms	1,382	1,879	2,179	2,367	3,904	3,822

Weapon Used	2006/7	2007/8	2008/9	2009/10	2010/11
Shotgun	128	157	137	141	157
Hand gun	792	881	493	504	483
Other firearms	2,091	2,203	1,131	1,268	1,309
All firearms	3,011	3,241	1,761	1,913	1,949

*Statistical data for air weapons is excluded from this chart.

---

[98] Firearms Act 1968, c. 27 § 51A, http://www.legislation.gov.uk/ukpga/1968/27/section/51A.

[99] MEMORANDUM TO THE HOME AFFAIRS COMMITTEE POST-LEGISLATIVE ASSESSMENT OF THE VIOLENT CRIME REDUCTION ACT 2006, Cm. 8327, 2011-12, at 10, *available at* http://www.official-documents.gov.uk/document/cm83/8327/8327.pdf.

[100] R v. Rehman, R v. Wood, [2006] Cr. App. R.(S.) 77, CA.

[101] Home Office, Statistical News Release, Homicides, Firearm Offences and Intimate Violence 2010/11: Supplementary Volume 2 to Crime in England and Wales 2010/11, Jan. 2012, www.homeoffice.gov.uk/publications/science-research-statistics/research-statistics/crime-research/hosb0212/hosb0212snr?view=Binary.

[102] Figures taken from *id.*

The following table lists the number of homicides that involved the use of a firearm, as reported by the Home Office:[103]

	2000/1	2001/2	2002/3	2003/4	2004/5	2005/6	2006/7	2007/8	2008/9	2009/10	2010/11
Firearm Homicides	62	90	57	61	62	38	52	47	35	33	52

Despite the country's stringent gun laws, newspaper reports indicate that illegal handguns can be purchased for £50–100 (approximately US$70–155).[104] In 2002 a Member of Parliament stated that there are some inner-city areas "in which it is now easier to buy an illegal gun than to find a taxi in the rain."[105] Newspapers reported that in the two years after the ban on handguns enacted after the Dunblane massacre the number of crimes in which handguns were carried increased by 40%.[106]

According to news reports, the source of illegal firearms entering Britain is diverse, with many originating from within the EU and even as close by as Northern Ireland, with allegations that since the ceasefire paramilitary groups have been disposing of their surplus weapons.[107] Reports also indicate that weapons are coming from as far afield as the US, Australia, and Argentina.[108] Customs officers have noted that there has been an increase in the amount of weapons originating from Central and Eastern Europe.[109] Regardless of the origin of these weapons, those that enter Britain are most commonly smuggled in by vehicles at ports, with estimates considering that 160 handguns enter the UK every year intended for criminal use.[110] However, in spite of this the numbers of weapons being intercepted has remained relatively low. In 2003 customs officers seized 126 handguns, 102 rifles, and 36 shotguns that were being smuggled into the country.[111]

Scotland Yard has expressed concern over the number of gun-related incidents, including

---

[103] Figures taken from *id.*

[104] Paul Lashmar, *Gun UK: A Teenage Girl is Dead and a Baby Wounded . . .*, THE INDEPENDENT ON SUNDAY (London), Oct. 17, 2004 (accessed via Lexis).

[105] *Gun Law Off-target*, DAILY TELEGRAPH (London), Aug. 13, 2002, at 19.

[106] *Id.*

[107] Lashmar, *supra* note 104.

[108] *Id.*

[109] *Id.*

[110] Burrell, *supra* note 1.

[111] Lashmar, *supra* note 104. *See also Ten Years of Operation Trident*, TIMEOUT LONDON (Feb. 19, 2009), http://www.timeout.com/london/things-to-do/ten-years-of-operation-trident-2.

those using prohibited weapons, to the point that it planned to increase the number of officers carrying firearms on the street. The increase in gun crime led the Metropolitan Police to start Operation Trident in 1998, which is aimed at reducing the number of firearms incidents.[112]

The Association of Chief Police Officers' lead officer on licensing has stated that the system of certification in Britain serves only to minimize the risk of gun crime and cannot completely eliminate it.[113] However, in the wake of the Sandy Hook shootings in the US former Home Secretary Jack Straw maintained that the gun laws introduced after the shooting in Dunblane have reduced the risk of massacres in Britain.[114]

Prepared by Clare Feikert-Ahalt
Senior Foreign Law Specialist

---

[112] Jason Bennetto, *Drug Gangs Force Police to Increase Firearms Officers*, INDEPENDENT (London), Jan. 30, 2004 (accessed via Lexis).

[113] Casciani, *supra* note 61.

[114] Rowena Mason, Connecticut School Shootings: Gun Controls Reduce Risk of Massacres, Says Jack Straw, THE TELEGRAPH (London), Dec. 16, 2012 (accessed via Lexis).

ISRAEL

FIREARMS CONTROL LEGISLATION AND POLICY

Summary

Israeli law regulates the issuance of firearms to both civilians and soldiers. Israel maintains restrictive policies with regard to issuing and renewing firearms licenses, and restricts their use.

The law designates persons holding certain positions, such as designated ministry employees, authorized community leaders, managers or owners of premises, and licensed guards and escorts, as eligible for firearms licenses based on security needs. Licensed private investigators, providers of guard services, and authorized escorts for field trips or camping trips may similarly be granted a license. The law also authorizes the issuance of firearms licenses to film producers and performers for purposes of gun possession or use during a performance.

Issuing a firearms license for private use to other persons requires proof of the existence of a cause that justifies the license. In addition to specific training and mental health requirements, applicants must prove that possession of a firearm is needed based on the location of their residence or employment, the type of occupation they are engaged in, or service in elite Israel Defense Force (IDF) reserve units.

Military firearms are issued to IDF soldiers. As a general rule, a soldier does not take his gun on home leave. Exceptions to this rule apply to soldiers who serve in combat units, those who serve in the West Bank or other specified areas, or who have obtained special authorization from high-ranking military officers based on their officer rank or for reasons of personal safety associated with their home or service location.

I. Introduction

There is no clear right to bear arms under Israeli law. In accordance with Israel's Firearms Law, 5709-1949 (the Law)[1] activities involving firearms, including the manufacture, trade, possession and use of firearms, require authorization. Accordingly, any act involving firearms for civilian use requires a special license issued by the Ministry of Public Security and approved by the police. Activities involving firearms for Israeli Defense Forces (IDF) use

---

[1] Firearms Law, 5709-1949, § 11, 3 LAWS OF THE STATE OF ISRAEL [LSI] 61 (5709-1949), as amended.

require authorization by the Minister of Defense.[2] The issuance of a license or authorization for firearms is based on restrictive criteria established by the relevant Ministry.[3]

The Law defines a "firearm" as

… a barreled instrument adapted to throw a bullet, projectile, shell, bomb or the like, capable of killing a person, and includes any part of, accessory to and ammunition for such an instrument, including a container that contains or may contain such material, excluding a container for tear gas.[4]

II. Licensing of Firearms to Civilians

A. Statutory Requirements

1. Proper Operation and Training

The Firearms Law requires the firearm subject to a license to be checked and approved as suitable for use prior to the issuance of a license.[5] The Law further requires the individual obtaining the license to have proper training in the use of the specific firearm he wishes to acquire or possess.[6] Firearms Regulations (Training for the Grant and Renewal of a License) 5752-1992[7] regulate training programs, their frequency, and certification of training, which is required as a precondition for the grant and renewal of firearms licenses. According to the Regulations, a person who possesses different types of firearms must undergo training for each one of them.

The Law requires shooting ranges and their supervisors to be licensed.[8] The Law further regulates the admission of trainees, including those operating firearms for sport purposes, into shooting ranges by requiring proof of minimum age, depending on the type of activity for which the training is sought, as well as recommendations from appropriate associations such as sport associations, for training in specific types of firearms.[9]

---

[2] *Id.* § 11.

[3] For the Ministry of Public Security policy regarding licensing, *see Criteria for Grant of a License for Personal Possession of a Firearm as Approved by the Minister on Aug. 4, 2011*, ISRAEL MINISTRY OF PUBLIC SECURITY (MOPS) (Aug 19, 2011), http://mops.gov.il/Pages/Firearm LicensingCriterion.aspx (in Hebrew).

[4] Firearms Law § 1 (translated by author, R.L.).

[5] Firearms Law § 5A.

[6] *Id.* § 5C.

[7] Firearms Regulations (Training for the Grant and Renewal of a License), 5752-1992, KOVETZ HATAKANOT (Subsidiary Regulations) No. 5415 p. 668 (in Hebrew).

[8] Firearms Law §§ 7, 7C.

[9] *Id.* § 7A1.

2. Persons Who May Obtain a License

The Law authorizes the Minister of Interior and the Minister of Defense (hereinafter licensing authorities) to issue licenses to

- the leader of a community for the protection of the people and property of, and traffic to and from, the community;[10]

- the owner or manager of an eligible establishment to protect the premises, its employees, and traffic;[11]

- an employee designated by a Minister for security purposes in connection with the functions of the employees of that ministry;[12]

- the producers of a film or a play, or people authorized by them to carry a licensed firearm during a performance;[13]

- the holder of a license for guard or private investigator services under conditions prescribed in the special license;[14] and

- escorts for field trips or camping trips, provided that the application is made in advance as prescribed by the licensing authority.[15]

3. Mental Health Requirements

The Law requires any physician, psychologist, mental health officer, or social worker to file a report with the Manager of the Ministry of Health regarding any patients under their care who would constitute a danger to themselves or to the public if they had access to a firearm. Such a report may be forwarded by the Manager to the IDF[16] or to state security agencies such as the police or prison authorities, who routinely inform the Ministry of Health of the names of their applicants for employment.[17]

License applications and information regarding the eligibility of applicants for employment with security agencies must be forwarded by licensing officials to the Manager, who will inform them of any records of the applicants' hospitalizations for mental health problems.[18]

---

[10] *Id.* § 9.

[11] *Id.* § 10.

[12] *Id.* § 10A.

[13] *Id.* § 10B.

[14] *Id.* § 10C.

[15] *Id.* § 10D.

[16] *Id.* § 11A(a).

[17] *Id.* § 11A(b).

[18] *Id.* § 11B.

4. Police Authority

A person who carries a firearm must carry his[19] license or authorization with him at all times and present them to any policeman who so requires.[20] A person who possesses a licensed firearm must deposit it at the police station at the place of his residence or occupation after expiration of his license. Special provisions apply to the seizure of firearms suspected of being involved in the perpetration of offenses.

5. Confiscation of Firearms and Revocation of Licenses

The Law imposes double penalties for committing offenses while using firearms.[21] In addition, a court that convicts a person of an offense against the Firearms Law may order the firearm to be forfeited to the state.[22]

In addition, the conviction of a person for a violent offense may, upon the prosecutor's request, result in an order for the cancellation of the person's firearm license and in license ineligibility for a period defined by the court. The conviction may also result in an order that the convicted person deposit his firearm at the police station close to his place of residence or business.[23] Such an order may also be prescribed by a court, upon a prosecutor's request, in cases involving convictions for domestic violence offenses.[24]

B. Ministry of Public Security Criteria for Licensing of Firearms

The Minister of Public Security is authorized to implement the Firearms Law.[25] According to information posted on the Ministry of Public Security (MOPS) website, the Ministry's policy is to limit the number of firearms available to the public, while giving preference to authorized organizations and their employees.[26] Indeed, whereas in the late 1980s during the first *Intifada* the number of private citizens who held firearms licenses reached 300,000, by June 2012 this number had been reduced to 170,000 and continues to decline.[27]

---

[19] Any reference to males in this report applies equally to females.

[20] Firearms Law § 13.

[21] *Id.* § 17.

[22] *Id.* § 18.

[23] *Id.* § 18A.

[24] *Id.* § 18B.

[25] *Id.* § 21. Note that implementation authorities were initially prescribed to the Minister of the Interior but were transferred to the Minister of Public Security on March 17, 2011, with firearms licensing authorities transferred to the head of the firearms licensing division in that Ministry on September 12, 2011. *See* YALKUT HAPIRSUMIM [Government Notices] No. 6214 p. 3162 (2001) *and* No. 6292 p. 6468 (2011), respectively.

[26] *See Criteria for Grant of a License for Personal Possession of a Firearm, supra* note 3.

[27] Tal Wolfowitz & Nitsan Shiri, *Deadly Weapon*, 1 DOMESTIC SECURITY 41 (June 2012), http://mops.gov.il/Documents/Publications/MopsNewsletter/MNL1June2012/MopsNewsletterFatalWeapon%20-p%2040-43.pdf (in Hebrew). *See also*, Yakov Amit, *History of Firearm Licensing in Israel*, MOPS,

According to the MOPS website, a person who wishes to obtain a firearm license must meet one of the criteria for issuance of a firearm license, as determined by the Minister in collaboration with security authorities. The current list of criteria is available on the Ministry's website[28] and is discussed below. A license is valid for a period of three years after which it must be renewed.[29]

The following discussion describes the evolution of criteria established by the MOPS from the mid-1990s to today.

1. Firearms' Licensing Criteria: 1995–2011

The Ministry's policy of restrictive licensing has evolved since the mid-1990s. A 1992 shooting at a psychiatric ward, killing four social workers, by a patient who as a security guard had a license to carry a weapon, prompted the appointment of the Cohen Inter-office Committee. The Committee reexamined the then-existing criteria for issuing firearms licenses and made recommendations that became the basis for new criteria adopted in 1995. According to these criteria, in addition to the criteria established by the Law, the issuance of firearms licenses is restricted to people who reside or work in dangerous geographic locations, those employed in lines of work requiring extra security, and groups involved in the country's public security.[30]

Further firearm licensing reform took place in 1999 and resulted in the introduction of additional preconditions. License applicants, accordingly, are required to complete proper firearms training and submit a health declaration verified by a family doctor attesting to their fitness to use a firearm. According to information posted on the MOPS website, the passage of the new restrictions has resulted in the reduction of the number of invalid licenses from 72,000 in 1999, to 33,000 after the initial introduction of the restrictions, and to less than 9,000 as of March 2012. Apparently, "[m]any of the people with invalid licenses are elderly individuals who are not aware of the new changes and requirements."[31]

The head of the MOPS Firearm Licensing Department, Yakov Amit, counted the sharp decline in the number of licenses, and the "[a]dvancement of capabilities" resulting from "the more stringent training requirements,"[32] as some of what he saw as accomplishments of the 1999 reform.

---

http://mops.gov.il/ English/AboutUsEnglish/Firearm/Pages/History_Firearm.aspx (last visited Dec. 17, 2012). Yakov Amit is the head of the Firearm Licensing Department at the Ministry of Public Security.

[28] *Criteria for Grant of a License for Personal Possession of a Firearm, supra* note 3.

[29] SHELI MIZRAHI, FIREARM LICENSES FOR PRIVATE CITIZENS: POLICY AND NUMERICAL DATA 2 n.10 (Knesset Information and Research Center, July 5, 2010), http://www.knesset.gov.il/mmm/data/pdf/m02587.pdf.

[30] Amit, *supra* note 27.

[31] *Id.*

[32] *Id.*

2. Firearms Licensing Criteria: August 2011–Present

New firearms licensing criteria were approved by the Minister for Public Security in August 2011. In addition to the criteria established by the Law (submission of a health form and training),[33] the new rules require proof of permanent residence and uninterrupted stay in Israel for a period of at least three years, and a basic knowledge of the Hebrew language.[34] They also establish minimum age requirements—twenty-seven for citizens with no military or national service ties, twenty-one for those who served in the Israel Defense Force (IDF) or national service, and forty-five for permanent residents who are not citizens.[35]

In addition, the 2011 criteria introduced a requirement of proof of "a cause that presumably justifies issuing a firearm license to an individual."[36] Such causes include residence or employment at locations that have been approved for firearms possession.[37] To obtain a gun license based on these grounds the applicant must submit proof that his life is centered in the approved municipality or that most of his work for three months preceding the application was performed there. A license based on these grounds is limited to "one gun and fifty additional bullets."[38]

Other causes that create a presumption of a justification for the issuance of firearms licenses to individuals include the transfer of explosives by a person licensed to do so, and the submission of invoices issued within the preceding three months or an income tax certificate attesting to the applicant's income from this occupation. A license based on this ground is similarly limited to "one gun and fifty additional bullets."[39]

High-ranking regular service officers at the captain ranking or higher in the IDF, or at a lieutenant or equivalent level in other security forces, who have served at least two years at this rank,[40] and reservists who belong to special reserve units, are similarly qualified for a restricted license for the possession of "one gun and fifty additional bullets."[41] An application for a license under these circumstances must include a recommendation by a unit commander at the rank of an IDF lieutenant colonel or higher, or the equivalent in other security services.[42]

---

[33] *Criteria for Grant of a License for Personal Possession of a Firearm, supra* note 3, at 2, items 3–4.

[34] *Id.* at 2, item 1.

[35] *Id.* item 2.

[36] *Id.*

[37] For example, dangerous locations requiring self-protection.

[38] *Criteria for Grant of a License for Personal Possession of a Firearm, supra* note 3, at 3, items 1–2. The text uses the term "אקדח" which means a gun, not the general term "כלי יריה" which means a firearm.

[39] *Id.* item 3.

[40] *Id.* item 4.

[41] *Id.* item 6.

[42] *Id.* items 4 & 6.

A gun license may also be issued to retired officers at the rank of lieutenant colonel or higher and to reservist officers at the rank of captain or higher, or to persons at equivalent ranks in other security forces. A license may also be issued to security officers in a public institution who were trained by the police and who have at least one year of experience on the job, and to other persons who are identified by the police or other security agencies as having a "special interest" for the purpose of gun possession. As in other cases, these licenses apply to the possession of "one gun and fifty additional bullets." Specific documentation and recommendations are similarly required.[43]

In addition to certain high-ranking security officers, firefighters and Magen David Adom[44] employees with at least one year experience may be eligible for a license for "one gun and fifty additional bullets."[45]

Instead of a license limited to "one gun and fifty additional bullets," an active sportsman/woman may qualify for a license for possession of a firearm that is recognized by the licensing authority as a firearm approved for sporting purposes, and for ammunition as determined by a shooting association.[46] Similarly, a license may be issued to a licensed hunter for a firearm recognized by the licensing authority as one used for hunting purposes, along with 700 bullets,[47] or to an authorized person for possession and use of a firearm that was similarly approved for "treatment of agricultural harm" and 700 bullets.[48]

As a general rule, an individual who qualifies for a license may be eligible for only one firearm. Possession of additional firearms may be licensed for special reasons, including when the additional firearm is an air or BB gun, when it is designed to be held as memorabilia, or when it is required for different fields of sports or for the prevention of harm to agriculture.[49]

III. Authorization for Possession of Military Firearms

A. Soldiers on Home Leave

The duties of soldiers to carry and safeguard personal weapons are regulated by orders issued by the IDF Central Command. As a general rule a soldier will not take his gun on home leave.[50] Exceptions to this rule apply to soldiers who

---

[43] *Id.* items 5, 6, 8 & 9.

[44] Magen David Adom is Israel's medical service association, equivalent to the Red Cross. For additional information, *see* the Magen David Adom website, http://www.mdais.com/271/ (last visited Dec. 20, 2012).

[45] *Criteria for Grant of a License for Personal Possession of a Firearm, supra* note 3, items 10-11.

[46] *Id.* item 12.

[47] *Id.* item 14.

[48] *Id.* item 13.

[49] *Id.* § 3.

[50] IDF Central Command Order No. 2.0101, Duty for Carrying and Safeguarding Personal Weapons, issued June 15, 1986, updated Oct. 11, 2007, § 5, http://dover.idf.il/IDF/pkuda/020101.doc (in Hebrew). The Order uses the term נשק, correlating to "weapon" in the English language.

- serve in combat units;

- serve in the West Bank or in other areas specified by an order for this purpose;

- were authorized by their unit officer at the rank of a colonel or higher for reasons of personal safety associated with their home or service location; or

- are officers whose request for a personal military weapon was approved by their unit officer at a ranking of colonel or higher.[51]

The IDF recognizes that personal weapons are an attractive target for theft by both terrorist and criminal elements.[52] According to news reports from September 2012, in an effort to prevent weapons theft IDF has prohibited soldiers belonging to a specific combat unit from carrying their personal weapons while on leave. According to IDF sources, soldiers of that unit were subjected to a very strict sorting procedure at the end of which a determination would be made with regard to soldiers' eligibility for carrying weapons while on home leave.[53]

B. Persons Belonging to Special IDF Units

Persons serving in special IDF programs that involve a combination of both military and other duties may be issued military weapons under special personal authorizations and subject to numerous conditions that include similar health and training requirements, authorizations from relevant authorities, and a temporary trial period before a weapon is issued by IDF. Such programs include the Yeshivat Ha-Hesder, for military and religious training, or the Nahal Brigade, which combines military service and the establishment of new agricultural communities.[54] Special requirements regarding safeguarding and storage are specified by the military order under which weapons can be distributed in these circumstances.[55]

Prepared by Ruth Levush
Senior Foreign Law Specialist

---

[51] *Id.* § 7.

[52] *Id.* § 2.

[53] Yoav Ziton, *Combatants on Condition, Depositing Weapons Before Leave*, YNET (Sept. 19, 2012), http://www.ynet.co.il/articles/0,7340,L-4283806,00.html (in Hebrew).

[54] *Nahal Brigade*, IDF, http://www.idf.il/1515-en/Dover.aspx (last visited Dec. 18, 2012).

[55] IDF Central Command Order No. 2.0107, Delivery of Military Weapons to Civilians, issued Mar. 1, 1981, updated Sept. 26, 2006, http://dover.idf.il/IDF/pkuda/020107.doc (in Hebrew).

JAPAN

FIREARMS-CONTROL LEGISLATION AND POLICY

Summary

Guns have been controlled in Japan since the late sixteenth century. After the Second World War, gun control became very strict. Many civilians have never seen a gun in their lives. In order for a person to own hunting guns and to hunt animals and birds with a gun, he or she must pay a hunting tax and obtain a gun-possession permit, hunting license, and hunting registration. The process for obtaining a gun-possession permit is cumbersome and time-consuming. The number of people who possess guns has been declining as a result of the very strict regulations.

The relationship between gun possession and crimes or suicides has not been studied in great detail. There are very few deaths by gunshot in Japan, which has a low homicide rate overall. The suicide rate, on the other hand, is very high, and many speculate that if Japanese people were able to possess guns more freely, the suicide rate would rise sharply. However, no scientific research has been conducted on that question.

I. History of Gun Control in Japan

Gun control was instituted in Japan soon after guns were introduced there, and the country has a long history of policies that restrict gun possession by members of the general public.

Guns were introduced to Japan through *wakō*[1] and Europeans in the mid-sixteenth century.[2] In 1588, the ruler of Japan, Hideyoshi Toyotomi, announced the Sword Hunt, which banned possession of swords and firearms by people who were not soldiers. "The measure had the double advantage from the ruler's point of view of preventing riots and distinguishing the peasant from the soldier."[3]

---

[1] *Wakō* are "any of the groups of marauders who raided the Korean and Chinese coasts between the 13th and 16th centuries." Wakō, ENCYCLOPÆDIA BRITANNICA ONLINE ACADEMIC EDITION (2013), http://www.britannica.com/ EBchecked/topic/634306/wako.

[2] TAKEHISA UDAGAWA, TEPPŌ DENRAI NO NIHONSHI [JAPANESE HISTORY OF THE INTRODUCTION OF GUNS] 26 (2006). It was widely believed in the past that guns were first introduced in Tanegashima, Japan by the Portuguese in 1543, but further studies concluded that guns were introduced by various foreigners.

[3] 2 GEORGE BAILEY SANSOM, A HISTORY OF JAPAN: 1334–1615 at 331 (1961).

During the Tokugawa period (1603–1867),[4] gun control was expanded. The Tokugawa Shogunate issued the following regulations and decrees:

Year   Regulation/Decree

1629:   The use of guns for the control of pests was permitted upon submission of a written declaration that the gun would be used properly.

1645:   The use of guns in Edo (Tokyo) was prohibited except by gun officials.

1662:   The possession of guns other than by hunters was prohibited. Hunters were registered and prohibited from renting out guns to others.

1676:   Crackdowns on illegal gun possessors would be conducted.

1685:   Persons who turned in or reported shooters of illegal guns would be rewarded.

1687:   Villages without hunters were allowed to rent guns.

1717:   Even hunters were prohibited from possessing guns in Edo and its outskirts. Guns could be rented for pest control for limited periods.

1729:   The rental conditions imposed in 1717 were tightened: the gun rental period would be for one year, a rental document would have to be submitted annually, and the number of boars and deer taken in the previous year had to be reported.[5]

The Meiji emperor was restored as head of Japan in 1868, and Japan was transformed from a feudal society into a modern country.[6] In 1872, the Meiji Government promulgated the Gun Control Regulation.[7] Under this regulation, only licensed merchants were allowed to sell guns (excluding military guns). Men who had formerly belonged to the soldier class and had owned military guns were required to report them to the authorities. These guns had to have newly carved numbers. The use of guns was thereafter basically limited to hunters.[8] The regulation, aimed at controlling guns and ammunition and disarming civilians, was intended to prevent "bad people from playing with guns."[9]

---

[4] Tokugawa period, ENCYCLOPÆDIA BRITANNICA ONLINE ACADEMIC EDITION (2013), http://www.britannica.com/EBchecked/topic/598326/Tokugawa-period.

[5] HARUYASU NAKASHIMA, JŪHŌ TŌKEN RUI TŌ NO TORISHIMARI [CONTROL OF FIREARMS AND SWORDS] 15–16 (1979).

[6] The Meiji Restoration and Modernization, ASIA FOR EDUCATORS (Columbia University, 2009), http://afe.easia.columbia.edu/special/japan_1750_meiji.htm.

[7] Jūhō torishimari kisoku, Dajōkan fukoku No. 28 (Jan. 29, 1872).

[8] Yoshinobu Endo, 1872 nen jūhō torishimari kisoku no seitei katei [Legislative Process of 1872 Gun Control Regulation], 62(2) J. HOKKAIDO U. EDUC. (HUMAN. & SOC. SCI.), 1, 4 (Feb. 2012), http://s-ir.sap.hokkyodai.ac.jp/dspace/bitstream/123456789/2858/1/62-2-zinbun-01.pdf.

[9] Id. at 2.

In 1899, gun and explosives regulations were integrated into one law, the Firearms and Explosives Control Law. In 1910, this law was completely revised. It contained the following provisions, among others:

- the manufacture and sale of guns and explosives were subject to government license;
- the sale of guns and explosives door-to-door or in outdoor markets was banned;
- when it was deemed necessary for maintaining public security, the government could control the transfer, transport, and possession of guns and explosives;
- the transfer of guns for military use was to be done only under government license; and
- the transfer, transport, and possession of handguns, shotguns, rifles, and swords were authorized only with the approval of the chief of the appropriate police station.[10]

Though the possession of guns by civilians were heavily regulated, it was possible for civilians to own guns, including handguns. This changed after the Second World War. Under the Allied Occupation, the Supreme Commander for the Allied Powers (SCAP) disarmed Japanese servicemen and issued several arms control directives in 1945 in order to safeguard against any possible danger that might arise from arms possessed by civilians.[11] In 1946, the Japanese government issued the Imperial Ordinance Concerning the Prohibition of the Possession of Guns and Other Arms, which banned the possession of firearms and swords by private citizens in principle, though the possession of hunting guns and artistic swords was allowed under license.[12]

When most of the arms had been collected from the general public and the post-war social disorder had settled, the SCAP arms control directives were rescinded,[13] and the Japanese government issued a new regulation in 1950. The 1950 Order Concerning Firearms and Swords broadened the exceptions to the general ban on the possession of guns and swords.[14] Thereafter, in addition for use in hunting, the possession of guns was permitted for the purpose of killing harmful animals and livestock, for emergency rescue activities, and for fisheries.[15] In 1955, the use of air guns and nail guns was added to the uses permitted in the regulation.[16] (Many accidents and

---

[10] NAKASHIMA, *supra* note 5, at 16–17.

[11] *Id.* at 17–18.

[12] Imperial Ordinance Concerning the Prohibition of the Possession of Guns and Other Arms, Imperial Ordinance No. 300 of 1946 (June 3, 1946).

[13] SCAPIN-2099: Instructions on the Surrender of Arms by Japanese Civilians (May 29, 1950). Information on the directive is available on the website of Japan's National Diet Library, *at* http://iss.ndl.go.jp/books/R100000002-I000006849593-00 (last visited Jan. 2, 2013).

[14] Order Concerning Firearms and Swords, Cabinet Order No. 334 of 1950 (Nov. 15, 1950). This Order prevailed after the Peace Treaty came into force on April 28, 1952, by legislation (Law No. 13 of 1952).

[15] *Id.* art. 3. *See* NAKASHIMA, *supra* note 5, at 21.

[16] Law No. 51 of 1955 (July 4, 1955).

crimes involving air guns had occurred in the late 1920s, and several youth organizations demanded air gun regulations because many of the accidents had involved youth.[17])

II. 1958 Law Controlling the Possession of Firearms and Swords

The 1950 Order was replaced by the Law Controlling the Possession of Firearms and Swords in 1958.[18] There were some changes made to the regulations in the 1950 Order, but the general prohibition of possession of guns by civilians was not changed. One of the changes implemented in the 1958 Law was the prohibition in principle of carrying guns and swords, regardless of whether the carrier was licensed to own the gun or sword. Previous years had seen notable gang fights in which guns and swords were used. A National Police Agency officer estimated that half of the guns and swords used in such gang fights were licensed and the other half were not.[19] With this amendment the government tried to prevent or reduce the use of guns and swords by gangs.[20]

The 1958 Law has frequently been amended following a public outcry after crimes or incidents involving guns, each amendment making the restrictions tighter. For example, when the police determined that most illegal guns were imported from abroad, a provision making the unauthorized importing of guns a crime was added to the law in 1965.[21] After an eighteen-year-old licensed to own two hunting rifles killed a police officer and went on a shooting spree against police officers in 1965, the age for owning a hunting rifle was raised from eighteen to twenty years old.[22] After replica guns were used for crimes in the 1960s, including airplane hijacking, the possession of replica handguns that appear real was also prohibited.[23] More recently, airsoft guns of more than a certain power began to be regulated by a 2006 amendment.[24] After five murders involving shotguns, a 2008 amendment further restricted the possession of such guns.[25]

---

[17] NAKASHIMA, *supra* note 5, at 22.

[18] Law Controlling the Possession of Firearms and Swords, Law No. 6 of 1958 (Mar. 10, 1958).

[19] Statement of Kunji Nakagawa, Minutes of Local Administration Committee, House of Councillors, No. 3, 28th Diet Session (Feb. 11, 1958), at 3.

[20] *Id.* at 2.

[21] Law No. 47 of 1965 (Apr. 15, 1965). Statement of Hideo Ohisu, Minutes of Local Administration Committee, House of Councillors, No. 4, 48th Diet Session (Feb. 9, 1965), at 4.

[22] Law No. 80 of 1966 (June 7, 1966). Statement of Yoshikazu Imatake, Minutes of Local Administration Committee, House of Councillors, No. 16, 51st Diet Session (Apr. 12, 1966), at 8.

[23] Law No. 48 of 1971 (Apr. 20, 1971). Statement of Takiichiro Hatsumura, Minutes of Local Administration Committee, House of Councillors, No. 7, 65th Diet Session (Mar. 2, 1971), at 8.

[24] Law No. 41 of 2006 (May 24, 2006). *See* Jigyō hyōkasho [Business Evaluation], National Safety Commission and National Police Agency (Mar. 2012), http://www.npa.go.jp/seisaku_hyoka/soumu/24juutouhou-hyoukasyo.pdf.

[25] Law No. 86 of 2008. *See* Hōmu sōgō Kenkyūsho, Kaitei Juhō tōken rui shoji tō torishimari hō [Law Controlling the Possession of Firearms and Swords, Second Edition] 11–12 (2012).

III. Possession and Use of Guns and Ammunition under the Current Law

The first article of the 1958 Law states that its aim is to provide control measures necessary to prevent danger and injury arising from *shoji* (possession) of guns, swords, etc.[26] *Shoji* means that an object is under the control of a person.[27] It includes storing and carrying.[28] The possession of guns and their parts is strictly limited to law enforcement officials, members of the Self-Defense Force, other public officials, and persons who have obtained permission from the government to use them for a specific purpose, such as hunters, target shooters, athletes who compete in national or international competitions, firearms dealers, manufacturers, firearm exporters, and antique-gun collectors.[29] The transfer, loan, and borrowing of guns and their parts are also restricted.[30] The term "guns" in this law means pistols, rifles, machine guns, hunting guns, other powder-charging firearms that have a mechanism for shooting metal bullets, and air guns with power specified by a Cabinet Office Ordinance.[31]

To obtain permission to possess a gun, a person must file an application with the Public Safety Commission of the prefecture where he or she lives specifying the gun to be in his or her possession and the purpose of its use.[32] The kind of gun permitted to be possessed is limited, depending on the purpose of the possession. Among the guns included are

- hunting guns (rifles and shotguns) or air guns, excluding air pistols, to be used for target shooting, hunting, or extermination of harmful birds and animals;

- special guns used in specific businesses, such as lifesaving, slaughterhouses, fisheries, and construction;

- guns for testing or research; and

- pistols and air pistols to be used in international athletic competitions when recommended by a person designated by Cabinet order.[33]

Possession of handguns by civilians is not allowed except for researchers using them for testing or research.

---

[26] Law Controlling the Possession of Firearms and Swords, Law No. 6 of 1958 (Mar. 10, 1958), *last amended by* Law No. 72 of 2011 (June 22, 2011), art. 1.

[27] Sup. Ct. Nov. 29, 1977, Case No. 1977 (a) 1069, 31-6 SAIKOŌ SAIBANSHO KEIJI HANREISHŪ [KEISHŪ] 1030.

[28] Tochigi Tsutomu and Nishida Masaki, Jūhō tōken rui shoji tō torishimari hō ihan jiken no shori ni kansuru jitsumu jō no shomondai [Practical Issues Dealing with Cases of Law Controlling Guns and Swords] 46 (2000).

[29] Law Controlling the Possession of Firearms and Swords arts. 3 & 4.

[30] *Id.* arts. 3-4, 3-7, & 3-10.

[31] *Id.* art. 2, para. 1. Enforcement Ordinance of Law Controlling the Possession of Firearms and Swords, Prime Minister's Office Ordinance No. 16 of 1958 (Mar. 22, 1958), *last amended by* Cabinet Office Ordinance No. 58 of 2012 (Sept. 14, 2012), art. 3.

[32] Law Controlling the Possession of Firearms and Swords art. 4-2.

[33] *Id.* art. 4, para. 1.

As of 2011, the total number of guns permitted to be possessed by civilians in Japan was 271,100.[34] The numbers have shown an annual decline: 839,086 in 1980,[35] 533,251 in 1990,[36] and 444,210 in 2000.[37] Details of the numbers for five recent years are as follows:[38]

	Year	2007	2008	2009	2010	2011
	Total	361,402	339,560	319,289	292,766	271,100
For Hunting	Rifles	41,193	39,862	38,772	36,818	35,006
	Others	253,437	237,046	221,640	201,633	185,165
Air Guns		33,331	31,759	30,527	28,198	26,612
For Construction		28,362	25,898	23,439	21,022	19,170
Other Guns		5,079	4,994	4,911	5,095	5,147

Those disqualified from possessing a gun according to Article 5 of the Law include

(1) a person less than 18 years of age (a talented athlete of age 14 years or over may be excepted);

(2) a person who has declared bankruptcy and the restrictions have not been removed;

(3) a person who has lost or may lose full mental ability through mental illness or specified health problems, or who has dementia;

(4) a person addicted to alcohol, narcotics, cannabis, opium, or stimulant drugs;

(5) a feebleminded person;

(6) a person without a fixed abode;

(7–11) a person whose license was revoked and a specified period has not elapsed;

(12) any person who has been sentenced to imprisonment and five years have not elapsed since his or her sentence was completed or remitted;

(13–14) a person who violated this Law or a related law and a specified period has not elapsed;

(15) a person who stalked another person and received a warning or restraining order;

---

[34] NATIONAL POLICE AGENCY, KEISATSU HAKUSHO [POLICE WHITE PAPER] 2012, Statistic 2-37, http://www. npa.go.jp/hakusyo/h24/toukei/01/2-37.xls.

[35] NATIONAL POLICE AGENCY, KEISATSU HAKUSHO [POLICE WHITE PAPER] 1981, Statistic 6-2, http://www. npa.go.jp/hakusyo/s56/s56s0602.html.

[36] NATIONAL POLICE AGENCY, KEISATSU HAKUSHO [POLICE WHITE PAPER] 1991, Statistic 5-5, http://www. npa.go.jp/hakusyo/h03/h03s0505.html.

[37] NATIONAL POLICE AGENCY, KEISATSU HAKUSHO [POLICE WHITE PAPER] 2001, Statistic 2-14, at 292, http:// www.npa.go.jp/hakusyo/h13/h130910.pdf.

[38] POLICE WHITE PAPER 2012, *supra* note 34, Statistic 2-37.

(16) a person who behaved violently and received a restraining order under the Domestic Violence Prevention Law;

(17) a person who is recognized by the [Public Safety] Commission as one who has committed violent acts as a member of a group or repeatedly; and

(18) a person who can be reasonably expected to harm another's life, body, or property, [be a threat to] public safety, or commit suicide.[39]

In addition, if a relative, including a *de facto* spouse, living with an applicant can be reasonably expected to pose a threat to the life or property of other persons or to public safety by using a gun or sword, the prefecture's Public Safety Commission may not permit the possession of a gun or sword.[40] There are exceptions and additional restrictions.

In order to possess a hunting gun or air gun, one must attend classes, held by the prefecture's Public Safety Commission, concerning the laws and regulations on possession of hunting or air guns and the methods of their use and safe storage.[41] In addition, in order to prevent a person without the skills to handle a gun from obtaining one,[42] the law requires an applicant for a gun-possession permit to take a skills test or complete shooting classes.[43] In the case of a rifle, permission for possession is not granted unless the person is a professional hunter; will use it to exterminate harmful animals and birds for the protection of his business; or has had a permit to possess a hunting gun for more than ten years.[44]

According to gun-shop websites, although obtaining a gun-possession permit the first time is cumbersome, it is not difficult if one follows the requisite steps.[45] The applicant for the permit must submit thirteen attachments, including photos, a medical certificate, a copy of his or her family register, certificates of completion of classes, etc., to the prefecture's Public Safety Commission.[46] The Public Safety Commission then gives an eligible person a permit certificate to

---

[39] Law Controlling the Possession of Firearms and Swords, Law No. 6 of 1958 (Mar. 10, 1958), *last amended by* Law No. 72 of 2011 (June 22, 2011), art. 5, para 1, items 1–18.

[40] *Id.* art. 5, para. 5.

[41] *Id.* art. 5-2, para. 1; art. 5-3, paras. 1 & 2.

[42] Ginō kōshū no jisshi ni tsuite [Regarding the Skills Class], National Police Agency, Public Safety Dept., Choho No. 152 (Nov. 18, 2009), at 1, http://www.npa.go.jp/jutoho/hoan20091118-04.pdf.

[43] Law Controlling the Possession of Firearms and Swords, art. 5-2, para. 3, items 3 & 4; art. 5-4; art. 9-5. The details of the test are prescribed in the Regulation on Skills Test, Skills Class and Shooting Class, Public Safety Commission Regulation No. 8 of 1978, *last amended by* Regulation No. 10 of 2009.

[44] Law Controlling the Possession of Firearms and Swords art. 5-2, para. 4, item 1.

[45] *Jūhō shoji ni tsuite* [*Regarding Possession of a Gun*], GUN SHOP MIYAKO, http://miyako-gun.com/初め ての方-1/ (last visited Jan. 17, 2013); *Jūhō shoji no hōhō* [*How to Possess a Gun*], GUNSMITH TAKIDA HIROSHI, http:// www.gunsmith.jp/kyoka.html (last visited Jan. 17, 2013).

[46] Law Controlling the Possession of Firearms and Swords art. 4-2; Enforcement Ordinance of Law Controlling the Possession of Firearms and Swords, Prime Minister's Office Ordinance No. 16 of 1958 (Mar. 22, 1958), *last amended by* Cabinet Office Ordinance No. 58 of 2012 (Sept. 14, 2012), arts. 9–11. *See also*, Ryōjū kūkiū no shoji kyoka tetuduki [Procedure for [Obtaining] Permission to Possess Hunting Guns and Air Guns], Metropolitan Police Dept., http://www.keishicho.metro.tokyo.jp/tetuzuki/gun/gun.htm (last visited Jan. 17, 2013).

possess a firearm,[47] which is valid for three years[48] and can be renewed every three years.[49] The permit becomes invalid, among other cases, when the person has been unable to take possession of the firearm within three months from the day the permit was granted or the person has lost possession of the firearm.[50]

Once the permit has been obtained, there are other provisions to be followed. Discharging a gun other than for the permitted purpose is prohibited.[51] The carrying or transporting of a gun is, in principle, prohibited unless the possessor does so for the permitted use of the gun or other legitimate reason.[52] When it is permitted, the possessor must cover the gun or put it in a case, and must not have bullets inside the gun.[53] When the possessor carries or transports the gun, he or she must carry the permit with him or her, which is subject to police inspection upon request.[54]

The person who has been authorized to possess a firearm must himself store it in a gun locker installed in accordance with the standards determined by the ordinance.[55] A young person aged fourteen years or older but younger than eighteen who is involved in competitive sport-shooting must store guns with a licensed person who has a gun-storage facility that meets the standards.[56] The Prefecture's Public Safety Commission may ask a person who stores guns about the storage situation at any time.[57] When the Commission recognizes the need to inspect the storage situation of hunting guns, such as to inquire about the possibility of their being stolen, it has the local police conduct an on-site inspection, with prior notice to the person storing the gun(s).[58] Further, under the authority of the Law Controlling the Possession of Firearms and Swords, the police may, with prior notice to gun owners, conduct nationwide inspections of gun owners' weapons and storage facilities.[59]

---

[47] Law Controlling the Possession of Firearms and Swords art. 7.

[48] *Id.* art. 7-2.

[49] *Id.* art. 7-3.

[50] *Id.* art. 8, para. 1.

[51] *Id.* arts. 3-13, 10, para. 2.

[52] *Id.* art. 10, para. 1.

[53] *Id.* art. 10, paras. 4 & 5.

[54] *Id.* art. 24.

[55] *Id.* art. 10-4; Enforcement Ordinance of Law Controlling the Possession of Firearms and Swords, Prime Minister's Office Ordinance No. 16 of 1958 (Mar. 22, 1958), *last amended by* Cabinet Office Ordinance No. 58 of 2012 (Sept. 14, 2012), art. 84.

[56] Law Controlling the Possession of Firearms and Swords art. 10-5; Enforcement Ordinance of Law Controlling the Possession of Firearms and Swords art. 84.

[57] Law Controlling the Possession of Firearms and Swords art. 10-6, para. 1.

[58] *Id.* art. 10-6, para. 2.

[59] *Id.* art. 13. *See* "17 man nin/30 man chō sōtenken" hōkokusho [Report on "The Comprehensive Inspection of "170,000 people/300,000 Guns"], "Comprehensive Inspection on Gun Administration" Project Team, National Police Agency (Apr. 3, 2008), http://www.npa.go.jp/safetylife/seikan48/siryou.pdf.

According to the Law, ammunition must be kept in a separate locked safe.[60] To buy ammunition, a separate permit from the Public Safety Commission is required under the Gunpowder and Explosives Control Law[61] unless the transaction is for three hundred (fifty in the case of rifle bullets) or fewer bullets.[62] Hunters cannot store more than eight hundred bullets.[63] The procedure for obtaining ammunition-purchase permits was tightened after the 2007 Sasebo shooting.[64] The applicant for a bullet-purchase permit is currently required to submit a "plan for bullet use."[65]

The Police have broad authority to supervise gun possession. When there is reasonable suspicion that a person is carrying or transporting a gun and he or she may be a threat to the life or property of other persons or to the public peace, judging from unusual behavior or the attendant circumstances, a police official may compel the person to produce the gun for inspection.[66] When the police deem it necessary, they may withhold the gun.[67] The gun will be returned to the original possessor within five days from the time of its surrender to the police unless the police find it was illegally possessed.[68]

At the time of a disaster or an incident that disturbs the public peace, a Public Safety Commission may prohibit or limit the delivery, transport, or carrying of firearms for which a permit has been obtained, for a limited area and period, by issuing a notice. The Commission may even order gun holders in the area to submit their guns provisionally and may keep them until the notice expires. The notice must be approved by the prefecture parliament within seven days from the day of notice.[69]

Quasi guns and gun-related accessories are also regulated. As briefly mentioned above, possession of airsoft guns are prohibited, except by certain public officials, if the bullet kinetic energy of the gun exceeds $3.4/cm^2$.[70] Even certain imitation models are banned. Except for

---

[60] Id. art. 10-4, paras. 3 & 4.

[61] Gunpowder and Explosives Control Law, Law No. 149, May 4, 1950, *last amended by* Law No. 121 of 1999, art. 17, para. 1 & art. 50-2.

[62] Id. art. 17, para 1, item 3; Ordinance on the Transfer, Import, and Sales of Bullets for Hunting Guns, Prime Minister's Office Ordinance No. 46 of 1966, *last amended by* Cabinet Office Ordinance No. 68 of 2009, art. 4.

[63] Gunpowder and Explosives Control Law art. 11, para. 1; Enforcement Regulation of Gunpowder and Explosives Control Law, Ministry of International Trade and Industry Ordinance No. 88 of 1950, *last amended by* Ministry of Economy, Trade and Industry Ordinance No. 39 of 2012, art. 15, para. 1(8).

[64] Philip Brasor, *Japan Faces Up to a World of Gun Crime*, THE JAPAN TIMES (Dec. 23, 2007), http://www. japantimes.co.jp/text/fd20071223pb.html.

[65] Jitsudan no kōnyū hōkoku genkakuka e [Report on the Stricter Purchase of Bullets], YOMIURI NEWSPAPER (Mar. 28, 2008) (on file with author).

[66] Law Controlling the Possession of Firearms and Swords art. 24-2, para. 1.

[67] Id. art. 24-2, para. 2.

[68] Id. art. 24-2, paras. 6–8.

[69] Id. art. 26.

[70] Id. art. 21-3; Enforcement Ordinance of Law Controlling the Possession of Firearms and Swords art. 100.

manufacturers or exporters, possession of a metal imitation pistol that has a shape bearing a marked resemblance to a real pistol is prohibited.[71] The possession of certain gun silencers, magazines, and barrels is also prohibited even when a person has permission to possess a gun.[72]

IV. Hunting

To hunt animals with a gun, a person must obtain a hunting license from the prefecture governor, along with a permit to possess a gun. Hunting licenses are prescribed under the Wildlife Protection and Hunting Law and are under the jurisdiction of the Ministry of Environment.[73] A hunting license may not be issued to a person who

(1) is younger than twenty years of age;

(2) may lose or has lost full mental ability through mental illness or specified health problems;

(3) is addicted to narcotics, cannabis, opium, or stimulant drugs;

(4) is feebleminded; or

(5) has violated the Hunting Law and has received and completed a certain penalty within the previous three years.[74]

A person must also pass a test to be licensed.[75] A hunting license expires after three years, and is renewable upon passing the suitability test.[76]

In addition to obtaining a hunting license, hunters must register themselves with the prefectures where they hunt, and pay a registration fee and hunting tax.[77] To be registered, proof of accident insurance that covers hunting accidents is also required. The Greater Japan Hunters' Association provides such insurance.[78]

The numbers of licensed hunters in Japan, including those using snares and guns, is generally decreasing, while their average age is increasing. As of 2010, there were approximately

---

[71] Law Controlling the Possession of Firearms and Swords art. 22-2.

[72] *Id.* art. 10-7.

[73] Chōjū no hogo oyobi shuryō no tekiseika ni kansuru hōritsu [Wildlife Protection and Hunting Law], Law No. 88 of 2002, *last amended by* Law No. 67 of 2006.

[74] *Id.* art. 40.

[75] *Id.* art. 41.

[76] *Id.* arts. 44 & 51.

[77] *See Hunter Registration Information*, FUKUOKA PREFECTURE, http://www.pref.fukuoka.lg.jp/d05/syuryousya-touroku.html (in Japanese; last visited Jan. 22, 2013).

[78] *2012 nen, kyōsai jigyōkara kyōsai hoken e* [*From Mutual Aid Program to Mutual Aid Insurance*], DAI NIHON RYŌYŪKAI [GREATER JAPAN HUNTERS' ASSOCIATION], http://www.moriniikou.jp/index.php?itemid=694&catid=8&catid=8.

[79] In 1980, approximately 450,000 hunting licenses were issued. Most of them were for hunting with guns. Recently, the number has been below 300,000, approximately 40% of whom hunt with snares.[80]

The declining number of hunters has become an issue as damage to farms and fisheries caused by wild animals has increased. The Special Measures Law to Prevent Damage by Birds and Animals to Agriculture and Fisheries[81] was enacted in 2007, under the jurisdiction of the Ministry of Agriculture, Forestry, and Fisheries (MAFF). One of the measures to prevent damage caused by wild animals was to support hunters.[82] After the 2008 amendment of the Law Controlling the Possession of Firearms and Swords was implemented, many licensed hunters complained that they were obligated by the amendment to take skills classes that include a shooting test.[83] Many of them, who were elderly and experienced, did not like the newly added test and threatened not to renew their licenses. Meanwhile, the damage caused to farms by birds and animals increased in 2010.[84] Accordingly, the Diet in 2012 amended the Special Measures Law to Prevent Damage by Birds and Animals to Agriculture and Fisheries,[85] so that hunters who renew their gun possession permits by December 2014 are exempted from the skills classes.[86]

V. Control of Gun Manufacturers and Dealers

The manufacture and sale of guns are regulated by the Weapons Manufacture Law and are under the jurisdiction of the Minister of Economy, Trade, and Industry.[87] The term "weapons" in this law includes explosives and firearms, such as pistols, rifles, hunting guns, bullets, and cartridges.[88] Any person intending to engage in the business of manufacturing weapons must obtain a permit from the METI for each factory or workplace.[89] To qualify, an applicant must

---

[79] Nenrei betsu shuryo menkyo shojisha sū [Numbers of Licensed Hunters by Age Group], Ministry of the Environment, http://www.env.go.jp/nature/choju/docs/docs4/menkyo.pdf (last visited Jan. 17, 2013).

[80] III Hokaku ni kansuru tōkei shiryō shūkei [Statistics on Hunting], Ministry of the Environment, at 84, http:// www.env.go.jp/nature/choju/capture/pdf/d1.pdf (last visited Jan. 22, 2013).

[81] Special Measures Law to Prevent Damage by Birds and Animals to Agriculture and Fisheries, Law No. 134 of 2007.

[82] *Id.* arts. 9 & 16.

[83] *Ryōjū tō o shoji shite iru minasan e* [*For People Who Possess Hunting Guns*], POLICE HEADQUARTERS OF KYOTO PREFECTURE, http://www.pref.kyoto.jp/fukei/site/seiki_j/jutoho/img/minasanhe.pdf (last visited Jan. 22, 2013).

[84] *Sankō shiryō* [*Reference*], MAFF, http://www.maff.go.jp/j/seisan/tyozyu/higai/pdf/sankou.pdf (last visited Jan. 22, 2013).

[85] Law No. 10 of 2012.

[86] Provisions attached to Special Measures Law to Prevent Damage by Birds and Animals to Agriculture and Fisheries, Law No. 134 of 2007, art. 3, *amended by* Law No. 10 of 2012.

[87] Buki tō seizō hō [Weapons Manufacture Law], Law No. 145, Aug. 1, 1953, *last amended by* Law No. 120 of 2007.

[88] *Id.* art. 2.

[89] *Id.* art. 3.

meet, among other things, the standards for facilities for the manufacture and safe storage of weapons as set forth in ministerial ordinances.[90]

Permits may be denied to

(1) a person who has been fined or given a more severe punishment on account of violating the Weapons Manufacture Law, where three years have not elapsed since his or her sentence was completed or remitted;

(2) a person with respect to whom three years have not elapsed since the day his or her permission to manufacture weapons was revoked;

(3) any person deemed unqualified to be a manufacturer because of a fine or more severe punishment imposed on him or her for violating other laws and regulations within the last three years;

(4) an incompetent person; and

(5) a business that has one of the aforementioned persons among its executive members.[91]

A person who intends to engage in the business of manufacturing hunting guns is also required to obtain a permit from the prefectural governor having jurisdiction over the factory or the workplace.[92] Any person who intends to operate a business to sell hunting guns must obtain a permit from the prefectural governor.[93] Bullets, cartridges, and blank cartridges are also subject to the Gunpowder and Explosives Control Law,[94] which includes regulations on storage and transportation.

VI. Offenses and Penalties

There are a number of offenses relating to guns that are prescribed in the Law Controlling the Possession of Firearms and Swords and that are separate from offenses committed using a gun, such as murder. The most severe penalty under the Gun Control Law is for the act of discharging a gun in a train, on a bus, or at a place used by large numbers of "unspecified" people. Such an act is punishable by penal servitude for a definite term of three years or more or for an indefinite term.[95] This punishment was established in 1995 to protect the general public by severely punishing gun fights in public places by gang members.[96] After the mayor of Nagasaki

---

[90] *Id.* art. 5.

[91] *Id.*

[92] *Id.* art. 17.

[93] *Id.* art. 19.

[94] Gunpowder and Explosives Control Law, Law No. 149, May 4, 1950, *last amended by* Law No. 121 of 1999.

[95] *Id.* art. 31, para. 1.

[96] Nishi, *Hasshazai towa* [*What Is Crime of Discharging*], YOMIURI ONLINE (Aug. 30, 1995), http://plus. yomiuri.co.jp/article/words/%E7%99%BA%E5%B0%84%E7%BD%AA.

City was shot to death by a gang member,[97] provisions were added to make the punishment even more severe. If the discharging of a gun is part of an activity of a group or organization, or is done to keep or gain advantage or profit for a group, the act is punishable by penal servitude for a definite term of five years or more or for an indefinite term and a fine not to exceed 30 million yen (about US$340,000).[98]

Any person who illegally possesses a gun is subject to a punishment of penal servitude for one year or more, but not to exceed ten years. If a person illegally possesses more than one gun, the penalty goes up to a maximum punishment of penal servitude for fifteen years. If any violator of the above provisions also carries, transports, or stores live cartridges, metal bullets, or explosives, the penalty is increased to penal servitude for three years or more.[99] If the discharging of a gun is part of an activity of a group or organization, or is done to keep or gain advantage or profit for a group, the penalty is increased.[100]

Any person who illegally imports firearms is punishable by penal servitude for not less than three years. Any person who imports firearms in order to make a profit is subject to penal servitude for a term ranging from not less than five years to life and a fine not to exceed 30 million yen (about US$340,000).[101] Any person who transfers, lends, or borrows handguns is subject to penal servitude for one year or more, but not to exceed ten years. Any person who commits these crimes in order to make a profit is punishable by penal servitude for not less than three years and a fine not to exceed 10 million yen (about US$113,000).[102]

Under the Weapons Manufacture Law, any person who illegally manufactures firearms is subject to penal servitude for three years or more. Any person who commits this crime in order to make a profit is subject to penal servitude for five years or more and a fine not to exceed 30 million yen (about US$340,000).[103]

VII. Crime Statistics

The total number of criminal cases involving the shooting of guns has declined over the last ten years. In 2001, the number was more than two hundred, but in 2010 the number was less than fifty.[104]

---

[97] Martin Fackler, *Killer of Nagasaki Mayor Linked to Japanese Gang*, THE NEW YORK TIMES (Apr. 18, 2007), http://www.nytimes.com/2007/04/18/world/asia/18iht-japan.4.5340098.html?_r=0.

[98] Law Controlling the Possession of Firearms and Swords art. 31, paras. 2 & 3.

[99] *Id.* art. 31-3, paras. 1 & 2.

[100] *Id.* art. 31-3, paras. 3 & 4.

[101] *Id.* art 31-2, paras. 1 & 2.

[102] *Id.* art. 31-4, paras 1 & 2.

[103] Weapons Manufacture Law, Law No. 145, Aug. 1, 1953, *last amended by* Law No. 120 of 2007, art. 31.

[104] MINISTRY OF JUSTICE, WHITEPAPER ON CRIME 2011, Chart 4-2-2-4, http://hakusyo1.moj.go.jp/jp/58/nfm/n_58_2_4_2_2.html.

The number of criminal cases involving handguns has also declined over the last ten years. In 2001, the number was eighty, but by 2010 the number was down to twenty. The number of criminal cases involving guns other than handguns has not changed. In 2010, the number was twenty-six.[105]

The following table shows the number of victims who were shot to death in recent years:[106]

Year	1991	1992	1993	1994	1995	1996	1997	1998	1999	2000
No.	31	21	30	38	34	17	22	19	28	23

2001	2002	2003	2004	2005	2006	2007	2008	2009	2010	2011
39	24	35	17	10	2	21	10	4	11	8

The crime rate in Japan is low compared with other countries. For example, according to Japan's 2011 White Paper on Crime, murder ratios in 2010 were 0.9 per 100,000 people in Japan, 2.8 in France, 2.7 in Germany, 2.1 in the United Kingdom, and 4.8 in the United States. The numbers of murders in 2010 were 1,103 in Japan, 1,746 in France, 2,218 in Germany, 1,167 in the UK, and 14,748 in the U.S.[107]

VIII. Suicides

Japan's suicide mortality rate is very high among OECD countries.[108] However, the rate of suicides by gun is quite low in Japan because guns are not easily accessible. Guns are not among the six major methods of committing suicide in Japan, which include hanging, leaping to one's death, and inhaling carbon monoxide.[109] Among police officers, there were fifty-four suicides committed using handguns between 1997 and 2007.[110] Many people who participate in online discussions on the issue of suicides have claimed that there might be more suicides if Japanese were able to possess handguns more freely. However, no credible research or studies have been done on this point.

---

[105] *Id.*, Chart 4-2-2-5

[106] Numbers were taken from each year's White Paper on Crime, *available at* http://hakusyo1.moj.go.jp/jp/nendo_nfm.html.

[107] WHITEPAPER ON CRIME 2011, *supra* note 104, Chart 1-4-2-1, http://hakusyo1.moj.go.jp/jp/59/nfm/n_59_2_1_4_2_0.html.

[108] "Suicide," *in* OECD, HEALTH AT A GLANCE 2011: OECD INDICATORS 35, http://www.oecd-ilibrary.org/social-issues-migration-health/health-at-a-glance-2011/suicide_health_glance-2011-9-en.

[109] Jisatsu shibō tōkei no gaikyō [Summary of Suicide Statistics], Ministry of Health, Labour and Welfare, § 7, http://www.mhlw.go.jp/toukei/saikin/hw/jinkou/tokusyu/suicide04/ (last visited Jan. 22, 2013).

[110] Kenji Ogata, *Keikan no kenjū jisatsu, Kotoshi sudeni 9nin* [*Police Officer Suicides by Handguns, Already 9 Cases This Year*], ASAHI NEWSPAPER (Nov. 15, 2008) (on file with author).

IX. Perception

Many civilians in Japan have never seen a gun in their lives. They are not familiar with guns.[111] It appears there is no demand among Japanese to relax gun control. Textbooks on the Law Controlling the Possession of Firearms and Swords simply state that the reason for the restrictions on guns is that they are inherently dangerous to people; therefore, to protect the safety of people, the possession and use of guns must be restricted.[112] There is no further discussion of why guns must be controlled. Even minor gun-related incidents that do not actually endanger other people can make the national news. For example, a national newspaper reported that a senior policeman forgot to remove one of the five bullets in his handgun and accidently discharged a bullet while examining the gun in a gun storage room before returning it. The bullet hit the wall of the room; no one was hurt, but the policeman will be punished for violating an internal regulation.[113]

Prepared by Sayuri Umeda
Foreign Law Specialist

---

[111] There are many private websites and blogs that state that people in Japan are not familiar with guns or have never seen or touched a gun. For example, one blogger on Yahoo Japan's Q&A website asked how he could touch a real gun for once, http://detail.chiebukuro.yahoo.co.jp/qa/question_detail/q1228937752 (in Japanese; last visited Jan. 29, 2012). Many recommended going to a shooting range abroad. *Id.*

[112] *E.g.*, HŌMU SŌGŌ KENKYŪSHO, *supra* note 25, at 1.

[113] *Jitsudan nukiwasureta ...* [*Forgot to Take Out a Bullet ...*], YOMIURI NEWSPAPER , Jan. 22, 2013 (on file with author).

LEBANON

FIREARMS-CONTROL LEGISLATION AND POLICY

Summary

There is no legal right under Lebanese law for anyone on Lebanese territory to bear arms. The government has wide latitude and discretion under the provisions of the Weapons and Ammunition Law to grant or refuse permits for the manufacturing, trading in, possession, and carrying of weapons and ammunition. However, Lebanon is notorious for the existence on its territory of several armed groups operating outside any legal framework.

I. Major Categories of Weaponry

The control of firearms in Lebanon is regulated by the Weapons and Ammunition Law, issued by a legislative decree dating back to 1959, which has been amended from time to time since that date.[1] According to this law, military equipment, weapons, ammunition, and explosives are divided into three categories:[2]

- The first category consists of military equipment, weapons, and ammunition intended for use in war on land, in sea, or in air which are or will become a part of the weaponry of the armed forces of every country; this weaponry includes those which are no longer in use but which could still be used only militarily and not for any other purposes.

- The second category consists of weapons and ammunition not intended for use by the military.

- The third category consists of explosives, gunpowder, and their accessories.

II. Classification of Weaponry into Nine Types

The law classifies all weaponry into the following types, which facilitate the legal regime applicable to each one:[3]

---

[1] Legislative Decree 137 of 12 June 1959 (Weapons and Ammunition Law), QAWANIN LUBNAN: MAJMU'AT AL'NUSUS AL-TASHRI'IYAH WA'AL-TANZIMIYAH.

[2] *Id.* art. 1.

[3] *Id.* art. 2.

First Type

A. Guns of all measurements and calibers with all their components intended for military use;

B. Machine guns of all kinds, measurement and calibers, and all their components;

C. Long and short canons of all kinds, measurements, and calibers including those made for aircraft and all of their components and parts;

D. All kinds of ammunition made to be used by the weaponry mentioned in A, B, and C;

E. Bombs, torpedoes, and land or sea mines of all kinds including any equipment related to them; and

F. All equipment related to military operations such as those made to attack airplanes and boats or to locate them.

Second Type

A. Combat vehicles, tanks, armored cars, and similar weaponry;

B. Naval vessels of all kinds, including aircraft carriers and submarines;

C. Water microscopes for submarines;

D. All kinds of combat aircraft including balloons and their parts and guns; and

E. Bases, yards, and armored or non-armored parts used for the manufacturing of the weaponry mentioned in A, B, and D above.

Third Type

Gear intended to protect against attacks, including protective clothing and masks.

Fourth Type

Weapons and ammunition that are not considered military weaponry, but could be used militarily, consisting of:

A. All kinds of pistols;

B. All kinds of ammunition for these pistols and all parts and components related to these pistols;

C. Weapons that can use the ammunition of military weapons referred to above and ribbed arms of all measurements and calibers;

D. All ammunition used in military weapons including certain hunting cartridges; and

E. Bayonets, swords, and spears, excluding those referred to in the seventh type.

Fifth Type

Firearms and ammunition of all calibers intended for hunting, which are not mentioned in the previous types and do not constitute a part of the weapons and ammunition referred to in paragraphs C and D of the fourth type and all handguns with particular barrels.

Sixth Type

Training weapons that fire by pressure without gunpowder.

Seventh Type

Antique and souvenir weaponry provided it is not usable and is not a part of the weapons referred to in paragraph C of the fourth type.

Eighth Type

Prohibited weapons, consisting of those not mentioned in the previous types and in particular: daggers, knives, brass knuckles, and similar items.

Ninth Type

A. All kinds of gunpowder;

B. All kinds of dynamite explosives; and

C. All kinds of explosive accessories and devices.

III. Permits to Possess and Carry Firearms

Firearms control in Lebanon is subject to two fundamental principles: (1) there is no constitutional right to bear arms; and (2) the government has wide latitude and discretion in granting permits to possess and carry firearms.

No one is permitted to acquire, possess, or transport weapons or ammunition of types 1 and 2, except in case of security disturbances or in the cases provided for in Chapter II of the decree related to the manufacturing and trading of these items in accordance with the requirements provided therein. The permit is issued by the Minister of National Defense. Members of the Lebanese military forces, the gendarmerie, and the police are allowed to transport such items within the scope of their duties in accordance with military laws and regulations.[4]

---

[4] *Id.* art. 25.

No person is allowed to carry or possess on the Lebanese territory any weapons or ammunition of type 4 except if he holds a permit issued by the army command. Such permits are given for one year and can be renewed.[5]

The *kaemaqam* (the highest official in the *qada*, the smallest administrative district in the country) has the right to issue permits relating to hunting weapons referred to in type 5. The permits to carry and possess type 5 weapons are personal, given only once, and do not expire except by death or the loss of its holder of any of the qualifications required by the legislative decree.

No permit can be issued for the possession and carrying of more than two weapons of type 4. Weapons of type 5 and their ammunition are not subject to this restriction. No hunting permits shall be issued except to those who hold permits to carry and possess weapons.[6]

No permit holder has the right to transfer or sell his permit, with or without compensation, unless the buyer has an authorization allowing him to do so. The permit holder must show his permit to any public authority officer upon request.[7]

Possession and carriage of weapons of type 6 are allowed and the identification papers serve in lieu of a permit.

Persons are permitted to acquire but not carry weapons of types 7 and 8. Permits for carrying such weapons are not issued under any circumstances, except for knives imported specifically for the use of scout organizations.[8]

No permits to carry or possess weapons of any types shall be issued except to people who are at least eighteen years old. However, permits for hunting weapons can be issued to those who are sixteen years old under the responsibility of their guardians. Permits can be issued provided that the applicant:

1. Has not suffered a mental illness;

2. Has not been sentenced to deprivation of his civil rights or convicted of a heinous felony or crime;

3. Has not been sentenced for carrying weapons or convicted of offenses against the security of state;

4. Has not, if a foreigner, been subject to a decision of revocation of residence or deportation; and

5. Has not been repeatedly convicted for violating this legislative decree.[9]

---

[5] *Id.* art. 24.

[6] *Id.* art. 28.

[7] *Id.* art. 30.

[8] *Id.* art. 27.

[9] *Id.* art. 29.

The permit shall be withdrawn from any person who fails to meet any of these requirements.[10]

Apart from permits for hunting weapons, the Ministry of National Defense has the authority to withdraw at any time a permit or stop its effects, based on reports of relevant authorities or public security needs. If the permit is withdrawn the weapon shall be confiscated and the permit fee shall not be returned.[11]

No trader or manufacturer is allowed to give anyone equipment, weapons, or ammunition of types 1 to 4 before making sure the concerned person is duly authorized to acquire them. The person acquiring these items must have a temporary permit stating the number of items he is authorized to obtain. The shop owner or manufacturer must inscribe in the specified place on the temporary permit the information related to the items to be sold, sign it, and stamp it with the seal of his commercial enterprise. He shall not deliver the items sold to the concerned person before the latter obtains the final permit.[12]

Any person who loses weapons or ammunition in his possession is required to notify the nearest office of gendarmerie, police, or general security, explain the circumstances surrounding the loss, give all pertinent information, and surrender his permit.[13]

Carrying a weapon without the relevant permit constitutes a criminal offense punishable by imprisonment from six months to two years for weapons of the first four types,[14] up to six months for weapons of the fifth, seventh, and eighth types,[15] and from one to six months for any violation of the Weapons and Ammunitions Law for which no specific penalty has been assigned.[16]

IV. Permits to Manufacture and Trade in Weaponry

No natural or legal person on the Lebanese territory can be involved in commercial or industrial activities of any kind related to equipment, weapons, and ammunition of any type without obtaining a bona fide permit issued by decree on the recommendation of the Ministers of Interior and National Defense.[17]

To obtain this permit, the person concerned must submit an application to the Ministry of Interior stating their

---

[10] *Id.* art. 31.

[11] *Id.* art. 32.

[12] *Id.* art. 37.

[13] *Id.* art. 39.

[14] *Id.* art 72.

[15] *Id.* art 73.

[16] *Id.* art 78.

[17] *Id.* art. 3.

- full name, date and place of birth, and identification card number;

- nationality;

- place of residency;

- occupation (weapons manufacturer or dealer);

- registration number with the Chamber of Commerce;

- address of the store or factory; and

- how the firearm is to be used, whether by a person or a company. In the latter case, the type of company, the commercial name, the names of the partners, directors, and heads of operations, agents, employees and, if it is a joint-stock company, the names of the Board of Directors and its members and their addresses must be stated.

The application must be accompanied by an extract of the police record of each of the persons mentioned in the preceding paragraph and a certificate of good conduct given by the commander of the gendarmerie or the police commissioner in the district where the person concerned resided during the last six months.[18]

No manufacturing or dealer permits that relate to the first five types of weaponry and explosives can be issued until the Ministry of National Defense has verified that the enterprise meets all technical qualifications required to insure the safety of peoples and neighboring buildings.[19]

Furthermore, no permit can be issued except to Lebanese citizens who have reached the age of twenty-one years, are free from mental illness, have not been prohibited by court order from carrying weapons, and have not been convicted of state security offenses.[20]

The holder of the permit must inform the Ministries of Interior and National Defense of any changes that occur during the lifetime of the permit, including changes concerning the company by-laws and its board of directors, the relocation of the premises, the stoppage of operations, and any changes in the equipment produced or traded.[21]

The permit may be issued for a maximum of five years and may be renewed for the same period. The permit will become void if its holder does not start the work in accordance with its terms within one year from the date of issuance.[22] The permit may be withdrawn immediately if any of the conditions of its issuance are no longer present.[23] Even where there is no fault on the

---

[18] *Id.* art. 4.

[19] *Id.* art. 6.

[20] *Id.* art. 7.

[21] *Id.* art. 8.

[22] *Id.* art. 9.

[23] *Id.* art. 10.

part of its holder, the Ministry of Interior or National Defense may withdraw the permit at any time for exceptional reasons or for public safety considerations. In such circumstances, raw materials, products, and equipment that are not suitable for any purpose other than the manufacturing of weapons and ammunition shall be confiscated to the benefit of the army, with fair compensation determined by a technical committee of four members appointed by the Ministry of National Defense and one expert chosen by the permit holder. Decisions made by this committee are subject to review by courts with jurisdiction to decide administrative cases.[24]

V. Illegal Armed Groups

While the law in Lebanon does not provide for a legal right to bear arms, and while the permits to possess and carry weapons are granted at the discretion of the executive branch, for the last few decades Lebanon has been home to several armed groups operating outside any legal framework or official government acquiescence. This situation, which is public knowledge, prompted the United Nations Security Council in 2004 to officially call for the disbanding and disarmament of all Lebanese and non-Lebanese militias.[25]

Prepared by Issam M. Saliba
Senior Foreign Law Specialist

---

[24] *Id.* art. 11.

[25] S.C. Res. 1559, U.N. Doc. S/RES/1559 (Sept. 2, 2004), http://www.un.org/ga/search/view_doc.asp?symbol=S/RES/1559(2004).

MEXICO

FIREARMS-CONTROL LEGISLATION AND POLICY

Summary

The right to bear arms in Mexico is granted in the Constitution. This right has been extensively regulated by the Federal Penal Code, the Federal Law on Firearms and Explosives (which greatly expands the provisions of the Federal Penal Code), and the Regulations of the Federal Law on Firearms and Explosives. The Federal Penal Code specifies the types of firearms that may be possessed or carried by citizens and restricts others for use by the armed forces. The carrying of firearms requires an individual or collective license, for which specific requirements must be met. Applicants for licenses to carry weapons are generally required to post a bond, provide a justification for the weapon, and submit evidence of good conduct, among other things. Licenses may be suspended or cancelled by the Secretariat of National Defense in certain circumstances, typically having to do with the license holder's conduct. Holders of licenses are restricted from carrying their firearms at or during specified public events, with certain exceptions for rodeos and gun-related events, or at any gathering where disputes are predictable. The Federal Law on Firearms and Explosives imposes restrictions on the manufacture, import, and export of firearms, and adds a long list of penalties for violations of its provisions to supplement those provided by the Federal Penal Code. The Law imposes stiff penalties for the smuggling of arms reserved exclusively for the armed forces. Mexico is a party to the Geneva Convention on Prohibitions or Restrictions on the Use of Certain Conventional Weapons.

I. Introduction

Like the United States, Mexico has a constitutional provision granting its citizens the right to bear arms, as well as legislation prescribing the limits on that right. Article 10 of the Constitution reads as follows:

Article 10. The inhabitants of the United Mexican States have the right to possess arms in their homes for their security and legitimate defense with the exception of those [weapons] prohibited by federal law and those reserved for the exclusive use of the Army, Navy, Air Force, and National Guard. Federal law shall determine the cases, conditions, requirements and places [under and] in which the inhabitants may be authorized to bear arms.[1]

---

[1] Constitución Política de los Estados Unidos Mexicanos, *as amended*, DIARIO OFICIAL DE LA FEDERACIÓN [D.O.], Feb. 5, 1917, errata, D.O., Feb. 6, 1917.

The above fundamental right has been extensively implemented and regulated by the Federal Penal Code,[2] as amended, and the Federal Law on Firearms and Explosives, as amended,[3] and its Regulations.[4] Additionally, penal laws of the several states may be applicable.

The carrying of firearms by certain government employees is also subject to the regulations of the government ministries that employ them.[5] Treaties play a role in Mexico's firearms restrictions, although largely in regard to the selection of weapons for the military.[6]

II. The Federal Penal Code: Prohibited Weapons

Articles 160–163 of the Federal Penal Code deal with prohibited weapons. Article 160 provides that persons who carry, manufacture, import, or store, without a legal purpose, instruments that can only be used to attack (*agredir*), and which have no application for work or for recreation, will be imprisoned for three months to three years, fined a sum of up to 360 days of the guilty party's net income,[7] and have their weapons confiscated. These crimes are punishable without prejudice to the provisions of the Federal Law on Firearms and Explosives.

Article 160 of the Federal Penal Code further provides that public employees may carry the arms needed to perform their duties, subject to applicable laws.

Article 161 states that licenses are required to carry or sell pistols or revolvers.

Article 162 imposes imprisonment from six months to three years plus a fine of 180 to 360 days of the guilty party's net income for the following persons:

I.- Whoever imports, manufacturers, or sells the weapons described in article 160; or whoever gives them away or sells them;

---

[2] CÓDIGO PENAL FEDERAL, *as amended*, D.O., Aug. 14, 1931, *available at* http://www.diputados.gob.mx/LeyesBiblio/pdf/9.pdf.

[3] Ley Federal de Armas de Fuego y Explosivos, Dec. 29, 1971, D.O., Jan. 11, 1972, *as amended*. The current text reflecting all amendments is available on the website of the Mexican Chamber of Deputies, *at* http://www.diputados.gob.mx/LeyesBiblio/pdf/102.pdf. The English translations of the Law contained in this report are provided by the author.

[4] Reglamento de la Ley Federal de Armas de Fuego y Explosivos, May 4, 1972, D.O., May 6, 1972.

[5] *E.g.*, Reglamento Interior de la Secretaría de Hacienda y Crédito Público, D.O. Sept. 11, 1996, *as amended*, art. 181(XIX) (dealing with the carrying of firearms by officials on official duty).

[6] Mexico is a party to the 1980 Geneva Convention on Prohibitions or Restrictions on the Use of Certain Conventional Weapons, http://untreaty.un.org/cod/avl/ha/cprccc/cprccc.html. This Convention prohibits or restricts the use of certain weapons, including fragmenting explosives, whose pieces cannot be located with the use of X-rays; booby traps; and certain incendiary weapons. Decreto de Promulgación de la Convención sobre Prohibiciones o Restricciones del Empleo de Ciertas Armas Convencionales que Puedan Considerarse Excesivamente Nocivas o de Efectos Indiscriminados y sus Tres Protocolos, D.O., May 4, 1982.

[7] Fines in terms of earnings of the convicted person are defined in the Federal Penal Code. CÓDIGO PENAL FEDERAL art. 29.

II.- Whoever places pistols or revolvers on sale without legal authorization;

III.- Whoever carries the weapons described in article 160;

IV.- Whoever without a legal purpose, and without the required permission, stockpiles arms; and

V.- Whoever without a license carries any weapon listed in article 161.

Additionally, any weapons involved in the above-described acts are to be confiscated.

Article 163 provides that the licenses mentioned in article 161 will be granted by the President through the designated department or secretariat, subject to the applicable laws and the following:

I.- The sale of weapons described in article 161 may only be made by mercantile establishments, and not by individuals; and

II.- Applicants for licenses to carry arms must meet the following requirements:

a). They must post bond in the amount set by the authority; and

b). They must prove their need to carry weapons as well as their prior history of honesty and prudence, with the testimony of five persons well-known to the authorities.

III. Federal Law on Firearms and Explosives: Firearms Restrictions

A. Registration and Possession

The President, through the Secretariats of Internal Affairs and National Defense, controls all arms in the nation. To that end, a Federal Arms Registry (*Registro Federal de Armas*) is to be established by the Secretariat of National Defense.[8]

Title Two of the Federal Law on Firearms and Explosives requires all firearms to be registered with the Secretariat of National Defense in the Federal Arms Registry.[9] Neither possession nor carrying of any arms prohibited by law or restricted to the exclusive use of the Army, Navy, and Air Force is allowed, except as provided in this Law.[10]

B. Permitted Firearms

Tools and utensils known to be used for farming or for any trade, profession, or sport are not considered prohibited arms, providing they are used at the work or sport site, or if it can be shown that they are being transported for the purpose of their use in work or sport.[11]

Possession or carrying of arms with the following characteristics is allowed, but subject

---

[8] Ley Federal de Armas de Fuego y Explosivos art. 4.

[9] *Id.* tit. 2.

[10] *Id.* arts. 7, 8.

[11] *Id.* art. 13.

to the terms and conditions set forth in the Federal Law on Firearms and Explosives:

I.- Semiautomatic pistols with a caliber not greater than .380 (9 mm.), but excluding .38 Super and .38 Commander [*Comando*] pistols and the 9 mm. Mauser, Luger, Parabellum, and Commander pistols, as well as similar 9 mm. models of other brands.[12]

II.- Revolvers with a caliber not greater than the .38 Special, excluding the .357 Magnum.[13]

Members of agricultural collectives [*ejidatarios y comuneros*] and other farm workers [*jornaleros del campo*] may possess and carry, outside of urban areas, any of the [permitted] arms mentioned above, or a .22 caliber rifle or shotgun of any caliber, except those with a barrel longer than 635 mm. (25) and those with a caliber greater than 12 (.729 or 18.5 mm.) [providing these have been licensed].[14]

Concerning hunting and target shooting, the Law provides that

[t]hose arms that hunters or target shooters may be authorized to possess in their homes and to carry, with a license, are the following:

I.- Pistols, revolvers, and .22 caliber rifles with revolving magazines (*de fuego circular*).

II.- .38 caliber pistols for Olympic or competition shooting.

III.- Shotguns of all calibers and models except those with barrels of less than 635 mm. (25), and those of a caliber greater than 12 (.729 or 18.5 mm.).

IV.- Three-barrel shotguns of the calibers permitted in the preceding section, with one barrel for metal cartridges of a different caliber.

V.- High-powered repeating or semiautomatic rifles, not convertible into automatics, with the exception of the .30 caliber carbine rifles, short carbines (*mosquetones*), and .223 caliber carbines, 7 and 7.62 mm., and Garand .30 caliber rifles.

VI.- High-powered rifles of calibers greater than those mentioned in the preceding section, for use abroad, with special permission, for the hunting of big game that do not exist among the national fauna.

VII.- Other sporting arms consistent with the legal rules for hunting . . . or the regulations of national or international target-shooting organizations for use in competitions.[15]

The Secretariat of National Defense is authorized to determine which target-shooting or hunting weapons and munitions may be possessed,[16] but, in regard to hunting weapons, it must obtain the opinion of other secretaries and agencies before making a determination.[17]

---

[12] *Id.* art. 9(I).

[13] *Id.* art. 9(II).

[14] *Id.* art. 9(II), para. 2.

[15] *Id.* art. 10(I)–(VII).

[16] *Id.* art. 19.

Application for approval of a type of hunting or target-shooting firearm may be made directly or through an association or club.[18]

For those who practice the sport of *charreria* (giving Mexican-style "cowboy" demonstrations), authorization may be granted to have revolvers of a caliber greater than .38, but only for the sake of authenticity of their costumes, and these revolvers must be carried unloaded.[19]

The destruction, loss, or theft of arms must be reported to the Secretariat of Defense, in compliance with regulations issued for this purpose.[20]

Articles 21–23 of the Law deal with gun collecting and museums. Gun collectors and private or public museums, with prior permission of the Secretariat of National Defense, may have collections of old and/or modern arms. They may possess arms prohibited by this Law if these are valuable (*tengan valor*) or have cultural, scientific, artistic, or historic significance. If a collection or museum not connected to a military institute of the nation has arms reserved for the exclusive use of the Army, Navy, and Air Force, written authorization from the respective branch of the military must also be obtained.[21]

Prior permission is required to acquire new arms for private collections, and these arms must be registered.[22] Disposing of arms in collections, either as a collection or individually, also requires prior authorization.[23]

IV. Gun Ownership

Under the Federal Law on Firearms and Explosives, arms may be kept in the home for the defense of the owner and those who live there, but such arms must be registered with the Secretariat of National Defense.[24] To make these controls effective, for purposes of the Registry, individuals may have only a single domicile for themselves and their family.[25] Anyone who acquires one or more arms is obligated to register it with the Secretariat of National Defense within thirty days, stating in writing the brand, caliber, model, and serial number if it has one.[26]

---

[17] *Id.*

[18] *Id.*

[19] *Id.* art. 10(VII), para 2.

[20] *Id.* art. 14.

[21] *Id.* art. 21.

[22] *Id.* art. 22.

[23] *Id.* art. 23.

[24] *Id.* art. 15.

[25] *Id.* art. 16.

[26] *Id.* art. 17.

Public servants and the chiefs of the federal police services and of those of the Federal District, the States, and municipalities are also obligated to register the arms under their control.[27] Prohibited arms for the purpose of this Law include those already listed in the Federal Penal Code.[28]

A. Licenses for Carrying Firearms

A license is required to carry arms, and articles 24–26 of the Law set forth the applicable requirements for obtaining a license.

Licenses are of two types: for officials and for private parties. Licenses for officials are valid so long as the person holds the position or job that provides the basis for issuing the license. Licenses for private parties must be renewed every two years.[29] Licenses for private parties may be issued individually for private individuals, or collectively for private legal entities.[30]

1. Individual Licenses

Licenses for individuals are for the exclusive use of that individual. Licenses are issued to private individuals who

A. earn their living by honest means,

B. have completed any military service obligation,

C. have no physical or mental impediment to their use of arms,

D. have not been convicted of any crime committed with the use of arms,

E. do not consume psychotropic or other prohibited drugs, and

F. demonstrate, in the judgment of the Secretariat of National Defense, a need to carry arms because of:

a) the nature of their occupation or employment,

b) the special circumstances of the place in which they live, or

c) any other legitimate reason.[31]

Licenses to private individuals for one or more firearms may also be issued for the purposes of target shooting or hunting, but only if the interested party is a member of a registered club or association and meets the first five requirements listed above.[32]

---

[27] *Id.* art. 18.

[28] *Id.* art. 12.

[29] *Id.* art. 25.

[30] *Id.* art. 26.

[31] *Id.* art. 26, para. I.

[32] *Id.*

2. Collective Licenses

Licenses are to be issued to private legal entities that are organized under Mexican laws, as follows:

> B. Licenses are issued to [private] security services which
>
> a) have authorization to operate as a private security service;
>
> b) have a favorable opinion from the Secretariat of Interior about their justification and need to carry arms; about the amount and characteristics of the arms; and about the places where they may carry them.
>
> C. Licenses are issued to other legal entities when special circumstances justify doing so, according to the discretion of the Secretariat of National Defense, for their internal security service and protection of their facilities. They must comply with the controls and supervision of the Secretariat.[33]

Foreigners may be authorized to carry arms only when, in addition to satisfying the conditions set forth above, they also have immigrant status or are tourists, and thus may be issued temporary licenses for sporting purposes.[34]

Licenses to officials may be issued either to individual officials or collectively. Collective licenses may be issued (a) to official dependencies and federal, public agencies under whose office the strategic installations of the country are placed, who must issue credentials, to be renewed every six months, to the individuals who will be using the firearms; and (b) to police departments.[35] These collective licenses are valid only for the number of persons on the police payrolls, and the police departments must issue credentials to the individuals who will be using these firearms. The request for issuance of collective licenses must be made by the Secretariat of Interior to the Secretariat of Defense.[36]

Members of the Army, Navy, and Air Force are exempt from the licensing requirement in those cases and circumstances specified by the Law and applicable regulations. Members of Federal Police institutions, the state police, the police of the Federal District and municipalities, and private security police may carry arms in those cases and circumstances established by the Law and applicable regulations.[37]

---

[33] *Id.*, para. II(B) & (C).

[34] *Id.* art. 27.

[35] *Id.* art. 29.

[36] *Id.*

[37] *Id.* art. 24.

B. Cancelling and Suspending Licenses

The Secretariat of National Defense has the power to issue, suspend, and cancel these licenses, with some exceptions, as provided in article 32, and must inform the Secretariat of the Interior about the licenses that it issues, suspends, or cancels.[38] A license may be cancelled if

I.- the holder makes bad use of the arms or license;

II.- the holder alters the license;

III.- the arms are used away from the authorized places;

IV.- the holder carries a firearm other than that licensed;

V.- the firearm's original characteristics are altered;

VI.- the issuance of the license was based on fraud, or, in the judgment of the Secretariat of National Defense, the reasons for the issuance of the license no longer exist; or because of a supervening cause, one of the requirements for its issuance is not longer met;

VII.- a court of competent authority has ordered it cancelled;

VIII.- the holder changes domicile without notifying the Secretariat of National Defense; and

IX.- the holder fails to comply with the requirements of this Law or its Regulations.[39]

Licenses to carry arms may be suspended when in the judgment of the Secretariat of National Defense suspension is necessary to restore the tranquility of a municipality or region.[40] Article 32 provides that the Secretariat of Interior has the power to issue, suspend, and cancel official individual licenses to carry firearms to federal employees and must provide notification of such activity to the Secretariat of National Defense for recording in the National Registry of Firearms.[41]

C. Restrictions on Licenses

Police credentials alone do not convey a right to carry arms unless there is a corresponding license to do so.[42] Licenses to carry arms must state the territorial limits in which they are valid. In the case of neighborhood guards or those of a specific place, the license sets forth exactly the area in which they are valid.[43]

Holders of licenses to carry arms are prohibited from carrying these arms to public demonstrations and public celebrations, assemblies or similar meetings, boards and meetings in

---

[38] *Id.* art. 30.

[39] *Id.* art. 31.

[40] *Id.*

[41] *Id.* art. 32.

[42] *Id.* art. 33.

[43] *Id.* art. 34.

which disputes are to be argued, or to any gathering for whatever purpose at which disputes are predictable, and are also prohibited from any act to obtain a result through using or threatening to use arms. Exceptions are made for parades and for sports events of *charreria* (rodeo), target shooting, and hunting.[44]

V. Gun Manufacturing and Import-Export Issues

Articles 37–67 of the Law deal with the manufacture, trade, importation, and exportation of firearms. Article 37 reserves to the President, acting through the Secretariat of Defense, the right to authorize the establishment of businesses to manufacture or trade in firearms. The Law covers businesses dealing in any of the permitted firearms mentioned in Articles 9 and 10 of the Law, as well as ammunition and explosives (including but not limited to many types specifically listed), plus detonators, fireworks, and related materials.[45]

Article 55 provides that arms that are imported under ordinary or extraordinary import authorization must be destined to the precise use that is stated in the import authorization; any modification or change that may be made to such destination requires a new permit.[46]

Exporters of firearms must show that they have an import permit from the country to which the firearms are to be shipped.[47]

When commercial shipments of firearms for import or export are in the possession of Customs, the interested parties must notify the Secretariat of National Defense, which must designate a representative to intervene at the Customs Office. Without meeting this requirement, the removal of the shipment from the Customs Office or its export out of the country cannot be permitted.[48]

Private parties who acquire arms or ammunition abroad must request an extraordinary permit to remove them from the Customs Office.[49]

VI. Smuggling Arms

The Federal Law on Firearms and Explosives supplements and greatly expands on the provisions of the Federal Penal Code. Article 84 of the Law may be translated as follows:

> Article 84.- Five to thirty years of prison and fines of twenty to five hundred days of the guilty party's net income will be imposed:

---

[44] *Id.* art. 36.

[45] *Id.* arts. 39, 41.

[46] *Id.* art. 55.

[47] *Id.* art. 56.

[48] *Id.* art. 57.

[49] *Id.* art. 58.

I.   Upon a person who participates in the clandestine introduction into the national territory of firearms, ammunition, cartridges, explosives, and materials that are reserved for the exclusive use of the National Army, Navy, and Air Force or are controlled in accordance with this Law.

II. Upon the public servant who, being obligated by his/her functions to prevent such introduction, does not do so.   Moreover, he/she will be fired from his/her employment or position and disqualified from performing any position or public commission; and

III. Upon a person who acquires the items referred to in paragraph one for commercial purposes.[50]

VII. Additional Infractions

The Law adds a very long list of penalty provisions separate from those listed in the Penal Code.[51]   The range of sanctions for violations of the Law are from one to forty-five years of imprisonment, fines from one to 750 days of the guilty party's net income, suspension or cancellation of the license, and confiscation of the weapons.[52]

VIII. Educational Campaign

Title One of the Law on Firearms and Explosives requires the federal executive branch as well as the governments of the states, the Federal District, and each local jurisdiction (*ayuntamiento*) to conduct permanent educational campaigns with the aim of reducing the possession, carrying, and use of weapons of every type.   In addition, the Law only permits advertising for sporting arms used in hunting or target shooting under the restrictions set forth in the Law.[53]

Prepared by Norma C. Gutiérrez
Senior Foreign Law Specialist

---

[50] *Id.* art. 84.

[51] *See* CÓDIGO PENAL FEDERAL arts. 160–163.

[52] Ley Federal de Armas de Fuego y Explosivos, tit. 2, arts. 77–91.

[53] *Id.* art. 5.

NEW ZEALAND

FIREARMS-CONTROL LEGISLATION AND POLICY

Summary

The New Zealand Police operate a firearms licensing system, but only certain classes of weapons are registered, namely handguns, military style semiautomatics, and restricted weapons. In order to possess these types of weapons license holders must also obtain license endorsements, which can be granted in limited circumstances. Permits to procure such weapons must also be obtained. The licensing system includes background and reference checks, as well as safety training and a written test. The Police inspect and approve firearm storage before issuing licenses and endorsements. Law changes in 1992 aimed at further restricting access to firearms included stricter firearm storage requirements, prohibiting the sale of ammunition to non-licensed persons, and new processes relating to mail order purchases of firearms and ammunition.

There are estimated to be about 1.1 million firearms in New Zealand—about one for every four people. The rate of deaths involving firearms has decreased in the past twenty years, including those resulting from assault, suicide, and accidents. The authors of one study suggested that the 1992 law changes contributed to a "detectable reduction in firearm suicides." Another study concluded that New Zealand has seen "the most pronounced decline in firearm homicide over the past two decades" compared to Australia and Canada.

I. Introduction

In New Zealand, the licensing of gun owners and restrictions on firearm sales are governed by the Arms Act 1983[1] and regulations made under that legislation: the Arms Regulations 1992[2] and the Arms (Restricted Weapons and Specially Dangerous Airguns) Order 1984.[3] Several provisions in these instruments were recently amended by the Arms (Military Style Semi-automatic Firearms and Import Controls) Amendment Act 2012.[4] The New Zealand Police (the Police) is the body responsible for administering firearms legislation. There is no

---

[1] Arms Act 1983, http://www.legislation.govt.nz/act/public/1983/0044/latest/DLM72622.html.

[2] Arms Regulations 1992, http://www.legislation.govt.nz/regulation/public/1992/0346/latest/DLM168889.html.

[3] Arms (Restricted Weapons and Specially Dangerous Airguns) Order 1984, http://www.legislation.govt.nz/regulation/public/1984/0122/latest/DLM95640.html.

[4] Arms (Military Style Semi-automatic Firearms and Import Controls) Amendment Act 2012, http://www.legislation.govt.nz/act/public/2012/0117/latest/DLM3653106.html.

right to own or possess firearms under New Zealand law, including for the purposes of self-defense.

The current legal regime for firearms can be characterized as a "licensing but no registration" system since the majority of firearms in the country do not need to be registered. A range of amendments aimed at further restricting access to firearms were introduced in 1992 following a massacre in which thirteen people were killed by a licensed gunman carrying semiautomatic firearms.

This report provides an overview of the history of firearms control legislation in New Zealand, sets out details about the licensing and registration systems, and discusses firearms dealing and importation restrictions. The final section of this report provides statistical information relating to firearm ownership and the number of deaths involving firearms.

II. History of Firearms Control Laws in New Zealand

A. Early Laws

Early firearms control laws in the mid-1800s in New Zealand were primarily aimed at preventing the acquisition of firearms by Māori.[5] The legislation included import restrictions as well as a rudimentary system of registration and licensing that was targeted at arms dealers. However, once the threat of armed conflict between Māori and the colonial government receded, the legislation became largely a "dead letter" by the turn of the century, and settlers could readily acquire firearms without registering them.[6] Another law was passed in 1908 that consolidated earlier legislation, by which time, in the predominantly rural society, "firearms were familiar and useful tools, which might be needed to protect the far-flung bounds of Empire, but did not pose a social problem calling for active control."[7]

Labor unrest prior to World War I led to the Police seeking greater controls for firearms, with limited success.[8] After World War I, the Police continued to push for statutory controls, particularly of handguns, which were being brought back to the country in large numbers by soldiers. In addition, political concerns regarding socialist revolutionary ideas likely contributed to the enactment of the more detailed Arms Act 1920, which included a system of permits to procure firearms and an obligation to register individual weapons. The Act also declared automatic pistols to be unlawful and required a license to possess other handguns, which could only be carried with a permit and for a "proper and sufficient purpose."[9] Later, in the 1930s,

---

[5] T.M. THORP, REVIEW OF FIREARMS CONTROL IN NEW ZEALAND: REPORT OF AN INDEPENDENT INQUIRY COMMISSIONED BY THE MINISTER OF POLICE 9 (1997), http://www.police.govt.nz/resources/1997/review-of-firearms-control/review-of-firearms-control-in-new-zealand.pdf.

[6] Id. at 10. See Arms Act 1860 (24 Victoriae 1860 No 38), http://www.nzlii.org/nz/legis/hist_act/aa186024v1860n38188/.

[7] THORP, supra note 5, at 10.

[8] Id.

[9] Id.; Arms Act 1920 (11 GEO V 1920 No 14), http://www.nzlii.org/nz/legis/hist_act/aa192011gv1920n14140/aa192011gv1920n14140.html.

pressure from farmers and sporting shooters led to some relaxing of the registration requirements for shotguns.[10]

The challenges and costs of maintaining an accurate and complete arms register were highlighted during the 1960s when increasing gun crime led the Police to try to make more frequent use of the register, resulting in the identification of widespread issues.[11] Following various reviews and discussions, the Police also determined in the 1970s that "a closer control of users was desirable to try to reduce access to firearms by unsuitable persons."[12] Although the Police did identify that the registration of firearms provided "an invaluable investigative aid," the agency saw the validation of existing records as an enormous and expensive task that would detract from other work.[13] The approach of focusing more on tighter screening of firearms license applicants rather than on registering firearms, a reversal of the approach that previously existed, gained political support and was formalized in the Arms Act 1983.[14]

B. 1983 Legislation

The original Arms Act 1983 provided for lifetime licenses that could be issued to persons over 16 years of age who were considered by police to be "fit and proper" to be in possession of a firearm. A firearms license allowed the holder to own as many firearms as he or she wished, including pistols and restricted weapons where the person obtained a special license endorsement to possess such weapons. There was no requirement for the registration of most weapons, apart from pistols and restricted weapons, for which an acquisition permit was also required.[15]

C. 1992 Amendments

While a number of features of the original 1983 legislation continue to apply today, the laws were amended in 1992 following the 1990 Aramoana massacre in which a thirty-three-year-old licensed gunman killed thirteen people using two "military-style semiautomatic" (MSSA) firearms before being shot dead by police.[16] The 1992 amendments and associated regulations included new restrictions on MSSAs, introducing a requirement to obtain a license endorsement to possess such firearms along with permits to procure them, similar to the existing requirements for handguns and other "restricted weapons." However, "[a] total ban on MSSAs was rejected in the face of opposition from user groups and the estimated cost of such a measure in terms of providing adequate compensation to current owners."[17]

---

[10] THORP, *supra* note 5, at 11.

[11] *Id.* at 13.

[12] *Id.* at 14.

[13] *Id.* at 15–16.

[14] *Id.* at 16.

[15] *Id.* at 16–18.

[16] *See id.* at 19–20.

[17] *Id.* at 20.

The 1992 amendment bill and accompanying regulations also required firearms licenses to be renewed every ten years; provided that ammunition sales only be made to firearms license holders; introduced a written permit system for mail order guns and ammunition; added tighter storage requirements along with inspections; and gave police powers to seize weapons in cases of domestic violence.[18]

D. 1997 Report and Subsequent Actions

Following the 1992 changes, and after two shootings by police officers in 1995, the government ordered an examination of internal police procedures for storing and using firearms.[19] The government also sought an independent review of firearms legislation, which subsequently took place in the context of gun massacres in Australia and the United Kingdom in 1996. The resulting 1997 report (the Thorp Report) recommended "radical reform of firearms laws,"[20] including restricting the number of handguns that a licensee can hold; banning all MSSAs; limiting magazine capacity for other semiautomatics; disqualifying persons convicted of certain offenses from holding a firearms license for a set period; and permitting the voluntary disclosure of relevant mental health information by health professionals.[21]

Many of the recommended changes in the 1997 report, including a return to a full firearms registry, were included in a bill that was introduced in 1999. However, due to intensive opposition during the parliamentary process, this bill did not advance.[22] A pared-down bill was later introduced in 2005, which was primarily aimed at enabling New Zealand to comply with the minimum legislative requirements of the Protocol against the Illicit Manufacturing of and Trafficking in Firearms, Their Parts and Components and Ammunition (supplementing the United Nations Convention against Transnational Organised Crime).[23] This bill also has not advanced.[24]

---

[18] *Id.* at 21–22; Arms Amendment Act 1992, http://www.legislation.govt.nz/act/public/1992/0095/latest/DLM278351.html.

[19] THORP, *supra* note 5, at 2.

[20] *Id.* at 237.

[21] *Id.* at 238–47 (Appendix 1: Recommendations). For an analysis of the Thorp Report, *see* Greg Newbold, *The 1997 Review of Firearms Control: An Appraisal*, 11 SOC. POL. J. OF N.Z. (1998), http://www.msd.govt.nz/about-msd-and-our-work/publications-resources/journals-and-magazines/social-policy-journal/spj11/1997-review-of-firearms-control-an-appraisal.html.

[22] *See* Kerry Williamson, *Why No Action on Guns!*, STUFF.CO.NZ (May 13, 2009), http://www.stuff.co.nz/national/politics/2405890/Why-no-action-on-guns; Kerry Williamson, *Registry Idea Shelved After Pro-Gun Lobbying*, STUFF.CO.NZ (May 16, 2009), http://www.stuff.co.nz/national/crime/2415864/Registry-idea-shelved-after-pro-gun-lobbying.

[23] *See* New Zealand Parliamentary Library, Bills Digest No. 1228: Arms Amendment Bill (No 3) 2005, http://www.parliament.nz/NR/rdonlyres/B1E7E92C-5473-4B6F-B0C4-E02B632A0C71/27184/1228Arms1.pdf.

[24] *See Arms Amendment Bill (No 3)*, NEW ZEALAND PARLIAMENT, http://www.parliament.nz/en-NZ/PB/Legislation/Bills/0/7/4/00DBHOH_BILL6590_1-Arms-Amendment-Bill-No-3.htm (last visited Jan. 9, 2013); ARMS AMENDMENT BILL (NO. 3): REPORT OF THE LAW AND ORDER COMMITTEE (Mar. 2012), http://www.parliament.nz/NR/rdonlyres/4C60851B-26DF-44F1-8F30-77BA5C3019D3/241315/DBSCH_SCR_5371_ArmsAmendmentBillNo32481_8853_5.pdf (recommending that the bill not proceed); Question for Written Answer 465 (2012), Hon. Phil Goff to the Minister of the Police (Feb. 15, 2012),

E. 2012 Amendments and Current Discussions

Amendments were passed in 2012 following a 2010 High Court finding against a Police interpretation of the definition of MSSAs that reclassified particular weapons as MSSAs.[25] The High Court decision created uncertainty about whether some semiautomatic firearms were MSSAs or not, particularly regarding an exclusion for firearms having a "sporting configuration," which included firearms that did not have certain features such as "a military pattern free-standing pistol grip."[26] The amendments covered four main areas: a clearer and more adaptable definition of MSSAs; an extension of regulation-making powers so that the Police can declare a firearm or type of firearm to be an MSSA; a right of appeal to enable firearms owners to challenge a classification of a firearm as an MSSA; and restrictions on the importation of airguns that have the appearance of being pistols, restricted weapons, or MSSAs.[27]

During the select committee process for the 2012 amendments, and in the Police annual report for that year, the Police indicated that it was considering the establishment of an advisory group "to improve communications between Police and the firearms community."[28] The annual report also stated that a review of the Arms Act 1983 is being conducted by the Police "to identify other amendments that could help to address operational issues that have emerged since the Act was last significantly amended in 1992."[29]

New Zealand is one of a small number of countries in which police officers do not routinely carry firearms.[30] The debate about arming officers reignites from time to time following incidents in which police officers are killed or injured, including most recently in

---

http://www.parliament.nz/en-NZ/PB/Business/QWA/d/3/5/QWA_00465_2012-465-2012-Hon-Phil-Goff-to-the-Minister-of-Police-Includes.htm (stating that the 2005 bill does not constitute the current Government's policy).

[25] *Lincoln v. Police* [2010] NZHC 183 (1 Mar. 2010), http://www.nzlii.org/nz/cases/NZHC/2010/183.pdf.

[26] *See* NEW ZEALAND POLICE, ARMS (MILITARY STYLE SEMI-AUTOMATIC FIREARMS AND IMPORT CONTROLS) AMENDMENT BILL – INITIAL BRIEFING, http://www.parliament.nz/NR/rdonlyres/4B9AE9E2-302B-47C4-BFF7-A75F8AC0904E/198543/49SCLO_ADV_00DBHOH_BILL10610_1_A191404_Initialbrie.pdf. For information on the passage of the bill along with associated documents, *see Arms (Military Style Semi-automatic Firearms and Import Controls) Amendment Bill*, NEW ZEALAND PARLIAMENT, http://www.parliament.nz/en-NZ/PB/Legislation/Bills/c/6/5/00DBHOH_BILL10610_1-Arms-Military-Style-Semi-automatic-Firearms-and.htm (last visited Jan. 9, 2013).

[27] *See* Arms (Military Style Semi-Automatic Firearms and Import Controls) Amendment Bill (2011), as Reported by the Law and Order Committee, http://www.parliament.nz/NR/rdonlyres/5D3298B7-7918-4574-8FA3-3072FC61B646/256278/DBSCH_SCR_5255_ArmsMilitaryStyleSemiautomaticFirea.pdf.

[28] NEW ZEALAND POLICE, ANNUAL REPORT 2011–2012, at 22 (2012), http://www.police.govt.nz/sites/default/files/resources/annual/new-zealand-police-annual-report-12.pdf. *See also* Letter, Kevin Kelly to Jacqui Dean MP paras. 2–8 (July 22, 2011), http://www.parliament.nz/NR/rdonlyres/24462618-0763-4A5E-9242-55A669725008/198547/49SCLO_ADV_00DBHOH_BILL10610_1_A198511_NewZealandP.pdf.

[29] New Zealand Police, *supra* note 28.

[30] *See* Peter Marshall, *The Debate About Arming Police*, NEW ZEALAND POLICE (July 14, 2010), http://www.police.govt.nz/blog/2010/07/14/debate-about-arming-police/24684; John Kelly, *Why British Police Don't Have Guns*, BBC NEWS MAGAZINE (Sept. 18, 2012), http://www.bbc.co.uk/news/magazine-19641398.

December 2012.[31] The current Police Commissioner has stated that, while he supports providing greater access to Tasers and firearms, including by having gun safes in more police vehicles, he does not support police officers routinely carrying firearms while on standard patrol.[32] In September 2012 he stated his belief that "routine arming of New Zealand Police would radically alter the relationship between police and public, without making the policing environment safer."[33]

III. Current Firearm Control Laws

A. Licensing System

All persons in possession of a firearm must hold a license in accordance with the Arms Act 1983.[34] Unlicensed persons may, however, be in possession of a firearm or ammunition if they are under the immediate supervision of a license holder.[35] General rules relating to firearms licenses include the following:

- Firearms license applicants are required to provide a photo, which is displayed on the license;[36]

- License holders are required to produce their license when required to do so by a member of the Police;[37]

- Persons in possession of a firearm must give their full name, address, and date of birth if requested by a member of the Police;[38]

- License holders are required to notify the Police of a change of address (Persons holding an endorsement as described below must also inform the Police of the

---

[31] *See, e.g.,* Michael Daly, *Armed Police Calls 'Scaremongering'*, STUFF.CO.NZ (Dec. 28, 2012), http://www.stuff.co.nz/national/crime/8124960/Armed-police-calls-scaremongering; Michael Daly & Jody O'Callaghan, *No Move to Arm Police Despite Attacks*, STUFF.CO.NZ (Dec. 29, 2012), http://www.stuff.co.nz/national/crime/8127288/No-move-to-arm-police-despite-attacks; Editorial, *Do Not Arm Police*, THE PRESS (Dec. 28, 2012), http://www.stuff.co.nz/the-press/opinion/editorials/8123653/Do-not-arm-police; Editorial, *Attacks on Police Unacceptable*, OTAGO DAILY TIMES (Jan. 4, 2012), http://www.odt.co.nz/opinion/editorial/241284/attacks-police-unacceptable.

[32] *See* Peter Marshall, *We're Not About to Short-Change Staff*, NEW ZEALAND POLICE (June 14, 2012), https://www.police.govt.nz/blog/2012/06/14/were-not-about-short-change-staff/31874.

[33] Peter Marshall, *A Question of Responsibility*, NEW ZEALAND POLICE (Sept. 20, 2012), http://www.police.govt.nz/blog/2012/09/20/question-responsibility/32757.

[34] *See generally, Firearms Safety – Firearms Licence*, NEW ZEALAND POLICE, http://www.police.govt.nz/service/firearms (last visited Jan. 9, 2013).

[35] Arms Act 1983, ss 43(3) and 43B(3).

[36] *See id.* s 34A; Arms Regulations 1992, reg. 30.

[37] Arms Act 1983, s 26.

[38] *Id.* s 40.

arrangements made for safe custody of the firearm during the shift to the new address);[39] and

• A person must notify the Police if any firearm is lost or stolen.[40]

The Arms Act and associated regulations are silent regarding the ownership or possession of firearms for the purposes of self-defense. However, the Arms Code (a firearms safety manual and guidance document produced by the Police and the New Zealand Mountain Safety Council (NZMSC) and provided to license applicants) states that

Self-defence is not a valid reason to possess firearms. The law does not permit the possession of firearms 'in anticipation' that a firearm may need to be used in self-defence.

Citizens are justified in using force in self-defence in certain situations. The force that is justified will depend on the circumstances of the particular case. Every person is criminally responsible for any excessive use of force against another person.

A firearm is a lethal weapon. To justify the discharge of a firearm at another person the user must hold a honest belief that they or someone else is at imminent threat of death or grievous bodily harm.[41]

1. Standard License

A standard firearms license allows the holder to obtain any number of sporting-type rifles and shotguns (referred to as "A category" firearms).[42] Any person over the age of 16 years may submit an application for a firearms license to the Police.[43] People aged 16 and 17 years must also hold a license in order to possess an airgun.[44] A member of the Police (Arms Officer) may issue a license if he or she is satisfied that the applicant is a "fit and proper person to be in possession of a firearm or airgun."[45]

Firearms licenses expire after ten years and can be renewed prior to their expiration.[46] A firearms license may be revoked if an Arms Officer considers that the holder is not a fit and proper person to be in possession of a firearm.[47] A license can also be revoked if an officer

---

[39] *Id.* s 34.

[40] *Id.* s 39.

[41] NEW ZEALAND POLICE, ARMS CODE 41 (Wellington, 2010), http://www.police.govt.nz/sites/default/files/services/firearms/NZP-Arms-Code-R3.pdf. *See also* THORP, *supra* note 5, at 102-103 for a discussion of firearms and self-defense under New Zealand law.

[42] ARMS CODE, *supra* note 41, at 42.

[43] Arms Act 1983, s 23(1).

[44] ARMS CODE, *supra* note 41, at 42.

[45] Arms Act 1983, s 24(1)(b).

[46] *Id.* s 25(1).

[47] *Id.* s 27(1)(a).

considers that it is "reasonably likely" that a firearm in the license holder's possession could be obtained by someone that is not a fit and proper person to possess a firearm.[48] Amendments to the legislation as a result of the Domestic Violence Act 1995 also provide for refusal or revocation of a license where the Police are satisfied that there are grounds for making an application for a protection order, or where such an order is in force.[49]

In applying for a license, a person must supply various details, including whether he or she has been convicted of any offense or been refused a firearms license, whether in New Zealand or any country, and the name and address of two referees (references): one a near relative of the applicant, and the other a person "of whom inquiries can be made about whether the applicant is a fit and proper person to be in possession of a firearm."[50]

The Arms Code states that

People who have

- a history of violence or
- repeated involvement with drugs or
- been irresponsible with alcohol or
- a personal or social relationship with people who may be deemed to be unsuitable to obtain access to firearms or
- indicates [sic] an intent to use firearms for self defence

may find it difficult to satisfy the Police that they are fit and proper to have a firearm.[51]

While there are no provisions that deal directly with psychiatric assessments of firearms license applicants, a history of mental illness may also provide reason for the Police to refuse or revoke a license on the grounds that the person is not fit and proper to possess a firearm.[52]

There is no set waiting period to obtain a firearms license. The Police set performance standards for various services and activities, with the target standard for firearm licensing in the 2011/2012 fiscal year being 90% of licenses issued within thirty days of receipt of the application. The reports for the last two years show that the average period is considerably longer, being 104 days in 2010/2011 and 120 days in 2011/2012.[53] During 2011/2012, the

---

[48] *Id.* s 27(1)(b).

[49] *Id.* s 27.

[50] Arms Regulations 1992, reg. 15(2).

[51] ARMS CODE, *supra* note 41, at 40.

[52] *See, e.g., id.* at 53 (recommending that license holders discuss with family or doctors any reasons, "including mental health problems," that may mean they will be judged unfit to hold a firearms license); THORP, *supra* note 5, at 166–76 (discussing the impact of mental illness on violence and options for reducing the risk of misuse of firearms by the mentally disordered), 252 (referring to a multiple shooting carried out by "a young man with a psychiatric history which had earlier resulted in the revocation of his firearms licence"), and 253 (referring to a shooting incident where the individual's license and firearms had previously been removed "as a police officer believed Radcliffe not a fit and proper person by reason of his mental illness.").

[53] NEW ZEALAND POLICE, *supra* note 28, at 40.

Police also revoked 599 firearms licenses from persons deemed no longer fit and proper to hold a firearms license. An additional seventy-nine licenses were revoked in response to actions under the Domestic Violence Act 1995.[54]

2. Pistols and Restricted Weapon Endorsements

A person must apply to the Police for a license endorsement if they wish to possess a pistol or "restricted weapon."[55] An Arms Officer can make the endorsement if he or she is satisfied that the applicant "is a fit and proper person to be in possession of the pistol or restricted weapon to which the application relates."[56]

A pistol is defined as "any firearm that is designed or adapted to be held and fired with 1 hand; and includes any firearm that is less than 762 millimetres [30 inches] in length."[57] "Restricted weapon" refers to any weapon, firearm or not, which is declared to be a restricted weapon by way of a government order.[58] Once a weapon is declared to be a restricted weapon, a person in possession of such a weapon or its parts must dispose of them or obtain a license endorsement within one month of the notification being published. Compensation can be paid if the items are surrendered to the Police.[59]

The Arms (Restricted Weapons and Specially Dangerous Airguns) Order 1984 provides a list of restricted weapons in a schedule. The list includes anti-tank projectors; grenade launchers; incendiary grenades; mines; rocket launchers; devices designed for the purpose of discharging toxic gas or smoke; and "machine carbines or guns, submachine carbines or guns, and machine pistols, of any kind whatsoever, including those operated by gas or compressed air and including all other firearms capable of full automatic fire."[60]

License endorsements with respect to pistols and restricted weapons can be obtained in limited circumstances, including where the applicant is a member of a pistol shooting club recognized by the Commissioner of Police (known as a "B" endorsement[61]); or is a "bona fide collector of firearms," or an approved employee or member of a broadcasting body, theater company, or cinematic or television production company, or a person to whom the weapon has

---

[54] Id.

[55] See Arms Act 1983, s 50 (offense of unlawful possession of pistol, military style semiautomatic firearm, or restricted weapon).

[56] Id. s 30.

[57] Id. s 2.

[58] Id. The Governor-General may make such a declaration under section 4 of the Act.

[59] Id. s 37.

[60] Arms (Restricted Weapons and Specially Dangerous Airguns) Order 1984, sch.

[61] ARMS CODE, supra note 41, at 43.

special significance as an heirloom or memento (known as a "C" endorsement[62]); or a licensed dealer (or an agent or employee of a licensed dealer) (known as an "F" endorsement[63]).[64]

Endorsements with respect to pistols are subject to conditions that the license holder "may use the pistol only for target pistol shooting on a pistol range approved by the Commissioner for the purpose," and that they actively participate in the pistol shooting club by taking part in range activities on at least twelve days each year.[65] Where an endorsement with respect to pistols or restricted weapons is granted to other categories of person described above, the endorsement is subject to a condition that no live ammunition be used under any circumstances.[66]

3. MSSA Endorsements

As noted above, the definition of an MSSA firearm in the Arms Act 1983 was amended in 2012. It is now expressed in the positive rather than the negative, is more detailed, and provides for greater flexibility. The definition states that an MSSA is

  (a) a semi-automatic firearm having 1 or more of the following features:
    (i) a folding or telescopic butt:
    (ii) a magazine designed to hold 0.22-inch rimfire cartridges that—
      (A) is capable of holding more than 15 cartridges; or
      (B) is detachable, and by its appearance indicates that it is capable of holding more than 15 cartridges:
    (iii) a magazine (other than one designed to hold 0.22-inch rimfire cartridges) that—
      (A) is capable of holding more than 7 cartridges; or
      (B) is detachable, and by its appearance indicates that it is capable of holding more than 10 cartridges:
    (iv) bayonet lugs:
    (v) a flash suppressor:
    (vi) a component of a kind defined or described by an order under section 74A as a pistol grip for the purposes of this definition; or
  (b) a semi-automatic firearm of a make and model declared by an order under section 74A to be a military style semi-automatic firearm for the purposes of this Act; or
  (c) a semi-automatic firearm of a description declared by an order under section 74A to be a military style semi-automatic firearm for the purposes of this Act; or
  (d) a semi-automatic firearm that has a feature of a kind defined or described in an order under section 74A as a feature of military style semi-automatic firearms for the purposes of this Act.[67]

---

[62] *Id.*

[63] *Id.* at 44.

[64] Arms Act 1983, s 29(2).

[65] Arms Regulations 1992, reg. 22(1).

[66] *Id.* reg. 22(2).

[67] Arms Act 1983, s 2 (as amended by Arms (Military Style Semi-automatic Firearms and Import Controls) Amendment Act 2012, cl. 4). The previous definition of an MSSA firearm was "(a) a firearm which, after being

An applicant for an MSSA license endorsement (known as an "E" endorsement[68]) must be over the age of eighteen years and must satisfy the Police that he or she is a "fit and proper person to be in possession of the military style semi-automatic firearm to which that application relates."[69]

B. Safety Training and Testing

The Arms Regulations 1992 require that all firearms license applicants undergo a firearms safety course conducted by a member of the Police or other approved person.[70] The NZMSC's Firearm Safety section is currently the sole organization authorized to deliver firearms safety training, with individual volunteer instructors approved by the Police.[71] The NZMSC also administers the Firearm Safety Test; a written test that must be passed to obtain a firearms license under the regulations.[72] The test is based on the contents and safety rules of the Arms Code and involves multiple choice questions. There is no fee for either the training or the test, and people can attend even if they are not applying for a license.[73]

C. Security Requirements

1. Standard Rules

The Arms Regulations 1992 set out conditions relating to safety precautions that apply to all licenses. These conditions require that license holders[74]

- not put a firearm in such a place that a young child has ready access to it;

- take reasonable steps to ensure that ammunition is not stored "in such a way that a person who obtains access to the firearm also obtains access to the ammunition," or, where ammunition is stored with the firearm, ensure that the firearm is not capable of being discharged;

- take "reasonable steps" to ensure that firearms are secured against theft, which includes using a lockable cabinet, container, or stout receptacle; or a lockable steel and concrete storeroom; or a display rack in which firearms may be immobilized and locked so that none can be fired; and

---

loaded, fires, ejects, and chambers a cartridge with each pull of the trigger; but (b) does not include— (i) a pistol; or (ii) a semi-automatic firearm that, with its magazine (if any), is maintained at all times in a sporting configuration."

[68] ARMS CODE, *supra* note 41, at 43.

[69] Arms Act 1983, s 30B.

[70] Arms Regulations 1992, reg. 14(a).

[71] ARMS CODE, *supra* note 41, at 1.

[72] Arms Regulations 1992, reg. 14(b).

[73] ARMS CODE, *supra* note 41, at 41.

[74] Arms Regulations 1992, cl. 19.

- ensure that no firearm in the holder's possession is left in an unattended vehicle.

The Arms Code states that the Police will ensure that an applicant can provide safe storage prior to granting a firearms license.[75]

The legislation provides that it is an offense, subject to a fine of up to NZ$5,000 (about US$4,200) and/or imprisonment of up to four years, to carry or be in possession of any firearm, airgun, pistol, restricted weapon or explosive "except for some lawful, proper, and sufficient purpose."[76] Carrying or possessing firearms or ammunition in a public place without a lawful purpose carries the same penalties.[77] A similar provision, with a lesser penalty, applies with respect to carrying an imitation firearm.[78] It is also an offense to carry a loaded firearm in a motor vehicle.[79]

2. Pistols, Restricted Weapons, and MSSAs

The Arms Regulations 1992 contain additional security requirements in relation to pistols, restricted weapons, and MSSAs.[80] The regulations allow the Police to inspect any pistol, restricted weapon, or MSSA "and the place where it is kept."[81] Persons entitled to possess such weapons must keep them in either[82]

- a steel and concrete strong room "of sound construction" and of a type approved (either generally or in the particular case) by a member of the Police;

- a room "of stout and secure construction capable of being secured against unlawful entry" that meets certain specified requirements; or

- a locked steel case, box, or cabinet of a type approved by a member of the Police that is bolted or securely fixed within a building (again in a manner approved by a member of the Police).

Where the weapon is stored in a steel case, box, or cabinet, ammunition must be stored separately.[83]

---

[75] ARMS CODE, *supra* note 41, at 40, 45.

[76] Arms Act 1983, s 45.

[77] *Id.* s 51.

[78] *Id.* s 46.

[79] Land Transport (Road User) Rule 2004, cl. 7.21, http://www.legislation.govt.nz/regulation/public/2004/0427/latest/DLM302188.html.

[80] Arms Act 1983, ss 32 & 33A; Arms Regulations 1992, reg. 28.

[81] Arms Regulations 1992, reg. 29(1).

[82] *Id.* reg. 28(1).

[83] *Id.* reg. 28(2).

In addition, all endorsements with respect to restricted weapons include a condition that the holder of the license "ensures that every restricted weapon in his possession is both rendered inoperable by the removal of a vital part and maintained, by reason of the removal of a vital part, in an inoperable condition."[84] It is also an offense for a person to carry a pistol or restricted weapon outside of the boundary of his or her property other than in accordance with the conditions endorsed on his or her license.[85]

D. Permits to Procure and Registration of Pistols, Restricted Weapons, and MSSAs

In addition to requiring an additional endorsement to possess a pistol, restricted weapon, or MSSA, a permit to purchase such a weapon must be obtained from the Police. These acquisition permits expire after one month.[86] A person who sells or supplies these firearms to someone that does not have a permit to procure the weapon is liable on conviction to a fine of up to NZ$4,000 (about US$3,350) and/or a term of imprisonment up to three years.[87]

An application for a permit to procure a pistol, restricted weapon, or MSSA must include various details, including a description of the weapon to be procured, its location, and the full name of the current owner.[88] Once a permit has been issued the holder must deliver it to the seller, who must write various details on the permit, including a description of the firearm and the number of his or her firearms license. The purchaser must then return the permit to the relevant Police office and produce the firearm for inspection.[89] All pistols, restricted weapons, and MSSAs are required to have a serial number or other number by which it can be identified.[90]

Although license holders are not required to report "A" category firearms to the Police, the Arms Code contains a recommendation that people record the make, model, and serial number of all firearms, and states that the Police can record the information in their database if requested.[91]

E. Dealer Licenses and Record Keeping

A dealer's license (known as a "D" license) can be issued where the Police consider the applicant to be a fit and proper person to carry on a business as a dealer or manufacturer of firearms.[92] A dealer's license is personal to the holder and cannot be transferred;[93] therefore, all

---

[84] Arms Act 1983, s 32.

[85] *Id.* s 36.

[86] *Id.* s 35.

[87] *Id.* s 44.

[88] Arms Regulations 1992, reg. 24.

[89] *Id.* reg. 26.

[90] *Id.* reg. 27.

[91] ARMS CODE, *supra* note 41, at 52 & 53.

[92] Arms Act 1983, s 5.

[93] *Id.* s 6.

employees or agents of a dealer must also hold a license.[94]   Dealer licenses must be renewed annually[95] and can be revoked at any time by the Commissioner of Police.[96]

A dealer's license applies to one place of business only.[97]   However, a special license of up to five days' duration can be granted to dealers for the purposes of a gun show at another location.[98]   A firearms dealer cannot take possession of a pistol or restricted weapon unless he or she obtains an import permit or permit to procure.[99]

The Arms Act 1983 requires that dealers comply with regulations regarding record keeping, and must permit any member of the Police to inspect and make copies of any records.[100]   Records must be kept of the details of each item received, manufactured, and sold, with each entry required to be made "at or immediately following the time of the transaction to which it relates" and every book kept for at least five years after the date of the last entry.[101]

It is an offense to sell or supply a firearm or airgun,[102] or ammunition,[103] to an unlicensed person. Furthermore, in order to sell firearms or ammunition through mail order, the seller must obtain a written order that has an endorsement from a member of the Police stating that the purchaser's firearms license has been inspected.[104]

It is also an offense to import any firearm, pistol, MSSA, restricted weapon, or restricted airguns,[105] or any parts of such weapons, without first obtaining a permit from the Police.[106]   Various details must be included in the permit application under the regulations.[107]   Permits expire twelve months after they are issued[108] and can be revoked at any time.[109]   The Police have

---

[94] *Id.* s 11.

[95] *Id.* s 8.

[96] *Id.* s 9.

[97] *Id.* s 7.

[98] *Id.* s 7A.

[99] *Id.* s 10.

[100] *Id.* s 12.

[101] The relevant regulations were amended by the Arms (Military Style Semi-automatic Firearms and Import Controls) Amendment Act 2012, s 15 (inserting new reg. 7 into the Arms Regulations 1992).

[102] Arms Act 1983, s 43.

[103] *Id.* s 43B(1).

[104] *Id.* s 43A. This provision does not apply to any pistol, restricted weapon, or MSSA.

[105] Added by section 5 of the Arms (Military Style Semi-automatic Firearms and Import Controls) Amendment Act 2012.

[106] Arms Act 1983, s 16.

[107] Arms Regulations 1992, reg. 10.

[108] *Id.* s 18A.

[109] *Id.* s 18(4).

broad discretion to refuse to grant such permits[110] and can require the importer to produce samples for testing.[111] Furthermore, in order to grant a permit to import a pistol, MSSA, restricted weapon, or restricted airgun,[112] or any parts, the Commissioner of Police must be satisfied that there are "special reasons" why the weapon to which the application relates should be allowed into New Zealand.[113] When these types of weapons are imported, the importer must ensure that each bear a serial number by which they can be identified[114] and must provide a written notice to the Police that includes this number.[115]

IV. Statistical Information

A. Number of License Holders and Firearms

Due to the fact that sporting-type rifles and shotguns are not formally registered, the total number of such firearms can only be estimated broadly.[116] Estimates for the total number of firearms in New Zealand have remained relatively steady since the mid-1990s. For example, in the context of the 1997 Thorp Report, it was estimated that, as of 1996 (when the population was about 4.17 million people[117]), there were between 700,000 and 1 million firearms in New Zealand, including 6,919 registered MSSAs.[118] The total figure included an estimated 10,000 to 25,000 illegal guns.[119] The report stated that about 3% of the country's firearms were handguns,[120] with handguns, restricted weapons, and MSSAs therefore making up a total of "no more than 4 percent of the total armoury."[121]

The 1997 Thorp Report also noted the difficulty of calculating the number of license holders at that time, about four years after the start of the implementation of the 1992

---

[110] *Id.* s 18(1)(b).

[111] *Id.* ss 18(1)(a) & 18B.

[112] Added by section 7 of the Arms (Military Style Semi-automatic Firearms and Import Controls) Amendment Act 2012.

[113] Arms Act 1983, s 18(2).

[114] Arms Regulations 1992, reg. 12.

[115] *Id.* reg. 13.

[116] *See* THORP, *supra* note 5, at 24–25 (discussing the issues with obtaining data on the number of firearms in New Zealand).

[117] STATISTICS NEW ZEALAND, NATIONAL POPULATION ESTIMATES – DECEMBER 2006 QUARTER (Feb. 2007), http://stats.govt.nz/~/media/Statistics/Browse%20for%20stats/NationalPopulationEstimates/previous-releases/national-population-estimates-dec06qtr-hotp.pdf.

[118] THORP, *supra* note 5, at 27. Note that this figure does not include MSSAs that were "sporterised" following the 1992 amendments. It was estimated that, as of 1996, between 33 and 44% of MSSAs were registered as such, making the total number of both registered and "sporterised" MSSAs between 16,000 and 21,000. However, Thorp considered this to be conservative, with the likely total being between 20,000 and 25,000. *Id.*

[119] *Id.* at 29–33.

[120] *Id.* at 34.

[121] *Id.* at 117.

amendments, which saw lifetime license holders needing to reapply for a ten-year license.[122] The report estimated that, given various available information, there would be about 206,000 license holders by 1999.[123] Thorp also noted that a draft United Nations report included the figures of 1.1 million firearms and 250,000 license holders for New Zealand, which he suggested should only be used as a "guide, to be considered along with any other information available."[124]

About ten years later, in 2006, the Police reported to Parliament that there were at that time 227,704 firearms license holders and about 1.1 million firearms in New Zealand, including about 8,500 registered MSSAs as well as nine anti-tank projectors and sixteen grenade launchers.[125] The Police spokesman stated that many of the larger firearms would likely be collectors' pieces or have nonexplosive shells. He also said that there was an active policy not to increase the number of MSSAs and that "[t]he people that are in possession of them are subject to rigorous vetting and their security must be of a higher standard. Very few new people get these licenses."[126]

The following year, in 2007, the Small Arms Survey research project estimated that there were approximately 850,000 to 1 million firearms in civilian ownership in New Zealand, with an average ownership rate of 22.6 firearms per 100 people (the twenty-second highest rate of the countries surveyed).[127]

The most recent information located is from May 2010, when the Police provided a breakdown of firearm numbers and license holders to the Gunpolicy.org website.[128] The statement records that at that time there were about 223,000 holders of a current firearms license, with this number fluctuating daily. Of these people, 3,477 held B endorsements (target pistol shooters); 3,689 held C endorsements (pistols and/or restricted weapons as a collector, heirloom, museum curator, or for theatrical performances); and 5,171 held E endorsements (MSSAs). There were also 457 dealers' licenses.[129] The population of New Zealand at the end of 2010 was about 4.39 million people.[130]

---

[122] *Id.* at 35–37.

[123] *Id.* at 35, 37, & 109.

[124] *Id.* at 109.

[125] *See* Mike Steere, *Kiwis Go for the Big Guns; 1,100,1000 Licensed Firearms*, THE DOMINION POST (Nov. 7, 2006), *available at* LexisNexis Library Express (by subscription).

[126] *Id.*

[127] Ch. 2, Annex 4: The Largest Civilian Firearms Arsenals for 178 Countries, *in* SMALL ARMS SURVEY 2007: GUNS IN THE CITY, http://www.smallarmssurvey.org/publications/by-type/yearbook/small-arms-survey-2007.html.

[128] E-mail from Inspector Joe Green, NZ Police Licensing and Vetting Manager (May 24, 2010), *available at* http://www.gunpolicy.org/firearms/citation/quotes/1893.

[129] *Id.*

[130] *National Population Estimates: December 2010 Quarter*, STATISTICS NEW ZEALAND (Feb. 14, 2011), http://stats.govt.nz/browse_for_stats/population/estimates_and_projections/NationalPopulationEstimates_HOTPDec10qtr.aspx.

In terms of firearm numbers, the 2010 information reported that there were about 36,000 pistols and 7,800 MSSAs in the possession of endorsement holders.[131] The increase in MSSAs compared to the figures in the 1997 Thorp Report were reported to be primarily due to the change of understanding of what constituted a "military pattern free standing pistol grip" during 2009 and early 2010.[132]

In November 2012, it was reported that "[h]undreds of illegal firearms are being seized each year in police raids."[133] According to a National Strategic Assessment paper obtained by the news media, "[r]esearch indicates there is already a large pool of illegally held firearms in New Zealand and that firearms of almost any type can be obtained relatively easily from within the criminal fraternity without needing to source illicit firearms from overseas."[134]

B. Firearm Deaths

There are various sources of information available regarding firearm deaths in New Zealand, including annual crime statistics produced by the Police and Statistics New Zealand, the National Injury Query System operated by the Injury Prevention Research Unit at Otago University,[135] and international studies. Analysis of the data from these sources may produce slightly different results due to differences in definitions and counting methods. The following sample of the available data and analysis is provided for information purposes and is not intended to be exhaustive.

1. Assault/Homicide

Using the National Injury Query System, a search for fatalities resulting from assaults involving firearms between 1988 and 2009 shows that the crude rate was 0.5 per 100,000 people in 1988 (a total of eighteen deaths), increasing to 0.7 in 1990 (twenty-four deaths, including thirteen people killed in the Aramoana shooting massacre). During the 1990s the rate ranged from 0.5 per 100,000 people in 1994 (seventeen deaths, including five members of the Bain

---

[131] E-mail from Inspector Joe Green, *supra* note 128. *See also* the Regulatory Impact Statement on the Arms (Military Style Semi-Automatic Firearms and Import Controls) Amendment Bill, written by the Police in 2010, which states that there were at that time approximately 7,800 MSSAs in the possession of firearms license holders and just over 227,000 firearms license holders. REGULATORY IMPACT STATEMENT: ARMS (MILITARY STYLE SEMI-AUTOMATIC FIREARMS AND IMPORT CONTROLS) AMENDMENT BILL paras. 3 & 9 (2010), *available at* http://www.treasury.govt.nz/publications/informationreleases/ris/pdfs/ris-police-aa-apr11.pdf.

[132] E-mail from Inspector Joe Green, *supra* note 128.

[133] Jared Savage, *Police Seize Hundreds of Illegal Guns a Year*, THE NEW ZEALAND HERALD (Nov. 6, 2012), http://www.nzherald.co.nz/nz/news/article.cfm?c_id=1&objectid=10845355.

[134] *Id.*

[135] *National Injury Query System*, OTAGO UNIVERSITY INJURY PREVENTION UNIT, http://ipru3.otago.ac.nz/niqs/index.php (last visited Jan. 10, 2013). This system enables database searches to be conducted for both fatal and non-fatal injuries arising from various causes and as a result of different "intents" (unintentional, self-inflicted, assault, undetermined intent, other), with breakdowns also possible by region, age, and gender. The system covers the years from 1988 to 2009. For further analysis of pre-1993 figures relating to firearm deaths and injuries, *see* Robert Norton & John Langley, *The Epidemiology of Firearm Injuries in New Zealand*, 4(3) NZ PUBLIC HEALTH REPORT (Mar. 1997), http://www.moh.govt.nz/moh.nsf/Files/pvol4no3/$file/pvol4no3.pdf.

family killed in a shooting massacre) down to less than 0.1 in 1998 (four deaths). Throughout the 2000s the rate was between 0.1 and 0.2 per 100,000 people, up until 2009 when the crude rate was 0.3 (twelve deaths).[136]

The results for deaths resulting from assaults involving all external causes also show some fluctuations in the rates over the period between 1988 and 2009 (e.g., 1.7 per 100,000 people in 1988, 2.3 in 1992, 1.3 in 1995 and 1999, 1.2 in 2004 and 2008, and 2.0 in 2009).[137] However, comparing the two sets of data shows that the percentage of assault deaths involving firearms dropped from 31% in 1988 to 14% in 2009.

Using the most recent crime statistics published by Statistics New Zealand to calculate the percentage of recorded murders involving firearms compared to total recorded murders produces the following results for the period from 1994 to 2011:[138]

- 1994: 16 (27.6%)
- 1995: 9 (23.1%)
- 1996: 9 (18.8%)
- 1997: 13 (21.7%)
- 1998: 4 (8.2%)
- 1999: 5 (11.1%)
- 2000: 7 (13.5%)
- 2001: 6 (11.8%)
- 2002: 10 (16.7%)
- 2003: 7 (15.9%)
- 2004: 4 (8.9%)
- 2005: 9 (14.8%)
- 2006: 9 (18.4%)
- 2007: 5 (10.4%)
- 2008: 7 (13.5%)
- 2009: 11 (16.9%)
- 2010: 7 (15.2%)

---

[136] *National Injury Query System* search Jan. 8, 2013 (1988 to 2009 New Zealand Fatalities, Firearm, Assault intent, both genders, all age groups, all regions).

[137] *Id.* (1988 to 2009 New Zealand Fatalities, all external causes, Assault intent, both genders, all age groups, all regions).

[138] *New Zealand Recorded Crime Tables*, STATISTICS NEW ZEALAND, http://www.statistics.govt.nz/ tools_and_services/tools/TableBuilder/recorded-crime-statistics/ASOC-offence-calendar-year-statistics.aspx#National (last visited Jan. 9, 2013). To build the relevant tables click "National Annual Recorded Offences for the Latest Calendar Years (ANZSOC)" then "Murder"; clicking "Murder" in the next table provides a breakdown by method. The United Nations Office on Drugs and Crime (UNODC) also reported the following results for the percentage of homicides by firearm in New Zealand, based on information provided by the Police: 1995: 22.5%; 1997: 19.7%; 1998: 7.5%; 1999: 10.0%; 2000: 13.5%; 2001: 11.8%; 2002: 16.7%; 2005: 14.8%; 2006: 18.4%; 2007: 10.4%; 2008: 13.5%. UNODC, Percentages of Homicides by Firearm, Number of Homicides by Firearm and Homicide by Firearm Rate per 100,000 Population, http://www.unodc.org/ unodc/en/data-and-analysis/homicide.html (click "Homicides by firearm") (last visited Jan. 9, 2013).

- 2011: 3 (7.7%)

The Police reported to Parliament in 2006 that firearms were involved in less than 1.3% of all violent offending in the previous year.[139]   In 2011, the crime statistics released by the Police and Statistics New Zealand showed that New Zealand's murder rate was the lowest in twenty-five years.[140]

A 2011 study that compared long-term firearm homicide trends in "three countries with similar social histories but different legislative regimes: Australia, Canada, and New Zealand," concluded that "the most pronounced decline in firearm homicide over the past two decades occurred in New Zealand."[141]

2. Accidental/Unintentional Deaths

A search for unintentional deaths involving firearms using the National Injury Query System shows that there were eighteen such deaths in 1988, a crude rate of 0.5 per 100,000 people. In 1992 the rate was 0.3, and since that time the rate has been below 0.1 in most years, ranging from zero deaths in this category in 1997 to seven in 2003 (a rate of 0.2). In 2009, there were four unintentional deaths involving firearms, a rate of less than 0.1.[142]   Comparing these results to the results for unintentional deaths involving all external causes[143] shows that about 1% of such deaths involved firearms in 1988. In 2009, this figure was just 0.3%.

3. Suicide/Self-inflicted Deaths

The results of the National Injury Query System search for self-inflicted deaths involving firearms between 1988 and 2009 shows that there were much higher rates of such deaths compared to those resulting from assaults or accidents involving firearms. However, the numbers reduced significantly over that period.

In 1988 there were 102 self-inflicted deaths involving firearms; a crude rate of 3.0 per 100,000 people. The rate dropped to around 2.0 per 100,000 people during the first half of the

---

[139] See Steere, supra note 125. For the most recent summary of overall offense statistics and trends see NEW ZEALAND POLICE, NEW ZEALAND CRIME STATISTICS 2011/2012 (Oct. 2012), http://www.police. govt.nz/sites/default/files/resources/crime-statistics/00-national-2011-12-crime-stats.pdf.

[140] See Michelle Cooke, Murder Rate at 25-year Low, STUFF.CO.NZ (Oct. 3, 2011), http://www.stuff.co.nz/ national/crime/5723405/Murder-rate-at-25-year-low.

[141] Samara McPhedran, Jeanine Baker, & Pooja Singh, Firearm Homicide in Australia, Canada, and New Zealand: What Can We Learn From Long-Term International Comparison?, 26(2) J. INTERPERSONAL VIOLENCE 348, 348 (2011). This paper referred to a 2008 report by Inspector Joe Green of the New Zealand Police entitled "Arms Control Strategies." A presentation relating to this report is available on the website of the New Zealand Council of Licensed Firearms Owners. Joe Green, Arms Control Strategies: Debunking the Myths (2008), available at http://colfo.org.nz/attachments/article/143/Arms-Control-strategies-&-myths-symposium-paper.pdf.

[142] National Injury Query System search Jan. 8, 2013 (1988 to 2009 New Zealand Fatalities, Firearm, Unintentional intent, both genders, all age groups, all regions).

[143] Id. (1988 to 2009 New Zealand Fatalities, all external causes, Unintentional intent, both genders, all age groups, all regions).

1990s, and by the 2000s had reduced further to being between 0.9 (thirty-six deaths in 2000) and 1.3 (fifty-one deaths in 2001). In 2009, the rate was 1.2, reflecting fifty-three deaths.[144] When compared to the results for self-inflicted deaths involving all external causes,[145] the results show that about 21% of self-inflicted deaths involved firearms in 1988. In 2009, this same figure was about 10.4%.

A study by staff of the Canterbury Suicide Project published in the Australian and New Zealand Journal of Psychiatry in 2006 analyzed the possible impact of the 1992 amendments to the firearm laws on firearm-related suicide in New Zealand. The study covered an eighteen-year period from 1985 to 2002. The authors stated that the figures "clearly suggest that the introduction of the 1992 firearms legislation led to a detectable reduction in firearm suicides."[146] The trends were most marked for youth suicide, with the authors calculating that the figures for fifteen to twenty-four years olds implied that, "when compared with the pre-legislation period, rates of firearm suicide were reduced by 39% in the implementation period [1993-1996] and by 66% in the post-implementation period [1997-2002]."[147]

In its advice on the Arms (Military Style Semi-Automatic Firearms and Import Controls) Amendment Bill, the Police discussed the impact of the new requirements relating to firearm storage and security under the Arms Regulations 1992. The agency referred to the above findings and further stated that "[d]espite firearms leaking to the criminal community the misuse of firearms continues to decline as a percentage of all violent crime, and across the board is either steady or reducing. The number of incidents remains relatively static. Non-intentional death and injury in the home has decreased to single figures."[148]

Prepared by Kelly Buchanan
Chief, Foreign, Comparative, and
International Law Division I

---

[144] *Id.* (1988 to 2009 New Zealand Fatalities, Firearm, Self-inflicted intent, both genders, all age groups, all regions). In comparison, self-inflicted deaths by suffocation increased from a crude rate of 4.2 per 100,000 people in 1988 to 7.0 in 2009, while self-inflicted deaths by poisoning decreased from a rate of 3.4 per 100,000 people in 1988 to 2.5 in 2009. *Id.*

[145] *Id.* (1988 to 2009 New Zealand Fatalities, all external causes, Self-inflicted intent, both genders, all age groups, all regions).

[146] A.L. Beautrais, D.M. Fergusson, & L.J. Horwood, *Firearms Legislation and Reductions in Firearm-related Suicide Deaths in New Zealand*, 40(3) Aus. & N.Z. J. of Psych. 253, 255 (2006).

[147] *Id.* A search of the National Injury Query System shows a crude rate of 4.9 self-inflicted firearm deaths per 100,000 people in this age group in 1988 (twenty-nine deaths) and a rate of 4.2 in 1992 (twenty-four deaths). The rates were lower throughout the rest of the 1990s and since 1999 the numbers of deaths have been in single figures, apart from in 2005 when there were ten deaths (a rate of 1.7).

[148] Letter, Kevin Kelly, *supra* note 28, para. 32.

NORWAY

FIREARMS-CONTROL LEGISLATION AND POLICY[*]

Summary

   The purchase, possession, and use of firearms are tightly controlled in Norway, whose laws and regulations were made more stringent with amendments to the Firearms Act in 2009 and the adoption of new Firearms Regulations in that year. Permission to acquire a firearm must be obtained from the local police chief and is limited to persons of "sober habits" who have reasonable grounds for having a weapon. Fully automatic weapons, some semiautomatic weapons, and firearms disguised as other objects are banned under the law. Certain types of weapons not covered by the Firearms Act's definition of firearms, such as stun guns, are also generally banned. In addition, the National Police Directorate may issue regulations prohibiting the acquisition, ownership, or possession of firearms deemed through their design or operation to be especially dangerous or inappropriate for use.

   There are also legal provisions, among others, on the licensing of firearms dealers and exporter/importers, the maintenance of a central firearms register, and the mandatory safe storage of firearms. The police have the authority to conduct inspections of privately stored firearms, after notifying the owner.

   Nearly 10% of Norway's populace own firearms, which are used chiefly for hunting purposes. The gun laws were apparently not extensively amended in the aftermath of the 2011 massacre in Oslo and on a nearby island in which seventy-seven people were killed, chiefly through the use of firearms; however, the country's Mental Health Act has been revised to include a new chapter on enhanced security in institutions that accommodate the severely mentally ill or persons at risk for serious violent behavior.

I. Background

   On Friday, July 22, 2011, twin attacks were carried out in the government district of Oslo, Norway, and at a Labour Party youth camp on nearby Utøya Island. As a result of the bombing in Oslo and the mass shootings on Utøya, seventy-seven Norwegians died and 242 were wounded, most of them young people. It was the worst massacre of its kind in the country's history. The suspected assassin, Anders Behring Breivik, confessed to the bombing

---

[*] At present there are no Law Library of Congress research staff members versed in Norwegian. This report has been prepared by the author's reliance on practiced legal research methods and on the basis of relevant legal resources, chiefly in English, currently available in the Law Library and online.

and the killings and claimed he acted alone.[1] In August 2012, a five-judge panel of the Oslo District Court declared Breivik was sane when he carried out the attacks and sentenced him, after two months of deliberation, to the maximum term of twenty-one years in prison, overriding the findings of a report by court-appointed psychiatrists that Breivik suffered from paranoid schizophrenia.[2] Breivik legally acquired his weapons and ammunition in 2010, having successfully applied for a firearms license for a 9 mm Glock 17 pistol and a self-loading carbine, a semiautomatic Ruger Mini-14 rifle. He stated on the application form for the permit that he would use the weapons for hunting deer.[3]

Some questioned the police response to the attacks, but the internal affairs unit of the police issued a statement on January 10, 2013, to the effect that "while there were serious shortcomings in the police's response, it had dropped its investigation into complaints filed by the families of two victims because there was no evidence police had broken the law."[4] There were also proposals that the gun laws, which had been tightened in 2009, be made even stricter.[5] While that has apparently not yet happened, the Mental Health Act was amended in 2012 to include a new fourteen-provision chapter on safety in regional security departments and especially high-security units for the mentally ill.[6]

II. Relevant Legislation

The Act Relating to Firearms and Ammunition (Firearms Act)[7] governs the use of firearms in Norway. The firearms law was tightened in 2009, with the enactment of Regulation

---

[1] *Norway Massacre*, FT.COM, http://www.ft.com/intl/indepth/norway-massacre (last visited Jan. 22, 2013) (a collection of news items on the massacre).

[2] Mark Townsend, *Breivik Verdict: Norwegian Extremist Declared Sane and Sentenced to 21 Years*, GUARDIAN (Aug. 24, 2012), http://www.guardian.co.uk/world/2012/aug/24/breivik-verdict-sane-21-years; Mark Lews & Sarah Lyall, *Norway Mass Killer Gets the Maximum: 21 Years,* N.Y. TIMES (Aug. 24, 2012), http://www.nytimes.com/2012/08/25/world/europe/anders-behring-breivik-murder-trial.html?pagewanted= all&_r=0; Mark Lewis, *Why Norway Is Satisfied with Breivik's Sentence*, TIME (Aug. 27, 2012), http://world.time.com/2012/08/27/why-norway-is-satisfied-with-breiviks-sentence/.

[3] *Norwegian Terror Suspect Admits Guilt*, RT (July 24, 2011), http://rt.com/news/breivik-utoya-shooting-arrest/; *see also Norway Shooting: Quotes From Anders Behring Breivik's Online Manifesto*, TELEGRAPH (Aug. 19, 2011), http://www.telegraph.co.uk/news/worldnews/europe/norway/8657727/Norway-shooting-quotes-from-Anders-Behring-Breiviks-online-manifesto.html; *Skaffet seg våpen på lovlig vis* [*Obtain Guns Legally*], BERGENS TIDENDE (July 24, 2011), http://www.bt.no/nyheter/innenriks/Skaffet-seg-vpen-p-lovlig-vis-2542413.html; *"Breivik Manifesto" Details Chilling Attack Preparation*, BBC NEWS (July 24, 2011), http://www.bbc.co.uk/news/world-europe-14270007.

[4] *Anger as Police Drop Breivik Response Probe*, THE LOCAL (Jan. 11, 2013), http://www.thelocal.no/page/view/anger-as-norway-police-drop-breivik-response-probe.

[5] *Panel Proposes Tighter Gun Laws After Massacre*, THE LOCAL (Dec. 6, 2011), http://www.thelocal.no/page/view/norway-panel-proposes-tighter-gun-laws-after-massacre#.UNSF0-SdN2A.

[6] Lov om etablering og gjennomføring av psykisk helsevern (psykisk helsevernloven) (July 2, 1999, as last amended effective July 1, 2012), LOVDATA, http://www.lovdata.no/all/nl-19990702-062.html.

[7] Lov om skytevåpen og ammunisjon mv. [våpenloven] [Act on Firearms and Ammunition, etc.] (Act No. 1 of June 9, 1961, as last amended June 19, 2009, in force Dec. 28, 2009), http://www.lovdata.no/all/hl-19610609-001.html; Act No. 1 of 9 June 1961 Relating to Firearms and Ammunition [English translation based on the Act as amended in 1990], LOVDATA, http://www.ub.uio.no/ujur/ulovdata/lov-19610609-001-eng.html.

No. 904 of June 25, 2009, on Firearms and Ammunition (Firearms Regulations).[8] In late 2012 Norway imposed addition restrictions on its weapons exports, in the aftermath of a report that firearms produced in the country were responsible for over 200 civilian deaths in the war against Iraq.[9]

III. Definitions

Firearms (*skytevåpen*) under the Firearms Act are weapons (*våpen*) that can fire bullets, shot, and other projectiles by means of gunpowder or other propellant or by means of a mechanical device; weapons or devices for launching or dispersing explosives, gas, flares, rockets, etc. (including flame throwers); and imitation weapons that can relatively easily be converted to fire live ammunition.[10] If rendered permanently unusable, however, a weapon is not a firearm under the Act's definition.[11] Weapons parts (*våpendeler*) include cartridges consisting of a projectile, case, propellant, and detonator; projectiles of any kind intended for launch or dispersal by a firearm; sleeves (*hylser*) fitted with a charge or igniter; hand grenades (*håndgranater*), bombs, rockets, mines, etc.; illumination- (*lys-*), incendiary- (*brann-*), poison- and teargas grenades (*bokser*); and poison and teargas for use in a firearm or in the other types of ammunition (except the sleeves).[12]

The Firearms Act does not apply to firearms, firearms parts, or ammunition intended for use by or belonging to the military or the police, or to ammunition destined for or belonging to Norway's Explosives Inspectorate.[13] It also does not generally apply to slaughter equipment, signal pistols and other signaling devices, or rescue and harpoon guns; to their parts; or to the ammunition used in them. The Ministry of Justice and Public Security may determine the extent to which the law should apply to air and spring guns and pistols.[14] The King may determine that it shall be illegal to import, sell, or own certain types of firearms or ammunition.[15]

The Firearms Regulations distinguish between weapons not considered firearms, and therefore not subject to control, and firearms of various types that are subject to control. The

---

[8] FOR 2009-06-25 nr 904: Forskrift om skytevåpen, våpendeler og ammunisjon mv. (våpenforskriften) [FOR 2009-06-25 No. 904: Regulation Relating to Firearms, Firearm Parts, and Ammunition, etc. (Firearms Regulations)] (June 25, 2009, in force July 1, 2009, as last amended Apr. 25, 2012, in force from May 1, 2012), LOVDATA, http://www.lovdata.no/for/sf/jd/xd-20090625-0904.html.

[9] *See* Constance Johnson, *Norway: New Restrictions on Weapons Exports*, GLOBAL LEGAL MONITOR (Dec. 7, 2012), http://www.loc.gov/lawweb/servlet/lloc_news?disp3_l205403425_text.

[10] Firearms Act, § 1, ¶ 1(a)–(c).

[11] *Id.* § 1, ¶ 2. Nor is a weapon a firearm if, because of its age or construction, it cannot be used as a firearm or if it cannot be easily repaired or adapted to use for shooting. *Id.*

[12] *Id.* § 3.

[13] *Id.* § 4.

[14] *Id.* § 5. The King may fully or partially except from the law or from some of its rules firearms, firearm parts, or ammunition other than those mentioned in section 5. *Id.* § 6.

[15] *Id.* § 6a. This includes weapons and the like not set forth under the definition of firearms in section 1. *Id.*

former include, for example, muzzle-loading firearms manufactured before 1890; 1885 model-year rifles or shotguns or pre-1871 model-year pistols or revolvers in a person's possession before the Regulations entered into force; and weapons that have been rendered permanently unusable by virtue of all their essential parts having been made permanently unusable and it being impossible for them to be removed, replaced, or modified in such a way that it would be possible to reactivate the weapon.[16] The Regulations provide details on the features of the two types of firearms, two-handed firearms (shotguns, rifles, and combination guns) and one-handed firearms (pistols and revolvers).[17] They further distinguish the firearms based on the way they function, i.e., single-shot, single shot repeater, single shot semiautomatic, or automatic action weapons[18] and sets forth definitions of measurement of a firearm and its parts.[19]

IV. Purchase, Ownership, Possession, and Use

A. Purchase and Acquisition

The Firearms Act stipulates that anyone intending to buy or otherwise acquire a firearm or firearm parts must have permission from the police commissioner[20] of the place of residence of the applicant or, if the applicant does not have residency in Norway, from the chief of police of their whereabouts.[21] According to the Act, "[p]ermission may only be given to reliable persons of sober habits who need or have other reasonable grounds for possessing firearms, and who can not be deemed unfit to do so for any special reason."[22] The applicant must also provide a written statement stating why he or she wants a firearm.[23]

Permission to acquire a firearm or firearm parts will generally not be granted to anyone under eighteen years of age; in exceptional cases, weapons may be stored by a guardian or another person who meets the permit requirements for anyone under eighteen but over sixteen years of age. The permit age for acquisition of revolvers or pistols or their parts is twenty-one.[24] An application submitted by a minor must be ratified by the guardian.[25] No one may assign or transfer firearms, firearm parts, or ammunition to a person under eighteen years of age without

---

[16] Firearms Regulations, § 1, ¶¶ 1–3.

[17] *Id.* § 2.

[18] *Id.* § 3.

[19] *Id.* §§ 4 & 4a.

[20] Firearms Act, § 7, ¶ 1.

[21] *Id.* ¶ 2.

[22] *Id.* ¶ 3.

[23] Simon Tisdall, *Norway's Gun Laws Prove Easy to Ignore*, THE GUARDIAN (July 24, 2011), http://www.guardian.co.uk/world/2011/jul/24/norway-strict-gun-laws-circumvented.

[24] Firearms Act, § 7, ¶ 4. The King may set a higher age limit (than eighteen) for other types of firearms and firearm parts, but it cannot be higher than twenty-one. *Id.* ¶ 6.

[25] *Id.* ¶ 5.

the prior consent of the competent police commissioner; such consent may not be granted, however, when the person is under sixteen years of age.[26]

Similarly, those who intend to buy or otherwise acquire ammunition must also have a police permit.[27] The permit will only cover a certain quantity of ammunition and may not be made valid for a period longer than three months.[28] The qualifications and age limit on the basis of which the permit will be granted are the same as those for firearms; the permits are granted by the police of the place of residence or the whereabouts (for nonresident claimants).[29]

The application for a permit to acquire and possess firearms or firearms parts is to be sent to the police of the locality where the natural or legal person applicant is located, in the prescribed form and signed and dated by the applicant (or by the guardian, if the applicant is under eighteen).[30] Applications from a legal person must also indicate the full name and address of the person authorized to submit the application and the weapons for which the legal person is responsible.[31] The acquisitions permit (*ervervstillatelsen*) is valid for twelve months, extendable by six months. The extension of the period of validity is given by signing the permit to that effect.[32]

A weapons dealer, including a manufacturer and a gunsmith, will only hand over weapons or weapons parts that are covered by the acquisitions permit and upon presentation of approved credentials.[33] Weapons dealers provide on the acquisitions permit complete information about the weapons issued. The dealer retains a copy of the permit along with an endorsement attached to the record he or she keeps on the purchase and sale of firearms, and immediately sends the permit to the police commissioner of the district of the place of the business. He or she returns the copy of the permit to the buyer.[34] The copy of the permit that the buyer receives back from the dealer constitutes permission to possess weapons or weapons parts until the regular firearms license is received.[35] Anyone who sells or otherwise transfers a weapon privately is to proceed in the same manner as a weapons dealer, with certain further specifications.[36]

---

[26] *Id.* § 29, ¶ 1 However, this provision does not preclude, without the specific consent of the police commissioner, the entrusting of the objects to persons under eighteen for short-term use under proper supervision, as long as the parents or guardian of the person consent to it. Nor does the provision preclude a person under eighteen from dealing with the objects in capacity of an employee, when reasonable precautions are observed. *Id.* ¶ 2.

[27] *Id.* § 13, ¶ 1.

[28] *Id.* ¶ 2.

[29] *Id.* ¶ 1.

[30] Firearms Regulations, § 26, ¶¶ 1 & 3.

[31] *Id.* ¶ 2.

[32] *Id.* § 27.

[33] *Id.* § 28, ¶ 1.

[34] *Id.* ¶¶ 2 & 3.

[35] *Id.* ¶ 4.

[36] *Id.* § 29.

B. Ownership and Possession

Anyone who wants to own or possess firearms must have permission granted by the police commissioner, in the form of a firearms permit (*våpenkort*). It can be set as a condition for the granting of the license that the right to hand over the weapon to another party for up to four weeks (under section 11 of the Act) shall not apply.[37] In special circumstances, permission to own or possess a weapon can be issued to cover a specified period of time.[38] Permission from the police commissioner is necessary in order to make a significant change in the character or nature of the firearm or to substantially modify its ownership or possession.[39] Except for eligible recipients specified in the Act's section 11, firearms or firearms parts may not be left with someone not authorized to possess them.[40]

The firearms permit or the loan declaration must be shown upon the request of the police; weapon holders must always have with them the firearms permit or loan declaration when carrying or transporting the firearm, firearm parts, or ammunition, or else those items may be taken into police custody until the applicable document is presented.[41]

The Firearms Regulations contain a lengthy chapter on the conditions for authorized acquisition and possession of firearms. It covers the requirements for natural persons, legal persons, law enforcement officials and officers, and third parties as well as for purposes of collection, animal slaughter, pest eradication and seal hunting, protection, heritage and sentimental value, a museum collection, shooting and gun collection organizations, and so on.[42]

The police commissioner will revoke the firearms permit if the holder is not "sober and reliable" or if there are special circumstances that cause the holder to be deemed unfit to have a firearm. The permit can also be revoked if the holder no longer needs to have the firearm or on other reasonable grounds.[43] Upon revocation of the permit under such circumstances, the firearm is to be immediately submitted to the police commissioner.[44] A license issued pursuant to the Firearms Act's provisions on the sale of firearms, firearm parts, and ammunition or on their production may be revoked by the issuing authority if the license holder no longer meets the conditions for obtaining a license or if he contravenes the rules governing the exercise of the license.[45]

---

[37] *Id.* § 8, ¶ 1. Under § 11, a firearms license holder may entrust the firearm to another person for up to four weeks, with the exception of revolvers or pistols, which can never be left in the hands of others unless the King determines otherwise. *Id.* § 11, ¶ 1.

[38] *Id.* § 8, ¶ 2.

[39] *Id.* ¶ 3.

[40] *Id.* § 12.

[41] *Id.* § 9.

[42] Firearms Regulations, ch. 3, §§ 10–25.

[43] *Id.* § 10, ¶¶ 1 & 2.

[44] *Id.* ¶ 4.

[45] Firearms Act § 35.

C. Prohibited Weapons and Ammunition

The Firearms Regulations make it illegal to acquire, hold, or possess firearms normally used as (a) weapons of war, (b) fully automatic weapons, and (c) firearms disguised as other objects.[46] The National Police Directorate (*Politidirektoratet*) (NPD) may issue regulations that prohibit the acquisition, ownership, or possession of firearms or types of firearms that through their design or operation are perceived to be especially dangerous or inappropriate for use.[47]

The acquisition, ownership, or possession of certain semiautomatic weapons is also banned by the Firearms Regulations. Semiautomatic weapons that can be easily converted to produce fully automatic fire are banned. Would-be owners of a semiautomatic weapon must obtain police approval for the weapon.[48] As a general rule, semiautomatic weapons approved pursuant to corresponding rules in another European Economic Area country (the twenty-seven European Union Member States plus Iceland, Liechtenstein, and Norway) will be approved by the NPD.[49]

In addition, there is a ban on certain weapons or similar equipment not covered by the definition of firearms in the Firearms Act. These include stun guns, pepper spray, and other products for self defense that have an equivalent effect; as well as flick knives, batanga knives, stilettos, brass knuckles, billy clubs, karate sticks, throwing stars, blow guns for firing arrows or other objects, slingshots, and other similar, especially dangerous items.[50] The police commissioner has the authority to waive this prohibition, however, in special circumstances.[51] Acquiring, owning, or possessing a crossbow is also prohibited, unless a permit has been obtained from the police commissioner and the applicant meets the personal qualifications required.[52]

Reportedly, many categories of weapons, including some powerful handguns, have also been banned from sale.[53]

Forbidden ammunition includes armor-piercing ammunition, incendiary and explosive munitions, and ammunition and projectiles with the power to expand for use in pistols and

---

[46] Firearms Regulation, § 5, ¶ 1. Types of weapons designed purely for military or police purposes fall under category (a).

[47] *Id.* § 6.

[48] *Id.* § 7, ¶¶ 1 & 2.

[49] *Id.* ¶ 3.

[50] *Id.* § 9, ¶ 1. This provision is not applicable to weapons specific to or belonging to the police or the military. *Id.* ¶ 2.

[51] *Id.* ¶ 4.

[52] *Id.* ¶ 3. This provision does not apply to crossbows acquired before January 1, 1993. The personal qualifications are set forth under section 10 of the Firearms Regulations, which makes reference to the Firearms Act requirements of sobriety, reliability, suitability, age, and reasonable grounds.

[53] Tisdall, *supra* note 23.

revolvers with central fire ignition (except when used for practice and competition shooting).[54] Even though these domestic controls are in place, there remains the possibility of acquiring materiel from abroad. While the sale of clips for hunting rifles that hold more than three bullets is reportedly banned in Norway, Anders Breivik wrote in his manifesto that he bought ammunition clips for his rifle from a small, undisclosed US supplier that had acquired the clips from other suppliers.[55]

V. Sale and Manufacture of Firearms

Anyone who wants to trade in firearms, firearm parts, or ammunition must have a license (*bevilling*) from the competent ministry. The license application is to be submitted to the police commissioner of the district where the applicant intends to conduct business.[56] The license may be limited to specific types of firearms and ammunition and may also be made subject to other conditions determined by the competent ministry.[57] The license is required to contain details of the holder's name and place of business, the scope of the license, and the conditions applicable to its use.[58] The license can only be granted to persons considered fit to trade in firearms and ammunition who have business and warehouse facilities that meet the rules in force on the storage of such goods.[59] The Act's provisions authorizing the purchase, acquisition, or lending of firearms, firearm parts, or ammunition do not apply to a trade licensee's purchase of such materiel for resale.[60]

The trade license must be dated and signed by the police commissioner or his attorney and state the scope of the license, the name and place of the business, the name and address of the store manager responsible, the name and address of the person who may become general manager of sales of firearms, etc., and the terms and conditions that apply to exercising the license.[61] Police districts maintain an ongoing record (*fortegnelse*) of all trade licenses, and a record of new and revoked licenses will immediately be entered in the central weapons register (*sentralt våpenregister*).[62]

Authorized firearms dealers may only make deliveries of their goods to persons who can present a valid and comprehensive permit (*tillatelse*), if such a permit is required for acquisition of the goods. The dealer must ensure that delivery is made to the right person.[63] Delivery to

---

[54] Firearms Act, § 8, ¶ 1.

[55] Reid J. Epstein, *Norway Shooter: Ammo Clips Were from U.S.*, POLITICO (July 28, 2011), http://www.politico.com/news/stories/0711/60154.html.

[56] Firearms Act, § 16, ¶ 1. The provision also applies to weapons used for slaughter, signaling devices, etc., described in section 5 of the Act, unless otherwise determined by the King. *Id.*

[57] *Id.* ¶ 2.

[58] *Id.* ¶ 3. Additional details are set forth in section 36 of the Firearms Regulations.

[59] Firearms Act § 17, ¶ 1.

[60] *Id.* § 19, ¶ 2.

[61] Firearms Regulations, § 37.

[62] *Id.* § 38. Section 98 of the Regulations addresses the central weapons register.

[63] *Id.* § 39, ¶ 1.

another dealer may only take place when that dealer can prove that he or she has a license to trade in those goods to which the order applies. Upon delivery, the supplier is required to give notification of that fact to the police commissioner of the district where the supplier has his or her place of business. The notification will also state the date of delivery, the name and address of the consignee, and the number, type or nature, trademark, model designation, caliber, mechanism type, and number of weapons or weapons parts or the quantity and type of ammunition supplied.[64] The police may direct the dealer to provide the notification in electronic form.[65]

Authorized dealers have an obligation to maintain a continuous record of all purchases, sales, loans, etc. of firearms and firearms parts that are subject to control. The record must state the date of receipt or delivery; the name of the seller or buyer; and the quantity, type or nature, trademark, model designation, caliber, mechanism type, and the numbering of weapons or weapons parts received or delivered.[66] Upon the sale, etc., of these goods the dealer is required to attach a copy to the record of the person's acquisition permit (or sales notice, if the sale is to another dealer). Upon a purchase, etc., from an individual, the dealer is required to attach a purchase notice. Upon importation, a copy of the vendor invoice and shipping slip must be attached.[67] Upon the import of firearms and firearms parts, the dealer is required to set up a list (*oppgave*) of such goods. Within ten days after the imported items arrived in stock, the dealer is required to send the list to the police commissioner of the district where the dealer has his place of business.[68] At the end of each quarter, the dealer is required to update the list of his inventory of firearms or firearms parts subject to control. The list must state the firearms' or parts' quantity, type or nature, trademark, model designation, caliber, mechanism type, and number and must be sent to the police commissioner.[69]

A dealer must immediately notify the police if he comes into possession of banned firearms or unregistered firearms that are subject to registration.[70]

Manufacturers of firearms or firearm parts for sale must be licensed by the competent ministry; this also generally applies to ammunition manufacturers.[71] Those who make firearms or firearm parts for their own use, or their own ammunition, must be at least eighteen years of age and have permission from the police commissioner of the district where they reside. The licensing provisions in the Act are also applicable to weapons manufactured in this manner.[72]

---

[64] *Id.* ¶ 2.

[65] *Id.* ¶ 3.

[66] *Id.* § 40, ¶ 1.

[67] *Id.* ¶ 2.

[68] *Id.* ¶ 3.

[69] *Id.* ¶ 4.

[70] *Id.* ¶ 5.

[71] Firearms Act, § 20.

[72] *Id.* § 21, ¶¶ 1 & 2.

Those who supply firearms are to mark the firearms and firearms parts with a unique brand as well as the manufacturer's name, the country of origin or manufacturing location, the serial number, and the year (if not part of the serial number).[73] Importers of firearms that are subject to registration must mark the firearms and firearms parts with a unique brand that indicates the country of import and the importer.[74] The Police Directorate has the authority to provide additional guidelines with reference to these provisions.[75]

VI. Import and Export

Anyone who imports or exports firearms, firearm parts, or ammunition must have a permit from the competent ministry. The permit will specify the nature and amount of the goods and the permit's period of validity, which is extendable.[76]

In general, an import permit may be granted only to those who have a license to trade in firearms, firearm parts, or ammunition. An import permit may also be granted to those who can manufacture such goods. For importation of the goods for private use only, a permit can still be given if it is one that meets the terms of the Act on purchase and acquisition of firearms and ammunition,[77] but the Act stipulates that the provisions on firearms licenses also apply to goods so imported.[78] The King may issue specific rules on the import and export of firearms, firearm parts, or ammunition that (1) a Norwegian citizen brings upon exit and entry of the country in connection with a temporary stay abroad, (2) a Norwegian hunting expedition brings to and from hunting areas outside Norway's territorial waters, and (3) a foreign citizen brings upon entering and exiting Norway in connection with temporary residence in the country.[79]

VII. Offenses and Penalties

Anyone who willfully or negligently violates the provisions in, or made pursuant to, the Firearms Act will be subject to a fine or to a term of imprisonment of up to three months, unless the offense entails a stiffer penal provision.[80] For violation of the Act's provision on securing firearms for purposes of transport and not displaying them in a public place without reasons for doing so[81] or for the illegal import, sale, acquisition, or possession of firearms or ammunition, the offender will be subject to a fine or up to two years of imprisonment.[82] If the offense is more serious, fines or imprisonment for a term of up to four years may be imposed. In determining

---

[73] *Id.* § 93, ¶ 1.

[74] *Id.* ¶ 2.

[75] *Id.* ¶ 3.

[76] *Id.* § 23, ¶¶ 1 & 2.

[77] *Id.* § 24, ¶¶ 1 & 2. The terms are those found under sections 7 and 13 of the Act.

[78] *Id.* § 24, ¶ 3.

[79] *Id.* § 25.

[80] *Id.* § 33 ¶ 1.

[81] Reasons set forth under *id.* § 27b, ¶¶ 1 & 2.

[82] *Id.* § 33 ¶ 1.

whether the offense is serious, particular emphasis is placed on the kind and number of weapons involved, or whether the action is for other reasons of a particularly dangerous or socially damaging nature.[83] The same punishments are applicable to complicity in these offenses.[84] The King may decide that a violation of the provisions on obtaining certain permits or licenses should not be prosecuted if the offender informs the police of the violation within a certain specified period of time.[85]

Under the General Civil Penal Code of 1902, as amended, anyone who, with the intent to commit a felony, procures, manufactures, or stores firearms, firearm parts, ammunition, or explosives, or special equipment to manufacture or use such objects, will be punished upon conviction with a term of imprisonment of up to six years. Under especially aggravated circumstances, a term of up to ten years' imprisonment may be imposed. The same penalty will apply to aiding and abetting such an offense.[86] One factor in determining whether the offense of aggravated robbery is punishable by a term of twelve years of imprisonment as opposed to five years is whether or not a gun or other particularly dangerous implement was used; if death or serious bodily harm or damage result, the offender is liable to a punishment of up to twenty-one years in prison.[87] Anyone who is guilty of careless conduct likely to endanger the life or health of others in the manufacture, use, storage, or handling of explosives or firearms may be subject to a prison term of up to one year; the same applies to aiding and abetting such conduct.[88]

Under its Penal Code of 2005, which differs from the General Civil Penal Code, Norway has a number of criminal law provisions that have not yet entered into force. Under one such provision, a fine or imprisonment for up to two years will be available to be imposed on those who intentionally or through gross negligence repeatedly or seriously contravene provisions on the illegal import, transfer, acquisition, or possession of weapons under the Firearms Act.[89] Another provision that has not yet been implemented stipulates that serious illegal involvement with firearms, ammunition, explosives, or other explosive substances is punishable by a fine or imprisonment for up to six years.[90] In addition, the careless handling of such materiel that is likely to endanger the life or health of another person will be punishable with a fine or a prison term of up to one year.[91]

---

[83] *Id.* ¶ 2.

[84] *Id.* ¶ 3.

[85] *Id.* § 34.

[86] The General Civil Penal Code, Act No. 10 of May 22, 1902 (as last amended by Act No. 131 of Dec. 21, 2005), § 161, *available at* http://www.ub.uio.no/ujur/ulovdata/lov-19020522-010-eng.pdf; Almindelig borgerlig Straffelov (Straffeloven) [The General Civil Penal Code] (Penal Code)], Act No. 10 of May 22, 1902 (as last amended June 22, 2012), LOVDATA, http://www.lovdata.no/all/hl-19020522-010.html.

[87] *Id.* § 268.

[88] *Id.* § 352, ¶ 1.

[89] Lov om straff (straffeloven) [Act on Punishment (Penal Code)], Act No. 28 of May 20, 2005 (as last amended by Act No. 44 of June 20, 2008), § 190, ¶ 1, LOVDATA, http://www.lovdata.no/all/nl-20050520-028.html.

[90] *Id.* § 191, ¶ 1.

[91] *Id.* § 188.

VIII. Miscellaneous Provisions

The Firearms Act stipulates that firearms and ammunition must be kept securely locked down,[92] and gun safes have become mandatory. [93] The police may inspect such stored weapons, with the inspection to be conducted in private after prior notification.[94] Authorized dealers also have the obligation to securely store firearms, firearm parts, and ammunition.[95] According to Norwegian news reports, before storage a gun's end cap must be removed; persons who do not have a gun safe must remove the weapon's components before storing it, basically disabling it; and the vital components of the weapon should be locked up separately.[96]

Firearms being transported must be emptied of ammunition, be secured against going astray, and normally be covered.[97] Firearms must not without reasonable grounds be in a public place.[98] These two provisions also apply to air and spring guns and imitation weapons easily confusable with firearms as well as to firearms that have been rendered permanently unusable.[99]

The Firearms Act gives the King the authority to issue regulations to implement and supplement the Act's provisions.[100] He also has the power to prescribe fees for trade licenses and for import and export licenses for firearms, firearm parts, or ammunition;[101] to provide that the owner or holder pay the expenses for destroying or rendering unusable firearms, firearm parts, or ammunition;[102] and to determine that there should be a central arms register and to establish rules for its implementation, including that the register be kept by electronic means. All the information in such a computerized register may be exempt from public disclosure. [103]

IX. Statistical Information

A news report that cited police figures current in 2011 indicated that there were 1,229,436 registered guns in Norway, owned by 484,298 persons (about 9.7% of the population),

---

[92] Firearms Act, § 27a, ¶ 1. Detailed rules for storage, according to this provision, are stipulated by the King. These rules may also apply to firearms, firearm parts, and ammunition referred to in section 5 of the Act, which covers such instruments as signal pistols, slaughter equipment, and rescue and harpoon guns. *Id.*

[93] Ann Simmons, *In Norway Gun Ownership Is Common; Violence and Homicide Are Not*, LOS ANGELES TIMES (July 23, 2011), http://articles.latimes.com/2011/jul/23/nation/la-naw-norway-gun-policy-20110724.

[94] Firearms Act, § 27a, ¶ 2.

[95] Firearms Regulations, § 42. The provision also sets forth the types of locks and alarms required for such storage.

[96] Simmons, *supra* note 93.

[97] Firearms Act, § 27b, ¶ 1.

[98] *Id.* ¶ 2.

[99] *Id.* ¶ 3.

[100] *Id.* § 31, ¶ 1.

[101] *Id.* ¶ 2.

[102] *Id.* ¶ 3.

[103] *Id.* ¶ 4.

with many of the weapons obtained for hunting purposes or held by Norwegians registered for civil defense duty or in the military reserves.[104] The Norwegian Rifle Association reportedly has 32,000 members in 520 clubs, according to the Norwegian Broadcasting Co. (NRK). The NRK has estimated that in addition to the legally held firearms, another half a million have been smuggled into Norway illegally.[105]

According to the *Los Angeles Times*, "[h]omicide—whether gun-related or otherwise—is rare in Norway, which reports one of the lowest per-capita homicide rates in Europe."[106] In 2010, there reportedly were eighty-seven gun-related deaths in Norway, with two being gun-related homicides (one of them a handgun homicide, the other a long-gun homicide). The annual rate of all gun-related deaths per 100,000 population was 1.78 in 2010, with the rate of homicides from firearms per that amount of population being 0.04 and the handgun homicide rate 0.02.[107]

A report released in 2010 by the Norwegian Ministry of Health and Care Services, which covered homicide in Norway during the period 2004–2009, assessed the role of mental illness in the actions of known perpetrators of homicide in the country. Among other findings, it pointed out that the victims were known to the assailant in more than 80% of the killings.[108]

Prepared by Wendy Zeldin
Senior Legal Research Analyst

---

[104] Aled Dilwyn-Fisher, *Police Want Stricter Gun Control*, VIEWS AND NEWS FROM NORWAY (Aug. 2, 2011), http://www.newsinenglish.no/2011/08/02/police-will-have-stricter-gun-control/.

[105] Simmons, *supra* note 93.

[106] *Id.*

[107] *Norway — Gun Facts, Figures and the Law*, GUNPOLICY.ORG, http://www.gunpolicy.org/firearms/region/norway (last visited Jan. 22, 2013), citing various sources, most notably World Health Organization, *Inter-Country Comparison of Mortality for Selected Cause of Death – Gun Homicide in Norway*, EUROPEAN DETAILED MORTALITY DATABASE (Copenhagen: WHO Regional Office for Europe, Aug. 8, 2011).

[108] Simmons, *supra* note 93. *See also* MINISTRY OF HEALTH AND CARE SERVICES, HOMICIDE IN NORWAY IN THE PERIOD 2004–2009, [Summary in English: NOU 2010:3] (May 3, 2010), http://www.regjeringen.no/pages/13400193/PDFS/NOU201020100003000EN_PDFS.pdf. For statistics on crime in general in Norway, *see Crime and the Justice [sic]. Tables*, STATISTICS NORWAY, http://www.ssb.no/english/subjects/03/05/a_krim_tab_en/ (last visited Aug. 1, 2011).)

RUSSIAN FEDERATION

FIREARMS-CONTROL LEGISLATION AND POLICY

Summary

While self-defense and protection of property is a constitutional right guaranteed to Russian citizens, Russian legislation on gun control is relatively strict, limiting the circulation of firearms to Russian citizens older than eighteen years of age with a registered permanent residence, and for the purposes of self-defense, hunting, and sports activities only. The acquisition of guns is based on licenses provided for a five-year period by local police departments at one's place of residence after a thorough background check, including a review of the petitioner's ability to store guns safely and an evaluation of his/her medical records. Mentally ill people and those who have been treated for substance abuse are not allowed to possess firearms.

Major issues related to gun control are regulated by the Federal Law on Weapons and implementing regulations issued by the federal government and varied executive agencies. Legislative assemblies of the Russian Federation constituent components can enact provincial laws related to the circulation of firearms so long as they do not contradict federal legislation. Individuals are allowed to have up to ten long-barreled guns in their possession, and more if they are collectibles. Individuals are not allowed to carry guns acquired for self-defense; a license only serves as a carrying permit for hunting and sport firearms when these guns need to be transported. Russian citizens may not own guns that shoot in bursts or have magazines with more than a ten-cartridge capacity. The legalization of short-barreled handguns is currently being discussed by the legislature.

I. Background

According to a report by the Russian Ministry of Internal Affairs (police),[1] at the end of 2012 there were more than 6.3 million nonmilitary weapons registered in the Russian Federation, with a population of 142.5 million.[2] This number includes 700,000 firearms with a rifled bore and 4.2 million firearms with a smooth bore. According to the same report, approximately twelve million guns are held illegally and are not registered.[3] In 2012, 7,500 crimes were

---

[1] Anatoly Malikov, *Will the Life of Russians be Safer if Gun Control Laws Are Stricter?*, VOORUZHEN.RU (Nov. 16, 2012), http://vooruzhen.ru/news/135/2721/ (in Russian; last visited Jan. 8, 2013).

[2] CIA: THE WORLD FACTBOOK: RUSSIA (2012), https://www.cia.gov/library/publications/the-world-factbook/geos/rs.html.

committed with the use of firearms.[4] This constituted less than .5% of all crimes registered in the country. At the same time, police investigated 26,500 crimes related to the illegal circulation of weapons.[5]

Most of the weapons used in crimes committed in Russia turned out to be unregistered or were acquired by a person who used it for criminal purposes.[6] While Russia maintains relatively restrictive gun control legislation and strict procedures regulating the purchase and storage of firearms by private individuals, there is a huge black market for weapons, and most weapons used by criminals are stolen military or police guns, guns sold by law enforcement personnel who seized illegal weapons from criminals and did not register the confiscation of those firearms, or firearms made from modified nonlethal guns.[7]

According to news reports, the legal sale of weapons as well as the illegal acquisition of guns has significantly increased in recent years, especially after terrorist attacks on a hospital, theater, and school in 2002 and 2004, and a number of more recent mass shootings in public places committed by criminals or mentally unstable people.[8] These guns were apparently purchased for self-defense in response to the presumed inability of the state authorities to defend individuals from terrorists and criminals,[9] which has provoked an ongoing public discussion about the necessity of additional gun control measures or further simplification of firearms laws and expansion of the types of weapons allowed for personal possession.

II. Current Gun Control Legislation

Russian legislation that regulates the acquisition, transfer, and use of firearms consists mainly of the Federal Law on Weapons,[10] which sets forth the major principles defining the rules for acquisition, possession, and use of firearms, and implementing regulations issued by the federal government and selected executive agencies.[11] Relevant provisions are also included in

---

[3] Malikov, *supra* note 1.

[4] RUSSIAN FEDERATION MINISTRY OF INTERNAL AFFAIRS, NOVEMBER 2012 CRIME STATISTICS REPORT, http://www.mvd.ru/presscenter/statistics/reports/show_117029/ (in Russian; last visited Jan. 18, 2013).

[5] *Id.*

[6] Maria Butina, *Pistols to Everyone*, SLON.RU (July 24, 2012), http://slon.ru/russia/vsem_korotkostvol-813158.xhtml (in Russian).

[7] *Medvedev is Against Legalization of Weapons*, NEWSRU.COM (Dec. 17, 2012), http://www.newsru.com/russia/17dec2012/guns_print.html (in Russian).

[8] *After Beslan Terrorist Attack the Russians Started to Buy Guns*, NEWSRU.COM (Sept. 16, 2004), http://www.newsru.com/russia/16sep2004/beslan4_print.html (in Russian).

[9] *Id.*

[10] Law No. 150 of Dec. 13, 1996, SOBRANIE ZAKONODATELSTVA ROSSIISKOI FEDERATSII [SZ RF] [COLLECTION OF RUSSIAN FEDERATION LEGISLATION] (official gazette, in Russian) 1996, No. 51, Item 5681 (hereinafter Federal Law on Weapons).

[11] Russian Federation Government Regulation No. 814 of July 21, 1998 on Regulation of Civilian and Service Firearms and Ammunition on the Russian Federation Territory, SZ RF 2012, No. 12, item 1410 (last amended Sept. 4, 2012); Order of the Internal Affairs Minister of the Russian Federation No. 288 of April 12, 1999,

specific legal acts, such as federal laws on education, licensing activities, state protection, and countering terrorism, as well as the Criminal Code of the Russian Federation.

It appears that the main goal of existing legislation is to regulate the circulation of guns depending on the weapon's functional purpose (e.g., self-defense, hunting, sports activities) and maintain a licensing system that allows government monitoring of all operations with legally acquired guns. The Law on Weapons establishes the criteria under which an individual who intends to acquire guns may apply for a permit issued by local police authorities and regulates the type and quantity of firearms an individual may have in his/her private possession. Existing legislation also applies to the circulation of ammunition and cartridges for firearms. Procedures related to the issuance of licenses for the acquisition of weapons and permits for their possession, carrying, use, exhibition, trade, and collecting are regulated by implementing regulations based on the background check requirements established by the Law on Weapons.

According to the Russian Constitution, "each individual has the right to defend his/her rights and freedoms by all means not prohibited by law."[12] This means that people may use weapons that they legally own to protect their life, health, and property when necessary.[13] Necessity is defined by criminal legislation; it is presumed that a person who engages in necessary defense may use all measures needed to stop an ongoing attack.[14] The use of a firearm in the case of necessary defense must be recognized as legal if the use was proportional to the degree of danger posed by the attacker and the level of damage prevented. However, the courts traditionally compare the actual damage inflicted by fighting parties and recognize as justifiable the defense of those individuals who suffered more damage than they inflicted.[15] Because of the broad distribution of more lethal weapons recently, injury to an attacker is more often very serious than before. Legal scholars have called for a review of the laws on necessary defense and related judicial decisions.[16] Also, unlike previous laws, the Law on Weapons allows the use of firearms for the protection of personal property. For many years, courts had viewed the health and life of an offender as more valuable than the property of a law-abiding citizen who defended such property with guns. Current law does not say what type of threat to private property would be enough to justify the use of firearms against an individual who commits a crime, however.[17]

---

on Implementation of the Government Regulation No. 814, BIULLETEN NORMATIVNYKH AKTOV [BULLETIN OF EXECUTIVE REGULATIONS], 1999, No. 32 (both in Russian).

[12] Constitution of the Russian Federation art. 45.2, http://pravo.gov.ru/export/sites/default/konstituciya/Konst_2011.pdf (official version; in Russian).

[13] Eduard Tumanov, Kommentarii k Federalnomu Zakonu ob Oruzhii [Commentaries to the Federal Law on Weapons] 138 (Moscow, 2010).

[14] Criminal Code of the Russian Federation art. 37, SZ RF 1996, No. 25, Item 2954.

[15] Andrei Kaplunov & Sergei Miliukov, Primenenie i Ispolzovanie Ognestrelnogo Oruzhiia [Application and Use of Firearms] 99 (St. Petersburg, 2003).

[16] Id.

[17] Id. at 100.

The Law on Weapons states that the use of weapons for necessary defense must not cause harm to third parties.[18] In a number of recently resolved cases, Russian courts found several police officers guilty of injuring bystanders when they used their service firearms to defend themselves and other individuals.[19] Additionally, the Law prohibits the use of firearms against women, individuals with obvious signs of disability, and minors when their age is apparent or known. An exemption would be a case where the aforementioned individuals are engaged in an armed or group attack. Each use of weapons that entails injury to an individual must be reported by the gun owner to the police immediately, and no later than within twenty-four hours.[20]

III. Types of Firearms Permitted for Individual Possession

The Law on Weapons defines three types of firearms based on the purpose for which they are used and their technical characteristics: civilian, service, and combat firearms, and edged weapons.[21] Manual combat firearms and edged weapons are intended for official operational tasks carried out by agencies and services, as defined by federal legislation. The list includes the armed forces, police, border protection services, tax police and customs, and some other agencies. "Service weapons" include weapons intended for use by officials of government agencies and employees of companies who have been permitted by law to bear, keep, and use arms for self-defense and for performance of the duties assigned to them for protecting individuals and their property, nature and natural resources, valuable and dangerous freight, and special correspondence.

This report focuses on the circulation of civilian weapons, which can be used by Russian citizens for purposes of self-defense, hunting, and sports activities. The definition of the "circulation" of weapons was provided by the Russian Supreme Court in 1996 and includes the production (research, development, testing, artistic finishing, and repair), trade, sale, transfer, acquisition, collection, exhibition, accounting for, possessing, carrying, shipment, and transport of weapons.[22] The distinguishing characteristic of civilian firearms is that such firearms cannot be fired in bursts or have a cartridge capacity of more than ten bullets.[23]

According to the Federal Law on Weapons, only Russian citizens can own civilian weapons in Russia. Foreign nationals are not allowed to own guns. They may receive police permits to acquire weapons based on requests from the embassies of the countries of their citizenship but are required to export their acquired weapons within five days after acquisition. Foreign hunters and sportsmen can bring their hunting and sporting weapons into the country for the duration of a hunting period or sporting event, as specified in their invitation.[24]

---

[18] Federal Law on Weapons art. 24.

[19] KAPLUNOV & MILIUKOV, *supra* note 15, at 347.

[20] Federal Law on Weapons art. 24.

[21] *Id.* art. 2.

[22] Ruling No. 5 of the Russian Federation Supreme Court Plenum, ROSSIISKAIA IUSTITSIIA, No. 8, 1996, at 34.

[23] Federal Law on Weapons art. 3.

[24] *Id.* art. 14.

Article 3 of the Federal Law on Weapons specifies the types of guns that can be used by individuals for self-defense, hunting, and sports activities. These include smooth-bore long-barreled firearms, smooth-bore long-barreled firearms if the rifled part of the barrel is no longer than 140 millimeters, and pneumatic weapons with power of up to 25 joules. Bearing long-barreled weapons for the purpose of self-defense is prohibited.[25]

An individual cannot have more than ten guns in his/her possession, with the exception of guns included in a registered collection of weapons. An individual's possession of weapons cannot exceed five hunting rifled-bore guns and five smooth-bore long-barreled guns.[26]

On the basis of a decree issued by the President, Prime Minister of the Russian Federation, or head of a federal military organization, Russian citizens can be awarded with weapons. This could include any type of civilian or short-barreled combat handgun. Award weapons are subject to possession and carrying requirements. Carrying permits must be issued by local gun registering authorities at the individual's place of residence following the registration of an award weapon by the owner within two weeks after receipt. A weapon that can be fired in bursts and one that is prohibited by law for circulation on the territory of the Russian Federation cannot be given as an award.[27]

IV. Prohibited Weapons

Special restrictions are imposed on the circulation of civilian weapons. Prohibited firearms are those with a cartridge capacity of more than ten bullets, those that can fire in bursts, those with a barrel length of less than 500 millimeters or an entire length under 800 millimeters, and those that can be shortened to a length of under 800 millimeters without losing their shooting capacity. Rifled-bore sporting guns and pneumatic guns with a pumping power of more than 7.5 joules and a caliber of more than 4.5 millimeters must be kept at shooting ranges.[28]

The list of prohibited firearms includes (1) those with shapes that imitate other objects; (2) cartridges with bullets for armor-piercing, incendiary, explosive, or tracer action; and cartridges with shot charges for gas pistols; (3) weapons and other objects whose destructive action is based on the use of radioactive radiation and biological factors; and (4) gas weapons charged with nerve-paralytic, toxic, and other substances not permitted for use by the government or gas weapons that can cause a medium degree of harm at a distance of more than one meter. Also, the sale and installation of silencers and sights for night vision are prohibited, with the exception of sights for hunting. The policy for using such sights has been specifically established by law. The Law on Weapons does not allow the shipping of weapons by individuals.[29]

---

[25] *Id.* art. 6.

[26] *Id.* art. 13.

[27] *Id.* art. 20-1.

[28] *Id.* art. 6.

[29] *Id.*

V. Acquisition and Possession of Firearms

Russian citizens have the right to acquire and possess weapons according to rules established by legislation. These rules allow citizens of the Russian Federation who are eighteen years of age and older to apply for a license that would allow an individual to possess weapons of a specific type as stated in the license. Legislative assemblies of Russian Federation constituent components can lower the mandatory age by no more than two years. Usually, such decisions are made in those regions where industrial hunting is conducted or in areas with a significant indigenous population that has historically been involved in hunting activities. Before applying for a license to acquire hunting weapons, an individual must be registered as a hunter and be a member of a hunting society.

Licenses are issued by local police departments at one's place of permanent residence and each license is issued separately for a specific type of weapon—hunting rifled-bore, hunting smooth-bore, and sporting firearms. Licenses have unified federal numbering and their specific series and numbers are assigned to particular Russian territories. Official licensing documents have eleven protection levels, complicating the manufacturing of false documents.[30] Each license allows the petitioner to acquire and keep up to five different of weapons.

Where hunting weapons are purchased for hunting purposes, a license will also include a carrying permit. Licenses are issued for a five-year period and can be renewed. Hunting weapons with rifled-bore barrels and combined weapons where smooth-bore and rifled-bore barrels can be interchanged can be acquired by those hunters who have five years of experience possessing smooth-bore long barrel guns. Until recently, individuals who were found to have violated hunting rules or rules related to the use, storage, or circulation of weapons were prohibited from acquiring rifled-bore long-barreled weapons.[31] Because the law did not specify the type of violation and the level of public danger that would trigger this ban, and did not define the length of the ban, the Constitutional Court of Russia held this restriction to be unconstitutional in June 2012, and ordered the legislature to provide for specific rules regarding the acquisition of these types of weapons.[32]

Individuals who acquire weapons for the first time are required to attend six and a half hours of classes on the safe handling of guns offered by organizations designated by the government of the Russian Federation and to pass federal tests on knowledge of safety rules.[33] A license for weapons acquisition is required in order to accept guns as a gift or inheritance. Tests must be retaken and passed when an individual applies for license renewal.

The following documents must be submitted to a local police department, together with the application for a gun license:

---

[30] Leonid Vedenov, Zakony Rossiis ob Oruzhii [Russian Laws on Weapons] 7 (Moscow, 2003).

[31] Federal Law on Weapons art. 13.10.

[32] Constitutional Court of the Russian Federation, Ruling No. 16-P of June 29, 2012, http://www.ksrf.ru/ru/Decision/Pages/default.aspx.

[33] Government Regulation No. 731 of September 5, 2011, ROSSIISKAIA GAZETA [ROS. GAZ.], Sept. 9, 2011, http://www.rg.ru/2011/09/09/perechen-oruzhie-dok.html.

- Statement that an individual has no medical contraindications for possession of guns

- Statements issued by boards monitoring psychiatric and substance abuse services within the administrative area where an applicant permanently resides that the applicant was not treated for mental illnesses or drug abuse

- Proof of Russian citizenship

- Two photographs

- Statement from a territorial police officer that weapons can be safely kept at the applicant's residence

- Hunter's card

- License fee

- Proof of no less than five-year possession of smooth-bore barrel guns if applying for a license to purchase rifled-bore barreled guns[34]

Applications are reviewed within one month; the applicant then has six months to purchase guns before the expiration of the license. Licenses are not issued to those who cannot guarantee secure storage of weapons, have a court record that has not expired, or have committed at least two minor violations of public order within a one-year period. Individuals without permanent residency in a specific location cannot acquire guns.[35]

A list of diseases preventing an individual from having weapons has been established by the federal government[36] and includes the following:

- Chronic and long-lasting psychiatric diseases with severe or continuing forms of relapses

- Addictions to alcohol, narcotics, or other toxic substances

- Vision problems of -5 or worse in one eye when another eye is worse than -2, or -7 in one eye if the person is blind in the other eye

- Absence of a thumb and index finger, or three fingers on one of the hands

The State Duma of the Russian Federation is currently debating a proposal to introduce a measures that would impose criminal responsibility on physicians for issuing false statements about the medical conditions of those who apply for a gun license.[37]

---

[34] Government Regulation No. 814 of July 21, 1998, Ros. Gaz., Aug. 20, 1998, *available at* http://base.consultant.ru/cons/cgi/online.cgi?req=doc;base=LAW;n=135139.

[35] *Id.*

[36] *Id.*

[37] Bill 191803-6, introduced Dec. 17, 2012, http://asozd2.duma.gov.ru/main.nsf/%28SpravkaNew%29?OpenAgent&RN=191803-6&02 (official website of the State Duma of the Russian Federation).

All weapons must be registered within two weeks after their acquisition. Registration must be conducted by the same police department that issued the license for acquisition. According to article 22 of the Law on Weapons, it is the gun owner's responsibility to make sure that his/her weapons are stored safely. The local police inspector is obligated under the Law to visit a gun owner's residence at least once a year and review the safety of weapons.[38]

VI. Public Discussions and Proposed Legislation

Measured by the number of registered guns in the possession of individuals, Russia is ninth in the world.[39] Even though legally acquired and registered weapons are traced to a minimal number of crimes committed with firearms,[40] there are ongoing public debates on whether to introduce stricter gun control legislation or simplify the rules for obtaining and possessing guns for self-defense. Proposals to allow individuals to acquire and carry short-barreled handguns for self-defense are being discussed by legislators.[41] Even though one such proposal contains restrictions on bearing handguns in public places and educational institutions,[42] it appears that it has more opponents than proponents among the lawmakers.[43] Among other gun-control proposals currently under discussion are measures that would increase the age for acquisition of guns from eighteen to twenty-one, and the creation of a national collection of bullet case samples in order to make it possible to identify a gun used in a particular shooting.[44] Other proposals would provide for new rules to expedite the licensing process[45] and allow individuals to prepare cartridges for their hunting guns.[46]

Among other measures being discussed are suggestions to equip weapons sold in Russia with biometric scanners, which would prevent the use of a gun other than by its owner,[47] and a

---

[38] TUMANOV, *supra* note 13, at 185.

[39] *Russians Have 13 Million Guns*, SAFEGUN.RU, http://safegun.ru/bulletin/1.html (in Russian; last visited Jan. 14, 2013).

[40] *Colt Made All Equal*, SAFEGUN.RU, http://safegun.ru/info/info-14.html (in Russian; last visited Jan. 14, 2013).

[41] Bill 576559-5, introduced July 8, 2011, reintroduced Aug. 7, 2012 (Bill 123846-6), http://asozd2.duma.gov.ru/main.nsf/%28SpravkaNew%29?OpenAgent&RN=576559-5&02.

[42] Bill 171032-6, introduced Nov. 13, 2012, http://asozd2.duma.gov.ru/main.nsf/%28SpravkaNew%29?OpenAgent&RN=171032-6&02.

[43] Malikov, *supra* note 1.

[44] Bill 171032-6, http://asozd2.duma.gov.ru/main.nsf/%28SpravkaNew%29? OpenAgent&RN=171032-6&02.

[45] Bill 79444-6, introduced May 23, 2012, http://asozd2.duma.gov.ru/main.nsf/%28SpravkaNew%29?OpenAgent&RN=79444-6&02.

[46] Bill 56262-6, introduced Apr. 16, 2012, http://asozd2.duma.gov.ru/main.nsf/%28SpravkaNew%29?OpenAgent&RN=56262-6&02.

[47] Vladimir Voloshin, *Guns Will Have Black Boxes*, IZVESTIIA (Oct. 5, 2012), http://izvestia.ru/news/536891 (in Russian).

ban on the sale of all types of weapons on Russian territory between January and April 2014, in order to secure the safety of the 2014 Olympic Games, which are to be held in Russia.[48]

Prepared by Peter Roudik
Director of Legal Research

---

[48] Draft of the President's Decree published on the website of the RF Ministry of Internal Affairs, http://mvd.ru/documents/public (last visited Jan. 14, 2013).

SINGAPORE

FIREARMS-CONTROL LEGISLATION AND POLICY

Summary

Singapore has one of the toughest gun control laws in the world. According to the Arms Offences Act, unlawful possession or carrying of firearms is punishable with imprisonment and caning. Using or attempting to use arms when committing a scheduled offense is punishable with death. The death penalty may also apply to the offender's accomplices present at the scene of the offense.

Any person proved to be in unlawful possession of more than two firearms will be presumed to be trafficking in arms until the contrary is proved. Trafficking in arms is punishable with either death or imprisonment for life and with caning.

Possessing any firearms or importing, exporting, manufacturing, repairing, or selling them, requires a license. Licensing officers have the authority to refuse to issue a license, or to suspend or cancel a license without giving any reason.

I. Introduction

Singapore has one of the toughest firearms control laws in the world, according to its former Minister for Law, Professor S. Jayakumar.[1] Jayakumar attributes the fact that Singapore has very few firearm offenses in a time when "we see rampant firearm offences as well as smuggling and trafficking in weapons in the region and elsewhere in the world" to the strict gun control laws, including a "mandatory death penalty for anyone who discharges a firearm in the course of committing a serious offence, even if no one is injured or killed."[2]

Singapore's primary statutes regulating firearms are the Arms Offences Act,[3] which relates to the unlawful possession of arms and ammunition and the carrying and using of arms,

---

[1] S. Jayakumar, The Confluence of Law and Policy: The Singapore Experience, Address at the Millennium Law Conference, Singapore (April 10-12, 2000), *cited in* CHAN WING CHEONG & ANDREW PHANG, THE DEVELOPMENT OF CRIMINAL LAW AND CRIMINAL JUSTICE IN SINGAPORE 13–14 (2001).

[2] *Id.*

[3] Arms Offences Act, Cap 14, STATUTES OF THE REPUBLIC OF SINGAPORE (rev. ed. 2008) (originally enacted as Act 61 of 1973), http://statutes.agc.gov.sg/aol/search/display/view.w3p;ident=66818397-627b-4a3b-8e5a-77ed7dc882f0;page=0;query=CompId%3A66818397-627b-4a3b-8e5a-77ed7dc882f0;rec=0;resUrl=http%3A%2F%2Fstatutes.agc.gov.sg%2Faol%2Fbrowse%2FtitleResults.w3p%3Bletter%3DA%3Btype%3DactsAll#legis.

and the Arms and Explosives Act,[4] which regulates the manufacture, use, sale, storage, transport, importation, exportation and possession of arms, explosives and explosive precursors, and gives effect to the Convention on the Marking of Plastic Explosives for the Purpose of Detection.

II. Arms Offences Act

The Arms Offences Act, which was first enacted in 1973, states that the act shall have effect without prejudice to the provisions of the Arms and Explosives Act, or any other written law in force in Singapore relating to the unlawful possession of arms or ammunition.[5]

A. Definition of Arms

An "arm" is defined by the Arms Offences Act to mean "any firearm, air-gun, air-pistol, automatic gun, automatic pistol and any other kind of gun or pistol from which any shot, bullet or other missile can be discharged or noxious liquid, flame or fumes can be emitted, and any component part thereof and includes any bomb or grenade and any component part thereof."[6]

B. Unlawful Possession of Arms and Ammunition

According to the Arms Offences Act, any person who is in unlawful possession of any arm or ammunition shall be guilty of an offense and shall on conviction be punished with imprisonment for a term of not less than five years and not more than ten years, and shall also be punished with caning with not less than six strokes.[7]

Any person who unlawfully carries any arm shall be punished with imprisonment for a term of five to fourteen years and with caning with not less than six strokes.[8]

Aggravated penalties apply if the offender of the above two provisions was previously convicted of a scheduled offense; such an offender is subject to imprisonment for a term of five to twenty years and caning with not less than six strokes.[9]

Committing any scheduled offense while armed is punishable with imprisonment for life and caning with not less than six strokes.[10]

---

[4] Arms and Explosives Act, Cap 13, STATUTES OF THE REPUBLIC OF SINGAPORE (rev. ed. 2003) (originally enacted as Ordinance 9 of 1913), http://statutes.agc.gov.sg/aol/search/display/view.w3p;page=0;query=Comp Id%3A6452e9c4-95f1-4a1f-a0d8-abe75f0c3c7b;rec=0;resUrl=http%3A%2F%2Fstatutes.agc.gov.sg%2Faol%2 \Fbrowse%2FtitleResults.w3p%3Bletter%3DA%3Btype%3DactsAll;whole=yes.

[5] Arms Offences Act § 11.

[6] *Id.* § 2.

[7] *Id.* § 3(1).

[8] *Id.* § 3(2).

[9] *Id.* § 3(4).

[10] *Id.* § 3(3).

C. Using or Attempting to Use Arms

Subject to certain exceptions,[11] any person who uses or attempts to use any arm shall be guilty of an offense and shall on conviction be punished with death.[12] A person who uses or attempts to use arms is presumed to have intended to cause physical injury to a person or property until the contrary is proved.[13]

A person convicted of using or attempting to use any arm while committing or attempting to commit any scheduled offense shall be punished with death, regardless of whether he intended to cause physical injury to any person or property.[14] Moreover, each of his accomplices present at the scene of the offense who may reasonably be presumed to have known that that person was carrying the arm shall be punished with death, unless such accomplice can prove that he took all reasonable steps to prevent use of the arm.[15]

D. Trafficking in Arms

Trafficking in arms is punishable with either death or imprisonment for life and with caning with not less than six strokes.[16] Any person proved to be in unlawful possession of more than two arms will be presumed to be trafficking in arms until the contrary is proved.[17] "Trafficking in arms" under the act means to import, manufacture or deal in arms in contravention of the provisions of the Arms and Explosives Act, or to lend, give, sell, hire or offer any arm to a person who is not licensed to possess such arm.[18]

E. Exemptions

The provisions on unlawful possession of arms or ammunition under the Arms Offences Act do not apply to the following exempted persons:

> (*a*) a member of any visiting force lawfully present in Singapore or of the police force or of a volunteer force or local force constituted under any written law for the time

---

[11] The exceptions are those set forth at Penal Code, Cap 224, §§ 76-106, STATUTES OF THE REPUBLIC OF SINGAPORE (rev. ed. 2008) ("General Exceptions"), http://statutes.agc.gov.sg/aol/search/display/view.w3p; ident=3dd117ef-fda3-4694-9c59-01d19b65475c;page=0;query=DocId%3A%22025e7646-947b-462c-b557-60aa55dc7b42%22%20Status%3Ainforce%20Depth%3A0;rec=0#P4IV_76- (other than the exception in section 95, which states: "Nothing is an offence by reason that it causes, or that it is intended to cause, or that it is known to be likely to cause, any harm, if that harm is so slight that no person of ordinary sense and temper would complain of such harm.").

[12] Arms Offences Act § 4(1).

[13] *Id.* § 4(2).

[14] *Id.* § 4A.

[15] *Id.* § 5.

[16] *Id.* § 6.

[17] *Id.* § 6(2).

[18] *Id.* § 2.

being in force in Singapore, when the member is carrying any arm in, or in connection with, the performance of his duty;

(*b*) any person who carries an arm as part of his official or ceremonial dress on any official or ceremonial occasion;

(*c*) any person licensed or authorized to carry or possess an arm under or by virtue of any written law relating to arms for the time being in force in Singapore; or

(*d*) a member of any organization or association specially authorized by the Minister by notification in the Gazette, when the member is carrying any arm in, or in connection with, the performance of his duty.[19]

III. Arms and Explosives Act

The Arms and Explosives Act, originally enacted in 1913, stipulates licensing requirements for arms, explosives, and explosive precursors. The Act also regulates related offenses, such as knowingly concealing firearms imported without a license, knowingly purchasing firearms from an unlicensed person, and offenses involving unmarked plastic explosives.[20]

A. Definition of Arms

"Arms" is defined by the Arms and Explosive Act to include:

(*a*) firearms, air-guns, air-pistols, stun guns, electronic dart guns, automatic guns, automatic pistols, guns or any other kind of gun from which any shot, bullet or other missile can be discharged or noxious fumes or noxious substance can be emitted, and any component part of any such arms;

(*b*) bayonets, swords, daggers, spears and spearheads; and

(*c*) such weapon, accessory, or other article or thing, as the Minister may, by notification in the *Gazette*, specify to be arms for the purposes of this Act or any part thereof.[21]

The definition of "arms" in the Arms and Explosives Act differs from that in the Arms Offences Act in that it includes bayonets, swords, daggers, spears, spearheads and additional articles that the authorized minister may specify.

B. Licensing Requirements for Firearms

In Singapore, any person who possesses, imports, exports, manufactures, or deals in firearms without a license shall be guilty of an offense. The Police Licensing and Regulatory

---

[19] *Id.* § 10.

[20] Arms and Explosives Act *passim*.

[21] *Id.* § 2.

Department issues two types of licenses: long-term licenses valid for two years and short-term licenses valid for fourteen days.[22]

Under the Arms and Explosives Act, no person in Singapore may, without a license, have in his possession or under his control any firearms, or import, export, manufacture, or deal in them.[23] "Deal in" under the Act means repair, sell, keep, or expose for sale.[24] Exemptions from the operation of the Act include certain activities carried out by order of the government, members of military, and police in the course of their duty or employment, and the like.[25]

The Arms and Explosives Act allows the licensing officer to refuse to issue a license to an applicant if he determines that the applicant is not a fit and proper person to hold such a license or if issuing a license would be contrary to the public interest.[26]

Licenses issued under the Act are subject to conditions. First, without any reason being given, the licensing officer may suspend or cancel a license. Second, a license expires after such period as is prescribed. Third, the license is generally not transferable.[27]

C. Minister for Home Affairs to Prohibit Exportation by Notification

Under the Arms and Explosives Act, the Minister for Home Affairs may, by notification published in the Gazette, prohibit for a stated period the exportation of firearms from Singapore, either absolutely or to any specified country, territory, or place outside Singapore; permit their exportation or removal subject to such conditions, limitations, or restrictions as he considers necessary; or permit their removal from place to place within Singapore.[28]

D. Penalties

Any person who has in his possession or under his control the proscribed firearms is liable on conviction to a fine and imprisonment for a term which may extend to three years.[29] Caning may also be imposed if the offender is proved to have possession or control of the arms, explosives, poisonous or noxious gas, or noxious substance for the purpose of committing an offense punishable under the Penal Code.[30] Importing, exporting, manufacturing, or dealing in the proscribed firearms without a license are also subject to a fine and to imprisonment for a term

---

[22] *Singapore Police Force – Arms and Explosives*, SINGAPORE CUSTOMS, http://www.customs.gov.sg/leftNav/trad/TradeNet/Singapore+Police+Force+-+Arms+and+Explosives.htm (last visited Jan. 15, 2013).

[23] Arms and Explosives Act § 13.

[24] *Id.* § 2.

[25] *Id.* § 3(1).

[26] *Id.* § 21F.

[27] *Id.* § 21G.

[28] *Id.* § 9.

[29] *Id.* § 13(3) & (4).

[30] *Id.* § 13(5).

not exceeding three years.[31] Knowingly concealing firearms that were imported unlawfully or without a license is punishable by imprisonment for up to three years and a fine.[32]

Prepared by Laney Zhang
Senior Foreign Law Specialist

---

[31] *Id.* § 13(2).

[32] *Id.* § 22(1).

SOUTH AFRICA

FIREARMS-CONTROL LEGISLATION AND POLICY

Summary

South Africa's current firearms regulatory framework consists of the Firearms Control Act (FCA) and its subsidiary legislation, which has been in place since 2004. This framework imposes strict substantive and procedural requirements for obtaining a competency certificate, license, permit, or authorization to possess a firearm, to deal in firearms, or to carry out other firearm-related activities, including running a firearms-training enterprise or a hunting business.

Some of these requirements are of universal application. For instance, a separate license must be issued for every firearm and applicants must obtain a competency certificate. To do so, an applicant should, among other things, be a "fit and proper person" with no recent conviction for certain crimes, be stable, and not have a proclivity for violence. Other requirements vary depending on the type and purpose of the specific license sought. For instance, a person wishing to obtain a license to possess a firearm for self-defense is required to demonstrate a need for the weapon and inability to achieve protection through other means. In addition, an eligible individual may obtain only one license of this class, which must be renewed every five years.

Limited, mostly secondary sources located for this report point to a decrease in firearms-related crimes since the FCA came into force, although none of the sources establish a direct causal effect.

I. Introduction

South Africa has a comprehensive firearms-control regulatory regime in place. It consists of the Firearms Control Act[1] of 2000 (FCA) and its subsidiary legislation, the Firearms Control Regulations (FCA Regulations).[2] Before these laws took effect in 2004, firearms were

---

[1] Firearms Control Act 60 of 2000 (FCA), *as amended*, 3 BUTTERWORTHS STATUTES OF THE REPUBLIC OF SOUTH AFRICA [BSRSA] (rev. ed. 2011). No online source for the current version of the FCA was located. The text of the original Act can be found on the website of the South African government, http://www.info.gov.za/view/DownloadFileAction?id=68229, along with the text of Firearms Control Amendment Act 43 of 2003, http://www.info.gov.za/view/DownloadFileAction?id=68021. The text of Firearms Control Amendment Act 28 of 2006 is available on the website of the South African Gunowners' Association (SAGA), http://www.saga.org.za/FCA%20Amendments%20ACT%202006%20gaz%2030210%2020070822.pdf.

[2] FCA 2000: Firearms Control Regulations (FCA Regulations), No. R. 345, GOVERNMENT GAZETTE [GG], No. 26156 (Mar. 26, 2004), http://www.info.gov.za/view/DownloadFileAction?id=161734, amended by the FCA,

regulated through the Arms and Ammunition Act 75 of 1969 (the 1969 AAA).[3] The designated regulatory authority is the National Commissioner of the South African Police Service (SAPS), which also functions as the National Commissioner of Registrar of Firearms (the Registrar).[4]

This regulatory regime has put in place stringent substantive and procedural limits on obtaining firearms. It imposes a ban on certain firearms designated "prohibited" firearms except in very limited circumstances.[5] It also imposes thorough requirements for obtaining a license for other firearms. For instance, a firearm for self-defense may be issued only if the applicant can demonstrate the need for a weapon and an inability to achieve protection through other means.[6] A person who meets these standards can be issued only one license for a five-year term, which may be renewed if the licensee continues to show compliance with all applicable requirements.[7] A person seeking a firearms license for dedicated sport shooting must be a member of an accredited hunting association.[8]

All applications for a firearms license must be accompanied by a competency certificate, which is issued only after it has been determined that, among other things, the applicant does not have a proclivity for violence or a substance-abuse problem and he or she completes training on the safe and efficient handling of firearms.[9] It also imposes equally strict rules on the safe custody of firearms.[10]

The regulatory regime also imposes stringent requirements on dealers. Among the notable obligations is a duty to keep records on all firearms and ammunition in stock and all firearms that the dealer holds on behalf of licensees, as well as the duty to link these three registers to a national database established by the Registrar.[11] A dealer must make available for inspection on request by any police official all firearms, ammunition, and records that he or she keeps.[12]

The impact of the current regulatory framework on firearms-related crimes is hard to ascertain. This is in large part because the SAPS has not released adequate statistical

---

2000: Amendment of the FCA Regulations, 2004, No. R. 696, GOVERNMENT NOTICES [GN], No. 27781 (Sept. 16, 2005), http://www.info.gov.za/view/DowloadFile Action?id=161672.

[3] Arms and Ammunition Act 75 of 1969, STATUTES OF THE REPUBLIC OF SOUTH AFRICA (Gov. Printer, 1969). Prior to that, the governing law was the Arms and Ammunition Act 28 of 1937 (1937 AAA), STATUTES OF THE UNION OF SOUTH AFRICA (Cape Times Ltd., 1937).

[4] FCA §§ 123 & 124.

[5] Id. § 4.

[6] Id. § 13.

[7] Id. § 24 & 27.

[8] Id. § 16.

[9] Id. § 9; FCA Regulations § 14.

[10] FCA Regulations § 86.

[11] FCA § 39; FCA Regulations § 37.

[12] FCA § 39.

information on the matter since the early 2000s.[13] In addition, while the FCA has been in effect since 2004, it appears that various key provisions have been implemented in increments, with some parts, particularly certain provisions added to the FCA through a 2006 amendment, implemented recently and others not yet put into effect. However, limited, mostly secondary sources located for this report point to a decrease in firearms-related crimes since the FCA went into force, although none of them establish a direct causal effect.

II. Definition of Firearm

The FCA adopts a broad definition of "firearm," which includes

- any device that can "propel a bullet or projectile through a barrel or cylinder by means of burning propellant, at a muzzle energy exceeding 8 joules (6 ft-lbs)";

- anything with the capacity to "to discharge rim-fire, centre-fire or pin-fire ammunition";

- any device that can be "readily altered" to be any of the above-listed firearms;

- any device designed to discharge any projectile of at least .22 calibre at a muzzle energy of more than 8 joules (6 ft-lbs), by means of compressed gas; or

- any barrel, frame, or receiver of a device mentioned above.[14]

However, the FCA excludes various devices that would otherwise be considered firearms under this definition. Explosive-powered tools designed for industrial application for splitting rocks or concrete, or for application in the mining or steel industry for removing refractory materials, are not considered firearms.[15] Also not considered firearms are stun bolts used in slaughterhouses, antique firearms,[16] air guns, tranquilizer firearms, paintball guns, flare guns, and deactivated firearms.[17] In addition, the FCA authorizes the Minister of Safety and Security (the Minister) to exclude any other device.[18]

---

[13] Lauren Tracy, *The Costs of Firearm Violence – A National Public Health Priority*, INSTITUTE FOR SECURITY STUDIES (May 17, 2012), http://www.issafrica.org/iss_today.php?ID=1484%2613; ADÈLE KIRSTEN, A NATION WITHOUT GUNS? THE STORY OF GUN FREE SOUTH AFRICA 6 (Univ. KwaZulu-Natal Press, 2008).

[14] FCA § 1.

[15] *Id.* § 5.

[16] An "antique firearm" was defined as "any muzzle loading firearm manufactured before 1 January 1900, or any replica of such firearm." *Id.* § 1. However, this definition was repealed by section 1(b) of the 2006 amendment to the FCA, which took effect in 2011. Commencement of Certain Provisions of the Firearms Control Amendment Act, 2006 (Act No. 28 of 2006), Proclamation No. 77, 2010, GG, No. 33871 (Dec. 17, 2010), http://www.info.gov.za/view/DownloadFileAction?id=137369.

[17] FCA § 5.

[18] *Id.* §§ 1 & 5.

III. The Right to Possess Firearms

In South Africa, the right to possess firearms is not guaranteed by law. The FCA imposes a general ban on the possession of firearms except in limited circumstances, and they may be possessed only with a license, permit, or authorization issued under the provisions of the FCA.[19]

Certain firearms are categorized as prohibited firearms and cannot ordinarily be possessed or licensed under the FCA. These include any

(a) fully automatic firearm;

(b) gun, cannon, recoilless gun, mortar, light mortar or launcher manufactured to fire a rocket, grenade, self-propelled grenade, bomb, or explosive device;

(c) frame, body, or barrel of such a fully automatic firearm, gun, cannon, recoilless gun, mortar, light mortar, or launcher;

(d) projectile or rocket manufactured to be discharged from a cannon, recoilless gun or mortar, or rocket launcher;

(e) imitation of any device contemplated in paragraph (b), (c), excluding the frame, body, or barrel of a fully automatic firearm, or (d); or

(f) [altered firearm].[20]

The FCA stipulates limited exceptions in which prohibited firearms may be licensed for private and public collections as well as for use in theatrical, film, or television productions.[21] However, the FCA Regulations impose rigorous requirements that need to be met for the proper utilization of these exceptions.[22]

The FCA also authorizes the Minister to add any firearm to the prohibited firearms category if doing so is "in the interest of public safety or desirable for the maintenance of law and order."[23]

---

[19] *Id.* § 3. Authorization for a muzzle-loading firearm requires a competency certificate. *Id.*

[20] *Id.* § 4. A "fully automatic firearm" is one "capable of discharging more than one shot with a single depression of the trigger." *Id.* § 1. An "imitation firearm" is anything that has the appearance of a firearm but is not capable of operating as such and cannot by superficial examination be identified as an imitation. *Id.* An "altered firearm" includes a firearm "(i) the mechanism of which has been altered so as to enable the discharging of more than one shot with a single depression of the trigger; (ii) the calibre of which has been altered without the written permission of the Registrar; (iii) the barrel length of which has been altered without the written permission of the Registrar; (iv) the serial number or any other identifying mark of which has been changed or removed without the written permission of the Registrar." *Id.* § 4.

[21] *Id.* §§ 4, 17, 18, & 19; *see also* Proclamation No. 77.

[22] FCA Regulations §§ 15–22.

[23] FCA § 4.

IV. Competency Certificates, Licenses, Permits, Authorizations, and Accreditations

An application for a firearm license, permit, or authorization may be made to the Registrar of Firearms by a natural or juridical person.[24] When the applicant is a natural person, the FCA requires that the person comply with all the necessary requirements set forth under its provisions, including providing a full set of fingerprints.[25] Significantly, the person must possess the relevant competency certificate, which is issued, among other things, only after the successful completion of training and a test on the efficient and safe handling of a firearm by an accredited training provider or the Safety and Security Training Authority.[26] If the applicant is a juridical person, the FCA requires that the entity be represented by a natural person who is to be identified in the license, permit, or authorization as the responsible person and who would be considered the holder of the license under the FCA.[27]

A. Accreditation

The FCA requires accreditation before a license for certain activities or businesses related to firearms can be issued.[28] These include

- public collectors or museums;

- hunting associations or sport-shooting organizations;

- collectors' associations;

- shooting ranges;

- those that provide training in the use of firearms;

- those that provide firearms for use in theatrical, film, or television productions;

- game ranchers;

- those that run hunting businesses;

- those that use firearms for business purposes; and

- government institutions.[29]

The FCA provides a list of minimum mandatory criteria that the Registrar must impose when reviewing an application for accreditation. These are

---

[24] *Id.* §§ 6 & 7.

[25] *Id.* § 6; FCA Regulations § 13.

[26] FCA § 6; *Application for a New Firearm License*, SOUTH AFRICA GOVERNMENT SERVICES, http://www. services.gov.za/services/content/Home/ServicesForPeople/Dealingwiththelaw/firearms/firearmlicence/en_ZA (last visited Jan. 28, 2013).

[27] FCA § 7.

[28] *Id.* § 8.

[29] FCA Regulations §§ 2–12.

a) trustworthiness and integrity;

b) suitability to perform the relevant functions in terms of the Act;

c) capacity to serve the purpose of the accreditation; and

d) capacity to advance the purposes of the Act.[30]

The FCA authorizes the Minister to issue additional criteria applicable to specific accreditations through regulations.[31] Accordingly, the Minister has issued additional accreditation criteria for each of the above-listed specific firearms-license applications.[32]

The Registrar may cancel an accreditation in certain instances, including if the holder of an accreditation fails to comply with any applicable criterion, is no longer qualified, or violates requirements under the FCA or terms of the accreditation.[33]

B. Competency Certificate

The FCA requires that an application to possess a firearm, trade in firearms, manufacture firearms, or be licensed as a gunsmith be submitted to a Firearms Officer for the area where the applicant currently maintains or will in the future maintain his or her residence or business.[34] A first-time application for a competency certificate may be granted only if the applicant

- is at least twenty-one years old;[35]

- is a citizen or a permanent resident;

- is a "fit and proper person" for the license he or she is seeking;

- is stable and does not have a proclivity for violence;

- does not have a substance-abuse problem;

- has no conviction within the five years immediately preceding the application for certain crimes related to violence, dishonesty, recklessness, or instability;[36]

---

[30] FCA § 8.

[31] Id.

[32] FCA Regulations §§ 2–12.

[33] FCA § 8.

[34] Id. § 9.

[35] The Registrar may waive this requirement for "compelling reasons," including if the underage applicant runs a business, is gainfully employed, or is a dedicated hunter, sports person, or private collector. Id.

[36] The FCA lists various specific crimes in this regard. These include a conviction under the FCA or the 1969 AAA for which the convicted person served a prison term without the option of a fine applied; for the unlawful use or handling of a firearm in any jurisdiction; for violence or sexual abuse for which he or she served a prison term with no option for a fine in any jurisdiction; for physical or sexual abuse within a domestic relationship in any jurisdiction; for fraud in relation to application(s) for a competency certificate, license, permit, or authorization under the FCA or the 1969 AAA; for an offense relating to substance abuse for which he or she served a prison term without the option of a fine in any jurisdiction; for dealing drugs for which he or she served a prison term with no

- has not "become or been declared unfit to possess a firearm" under the FCA or the 1969 AAA within the five years preceding the application; and

- has completed all the required tests on his understanding of the FCA, the training and test for the safe and effective use of a firearm, and all other applicable training and tests for the specific license he or she is seeking.[37]

Competency certificates are not permanent. A competency certificate to possess a firearm, trade in firearms, manufacture firearms, or open a gunsmith business is valid for as long as the license to which it relates remains valid, unless the certificate is terminated or renewed.[38] A competency certificate relating to a muzzle-loading firearm is issued for ten years.[39]

The FCA Regulations impose additional requirements. For instance, it requires anyone who provides a recommendation on behalf of any applicant to attest that the applicant

- is a fit and proper person to be issued a competency certificate, license, permit, or authorization;

- is in stable mental condition and does not have a propensity for violence; and

- does not suffer from a substance-abuse problem.[40]

Upon receiving an application for a competency certificate, the Registrar may launch an investigation for the purpose of determining whether the applicant is a fit and proper person, is in stable mental condition, or has a tendency for violence or a substance-abuse problem. An investigation would be launched if in the five years preceding the application the applicant, among other things,

- has been served with a protection order or accused of domestic violence, necessitating a police visit to his or her residence;

- has been denied a license, permit, or authorization for a firearm;

- has attempted suicide, suffered major depression or emotional problems, or had a substance-abuse problem;

- has been diagnosed or treated for depression, substance abuse, or behavioral or emotional problems;

---

option of a fine; for any offense under the South African Domestic Relation Act 116 of 1998 for which he served a prison term with no option of a fine; for an offense relating to "negligent handling of a firearm"; for an offense under the Explosives Act 26 of 1956 for which he or she served a prison term with no option of a fine; or for sabotage, terrorism, public violence, arson, intimidation, rape, kidnapping, or child stealing in any jurisdiction. *Id.* All of the above-listed offenses also include conspiracy, incitement, or attempt to commit such offense. *Id.*

[37] *Id.*; FCA Regulations § 14.

[38] FCA §§ 10 & 10A.

[39] *Id.* § 10.

[40] FCA Regulations § 13.

- has been reported to the police or social services for threatening or attempting violence or other conflict anywhere;

or if in the two years preceding the application the applicant

- went through a divorce or separation from a partner in which violence was alleged, or
- was fired or laid off from his or her job.[41]

In the course of investigating an applicant for a competency certificate, the Registrar may require the applicant to submit a doctor's certificate regarding the applicant's dependence on intoxicating or narcotic substances[42] and/or a report compiled by a psychiatrist or psychologist on the applicant's mental condition or propensity for violence.[43]

C. Licenses to Possess Firearms

The FCA requires that the Registrar issue a separate license in respect of each of the following firearms: firearms for self-defense; restricted firearms for self-defense; firearms for occasional hunting and sport shooting; firearms for dedicated hunting and dedicated sport shooting; firearms for private collection; firearms for public collection; firearms for business purposes; firearms for temporary possession.[44] The Registrar may issue an additional license with respect to a single firearm to everyone who resides in the same premises as the license holder.[45]

1. License to Posses a Firearm for Self-Defense

In this category, the Registrar may issue a license for any shotgun that is not fully or semiautomatic or for a handgun that is not fully automatic.[46] While any natural person is eligible to apply, a license is issued only if the applicant "needs a firearm for self-defense" and cannot "reasonably satisfy the need by means other than the possession of a firearm."[47] A person is permitted to hold only one license of this kind.[48]

---

[41] *Id.* §§ 14 & 124.

[42] FCA Regulations § 14.

[43] *Id.*

[44] FCA § 11. However, the FCA permits the issuance of a single document containing licenses with respect to more than one firearm.

[45] *Id.* § 12. However, this only applies to firearms licensed for self-defense as well as hunting and sports-shooting. *Id.*

[46] *Id.* § 13.

[47] *Id.*

[48] *Id.*

A license in this category is issued for a five-year term and may be renewed provided that the licensee continues to comply with all the applicable requirements.[49]

2. License to Possess a Restricted Firearm for Self-Defense

A restricted firearm includes any semiautomatic rifle or shotgun that cannot be readily converted into a fully automatic firearm, or any firearm declared as such by the Minister.[50] The Registrar may issue a license for a restricted firearm to any natural person if he or she can demonstrate that a license to possess a firearm for self-defense (see section C(1) above) "will not provide sufficient protection" and submits "reasonable information to motivate the need for a restricted firearm for self-defense purposes."[51]

A qualifying person can hold only one license for a restricted firearm for a two-year term, which can be renewed if the licensee continues to be in compliance with all applicable rules.[52]

3. License to Possess a Firearm for Occasional Hunting and Sport Shooting

In this category, the Registrar may issue a license for any handgun (which is not fully automatic) or a rifle or shotgun (which is not semi- or fully automatic) that is not a restricted firearm, or a barrel, frame, or receiver of any of these firearms.[53]

There are limitations on the number of licenses that may be issued in this class. Any natural person who is an occasional hunter or sports person is eligible for a maximum of four ten-year-term licenses.[54] The number of licenses that can be issued may be less depending on whether the applicant holds a license of a different class. For instance, an applicant who has a license to possess a firearm for self-defense can be issued a maximum of three licenses in this category.[55] In addition, an applicant cannot be licensed for more than one handgun.[56]

A license in this class is issued for a ten-year term and may be renewed if the licensee is in compliance with all the applicable rules.[57]

---

[49] *Id.* §§ 24 & 27.

[50] *Id.* § 14.

[51] *Id.*

[52] *Id.* §§ 14, 24 & 27.

[53] *Id.* § 15.

[54] *Id.*

[55] *Id.*

[56] *Id.* § 15.

[57] *Id.* §§ 24 & 27.

4. License to Possess Firearm for Dedicated Hunting and Dedicated Sports Shooting

The Registrar is authorized to license the following kinds of firearms in this category: a handgun, rifle, or shotgun that is not fully automatic; a semiautomatic shotgun with the capacity to fire a maximum of five shots before it has to be reloaded; or a barrel, frame, or receiver of any of these firearms.[58]

The FCA imposes certain requirements for applicants in this category. In order to be licensed, an applicant should be a member of an accredited hunting association or sport-shooting organization and the license application should include a sworn statement or a solemn declaration from a chairperson of the association or organization indicating that the applicant is a registered member.[59]

A license in this category is issued for a ten-year term and can be renewed if the licensee continues to be in compliance with all applicable requirements.[60]

5. License to Posses a Firearm in a Private Collection

Any firearm, including a prohibited firearm, can be licensed in this category.[61] However, the firearm must be one approved for collection by an accredited collectors association; the applicant must be a member of an accredited collectors association; and the license application must be accompanied by a sworn statement or solemn declaration from the chairperson of the association verifying the applicant's membership.[62] The firearm must be at least fifty years old and have an attribute of collectability that is of historical, cultural, artistic, technological, heritage, or scientific value.[63]

This type of license is issued for a ten-year term and may be renewed if the licensee is in compliance with all applicable requirements.[64]

---

[58] *Id.* § 16.

[59] *Id.*

[60] *Id.* §§ 24 & 27.

[61] *Id.* § 17.

[62] *Id.*

[63] FCA Regulations § 15. A prohibited firearm that does not meet the age and collectability standards may still be licensed if its production has been discontinued for at least ten years, and it will likely become of collectable interest from a historic, technological, scientific, heritage, educational, cultural, or artistic perspective; it is part of a commemorative issuance or limited edition; it will fit in as part of a demonstrable theme of future value, where the likelihood of such future value can be sufficiently demonstrated or motivated; it is proven or generally accepted to be associated with famous or infamous people or events; it is currently considered to be nationally or internationally scarce or rare for an acceptable reason; its design materials or method of manufacture are unusual or unique and of historic interest; it is a significantly valuable example of custom or one-off building by a well-known gunmaker or gunsmith; it is a prototype or part of a limited production run; it is a replica of a well-known historical firearm; or it is an investment-grade firearm or device of significant value. *Id.*

[64] FCA §§ 24 & 27.

Both the FCA and FCA Regulations impose rigorous safety requirements for holders of licenses in this category. A storage place is specified in every license, and the licensee is required to store the firearm at the specified place.[65] The licensee may put the firearm on public display provided that

(a) the firearm is unloaded;

(b) the firearm, if it is a handgun, is displayed in a lockable display cabinet; or

(c) where the firearm is on open display, it must be rendered inoperable by means of a secure locking device; or

(d) the firearm is securely attached to a non-portable structure on which, or in which, it is displayed by a metal attachment, chain, metal cable or similar device in such manner that the firearm cannot readily be removed; and

(e) the firearm is not displayed with, and is not readily accessible to, ammunition that can be discharged from it, except where such firearm or ammunition is displayed in a locked display cabinet or similar device.[66]

6. License to Posses a Firearm for Business Purposes

The Registrar may issue a license for any firearm other than a prohibited firearm to a security service provider who holds a firearms competency certificate,[67] or anyone accredited to provide training for use of firearms; to provide firearms for use in theatrical, film, or television production, to conduct a hunting business; or to be a game rancher.[68]

The FCA and FCA Regulations impose rigorous restrictions with regard to licensees providing firearms for use by other people. For instance, a person holding a license to possess a firearm for a business purpose can provide the firearm for use by another person only if it is for business use as specified in the license and the person carries valid official identification documents and a written authorization document issued by the holder of the license detailing the specifications of the firearm; its intended use and period of use; and the reason for its use and place of use.[69] The holder of a license in this category is required to keep a register of all firearms.[70]

The term of licenses issued in this category is five or ten years, depending on the specific type. Firearms licenses issued to a game rancher or to hunting businesses have a ten-year term,

---

[65] *Id.* § 17.

[66] FCA Regulations § 16.

[67] *Id.*

[68] FCA § 20. A prohibited firearm may be issued to a person accredited to provide firearms for use in theatrical, film, or television productions, but additional conditions apply. *Id.*

[69] FCA Regulations § 21.

[70] FCA § 20; FCA Regulations § 22.

whereas all other licenses are issued for a five-year term.[71] All licenses are eligible for renewal provided the applicant remains in compliance with all applicable requirements.[72]

7. Temporary Authorization to Possess a Firearm

A temporary authorization can be issued to anyone, including an alien.[73] Among other things, applicants are required to submit a written motivation for their use of the firearm, including information on steps they plan to take to ensure the safe custody of the firearm, and a declaration that they have the capability to ensure safe custody of the firearm.[74] An authorization of this kind is valid for "the firearm and period and specific use specified in the authorization."[75] The Registrar may require an applicant to complete any relevant training.[76]

D. Termination of a Firearms License

Any of the licenses discussed above may be terminated under certain circumstances. A license may terminate if the period of time for which it is issued expires, the holder of the license surrenders it, or if the license is cancelled under provisions of the FCA.[77] Significantly, it may be terminated if the holder of the license "becomes or is declared unfit to possess a firearm."[78]

A person may be declared unfit to posses a firearm by the Registrar. The Registrar may declare someone unfit if a final protection order has been issued against him or her under the Domestic Violence Act.[79] Before taking any action, the Registrar is required, among other things, to ensure that the person is afforded due time and opportunity to challenge the allegations made against him or her, as well as to request the appearance of and examine anyone who has made a statement against him or her.[80]

In addition, a conviction for certain crimes automatically renders a person unfit to possess a firearm unless the court that convicted the person says otherwise.[81]

---

[71] FCA § 27.

[72] *Id.* § 24.

[73] *Id.* § 21.

[74] FCA Regulations § 23.

[75] *Id.* § 24.

[76] *Id.*

[77] FCA § 28.

[78] *Id.*

[79] *Id.* § 102. Additional factors for declaring a person unfit have also been enacted although they have yet to take effect. Under these additional factors, a person may be declared unfit based on information provided under oath or affirmation that he has threatened to take his own life or the life of another person with a firearm or other weapon; he has mental problems, a propensity for violence, or a substance-abuse problem; he has failed to take the required steps to ensure the safekeeping of a firearm; or he has provided false or misleading information in response to any requirement under the FCA. *Id.*

[80] *Id.*

[81] *Id.* § 103.

If a person is declared unfit, all competency certificates, licenses, authorizations, and permits issued to him are automatically terminated and remain so even during an appeal process, if any.[82]   In this situation, a person is required to surrender any competency certificates, licenses, authorizations, and permits to the nearest police station immediately.[83]

E. Firearms Dealers

A person may not trade in firearms or ammunition without a license.[84]   In order to be issued a dealer's license, an applicant must be a "fit and proper person to trade in firearms."[85]   A dealer's license is issued for a one-year term and may be renewed if, among other things, the licensee continues to be in compliance with all applicable requirements.[86]   While a dealer's license is not transferrable, another person who has a competency certificate may engage in trade on behalf of a licensed dealer.[87]

There are various duties associated with a dealer's license. Dealers must follow specific record-keeping requirements and keep a register of every firearm and all ammunition they have in stock, regardless of the source, in a Firearms Stock Register and an Ammunition Stock Register.[88]   They must also keep a record in a separate Firearms Safe Custody Register of all the firearms they receive and hold on behalf of any licensee.[89]   Dealers are also required to establish a workstation linking all these registers to the central dealers' database established by the Registrar,[90] as well as make available for inspection by any police official any firearm or ammunition in stock, their dealer's license, and any register they keep.[91]   In addition, when

---

[82] Id. § 104.

[83] Id.

[84] Id. § 31.

[85] Id. § 32.

[86] Id. §§ 35 & 12. The term of a license in this class was extended from one to five years in 2006, however, the amending provision has yet to take effect.

[87] Id.; FCA Regulations § 31.

[88] FCA § 39; FCA Regulations § 37.

[89] FCA Regulations § 37.

[90] FCA § 39; FCA Regulations § 37. Section 40 of the FCA Regulations provides that the central database is to contain

> (a) the information and supporting documents submitted by an applicant on the prescribed form under regulation 13 regarding a competency certificate, dealer's licence, authorisation, renewal or copy thereof, as well as, the relevant information in respect of the suspension or termination thereof;
>
> (b) the information on a competency certificate, license, authorisation, permit and a renewal or copy thereof, that were issued or refused as a result of an application; and
>
> (c) the details and information submitted by a dealer in respect of the acquisition, transfer and disposal of a firearm or ammunition effected under the Act.

[91] FCA § 39.

approached by a holder of a license for possession of a prohibited firearm, dealers are required to seek and obtain a written confirmation from the Registrar before transferring such firearm.[92]

F. Safe Custody of Firearms

When license holders do not have their firearm on their person, they must store the firearm and its ammunition in a safe or a strong room that meets the requirements of the South African Bureau of Standards (SABS), standards 953-1 and 953-2.[93] The same requirement applies to dealers.[94]

A person who is licensed to possess a firearm may store a firearm licensed to another person if he or she obtains written permission from the person to whom the firearm is licensed, the authorization is endorsed by a relevant Designated Firearms Officer, and the firearm is stored in a safe that meets the above standards that is located at a place stipulated in the written permission.[95]

G. Firearm-free Zones

The FCA authorizes the Minister, in consultation with certain authorities, to declare any place to be a firearm-free zone if doing so is in the public interest and in accordance with the provisions of the FCA.[96] The FCA states that unless specifically permitted, no one may allow, carry, or store any firearm or ammunition in a firearm-free zone.[97]

The FCA gives police broad search and seizure powers in firearm-free zones. Police officials may conduct warrantless searches of any building or premise within a firearm-free zone if they have a "suspicion on reasonable ground" regarding the presence of a firearm or ammunition.[98] They may also search without a warrant any person in a firearm-free zone.[99] In addition, the police may seize any unauthorized firearm or ammunition in a firearm-free zone.[100]

Any owner or lawful occupier of any premise can apply to have the premise declared a firearm-free zone.[101] The application must include reasons for seeking the declaration,

---

[92] FCA Regulations § 31.

[93] *Id.* § 86; *see also* Peter Smith, *Safekeeping and the FCA: Safes and Strong Rooms and the Firearms Control Act*, SOUTH AFRICA ARMS AND AMMUNITION COLLECTORS ASSOCIATION – GAUTENG, http://www.saaaca. org.za/?page_id=833 (last updated Jan. 7, 2012).

[94] *Id.*

[95] FCA Regulations § 86; FCA § 124.

[96] FCA § 140.

[97] *Id.*

[98] *Id.*

[99] *Id.*

[100] *Id.*

[101] FCA Regulations § 109.

availability of the capacity to maintain the premise as a firearm-free zone, and a means for informing the public of the premise's status as a firearm-free zone.[102]

V. Offenses and Penalties

A. Under the FCA

Violation or failure to comply with the provisions of the FCA or the terms of a license, permit, or authorization is an offense.[103]

Failure to lock a firearm in a safe, strong room or device as required by law is an offense.[104] A person also commits an offense if he or she loses possession of a firearm by failing to take the necessary steps to ensure is safekeeping.[105]

The FCA also stipulates various offenses regarding the use of competency certificates, licenses, permits, or authorizations. It makes it an offense to fraudulently alter, use, or possess any fraudulently altered document.[106] It is also an offense to use any document issued to someone else or to allow the use of such document by another person.[107] In addition, it criminalizes supplying false information in any document required for submission under the FCA, or while acquiring any of these documents or filling out registers.[108]

Additionally, failure to report the loss, theft, or destruction of a firearm to the police is considered an offense, whether by the person licensed to possess the firearm or anyone who was in possession of the firearm when it was lost, stolen or destroyed.[109]

The FCA states that a person convicted of an offense under its provisions may be subject to a fine or imprisonment.[110] The maximum possible prison term for each offense is spelled out in great detail, the terms ranging from two to twenty-five years.[111] In addition, if the penalty stipulated for the offense in question is a fine or prison term of up to five years, additional administrative fines are imposed.[112]

---

[102] *Id.*

[103] FCA § 120.

[104] *Id.*

[105] *Id.*

[106] *Id.*

[107] *Id.*

[108] *Id.*

[109] *Id.*

[110] *Id.*

[111] *Id.* § 121.

[112] *Id.* §122.

B. Under the FCA Regulations

Anyone who violates or fails to comply with the FCA Regulations commits an offense.[113] Anyone who makes a false claim with regard to his or her accreditation or that of another person, or provides any false information while providing information required by the Regulations also commits an offense.[114] A conviction under the Regulations is punishable by a fine and/or imprisonment of up to one year.[115]

VI. Statistical Information

Before the FCA took effect in 2004, there were an estimated 4.5 million registered firearms in South Africa, of which around 3.5 million (78%) were held by individuals.[116] Around 190,000 licenses were issued annually from 1994 through 1999, and over 13,000 individuals had more than ten firearms to their name.[117] The years since 2004 have seen a drop in the number of legal firearms possessed, with a figure of 3.7 million registered firearms recorded in 2008.[118]

All the same, it appears that South Africa remains among the countries with the highest firearms circulation. A 2007 survey ranked South Africa seventeenth in the world in private firearms holdings.[119] At that time, in addition to registered firearms, the country had an estimated 500,000 to 4 million illegal firearms in circulation.[120] In comparison, the combined holdings of firearms by the police and army were said to be around 570,000.[121]

Before the FCA took effect, firearms-related crimes were very high. In 1994, 26,832 murders were committed, 11,134 of which involved firearms.[122] While the country saw a decline in overall murders from 1994 through 2000, there was an 8% increase in the number of firearms-related murders, from 41% of all murders in 1994 to 49% in 2000.[123] The number of

---

[113] FCA Regulations § 110.

[114] Id.

[115] Id.

[116] Robert Chetty, *Firearm Distribution in South Africa, in* FIREARM USE AND DISTRIBUTION IN SOUTH AFRICA 32, 33 (National Crime Prevention Centre, 2000).

[117] Id.

[118] KIRSTEN, *supra* note 13, at 4.

[119] Aaron Karp, *Completing the Count: Civilian Firearms, in* SMALL ARMS SURVEY 39, 47 (Graduate Institute of International Studies, 2007), http://www.smallarmssurvey.org/fileadmin/docs/A-Yearbook/2007/ en/full/ Small-Arms-Survey-2007-Chapter-02-EN.pdf.

[120] Id., Annexe 3; KIRSTEN, *supra* note 13, at 6.

[121] KIRSTEN, *supra* note 13, at 4.

[122] Id. at 6.

[123] Id.

crimes committed with firearms, which had accounted for 48% of all crimes in 1995–96, jumped to 63% by 1998.[124]

Accurate information on the distribution of and crimes committed with firearms after the FCA took effect in 2004 is difficult to obtain. This is in large part because the South African Police Service (SAPS) reportedly stopped releasing data on the subject in the early 2000s.[125] In addition, it appears that South Africa is still fine-tuning its firearms regulatory regime; the FCA has been implemented incrementally, and various key amendments made to it in 2006 took effect only recently, with more yet to come.[126]

Nevertheless, the limited number of sources located for this report suggest that there has been a general decline in firearms-related crimes since 2004. A recent statistical report issued by SAPS showed cases of illegal possession of firearms and ammunition exhibiting a slight decline. In 2004–2005, 15,497 cases of illegal possession of firearms and ammunition were reported, while in 2011–2012 the number of similar cases was down to 14,461.[127] Recent SAPS data also shows an overall decline in the prevalence of contact crimes (murder, attempted murder, sexual offenses, assault, robbery with aggravated circumstances, and common robbery) since 2004.[128] For instance, from 2003–2010, there was a marked downward trend in murders (with an 8.6% decrease) and attempted murders (which declined by 6.1%).[129] Since the FCA took effect, firearms-related offenses are said to have fallen by 21%.[130]

However, it appears that that the causal effect of the FCA on the decline in firearms-related crimes has yet to be established.[131]

Prepared by Hanibal Goitom
Foreign Law Specialist

---

[124] Stephen Burrow et al., *The Extent of Firearm Deaths and Injuries in South Africa, in* FIREARM USE AND DISTRIBUTION IN SOUTH AFRICA 51 (National Crime Prevention Centre, 2000).

[125] Tracy, *supra* note 13; KIRSTEN, *supra* note 13, at 6.

[126] *See* Commencement of Certain Provisions of the Firearms Control Amendment Act, 2006 (Act 28 of 2006), No. 77, 2010, GG, No. 33871 (Dec. 17, 2010), http://www.info.gov.za/view/DownloadFileAction?id=137369; *see also* Commencement of Certain Provisions of the Firearms Control Amendment Act, 2006 (Feb. 17, 2012). http://www.info.gov.za/view/DownloadFileAction?id=160124.

[127] *Illegal Possession of Firearms and Ammunition in RSA for April to March 2004/2005 to 2011/2012*, CRIME RESEARCH AND STATISTICS – SOUTH AFRICA POLICE SERVICE, http://www.saps.gov.za/ statistics/reports/crimestats/2012/categories/illegal_pos_firearm_ammunition.pdf.

[128] Lauren Tracy, *South Africa: Implementing The Firearms Control Act – A Complete Failure Or Work In Progress?*, INSTITUTE FOR SECURITY STUDIES (July 11, 2011), *available at* http://allafrica.com/stories/20110711 1819.html.

[129] *Id.*

[130] Ntombi Dyosop, *Did Gun Control Cause Fall in Gun Crime? The Data Backs the Claim*, AFRICA CHECK (Dec. 15, 2012), http://www.africacheck.org/reports/did-gun-control-cause-fall-in-gun-crime-the-data-backs-the-claim/.

[131] *Id.; see also* Tracy, *supra* note 13.

SPAIN

FIREARMS-CONTROL LEGISLATION AND POLICY

Summary

    The regulation of guns in Spain is highly restrictive. The bearing of arms by civilians is not considered a right but a privilege that may be granted by the government if legal conditions are met. Guns are regulated by the Ministry of the Interior through the General Directorate of the Civil Guard. Different types of licenses are required according to the type of weapon to be used. Firearms licenses for personal security are restricted to those who can prove that a real danger to their security exists. Automatic weapons are strictly forbidden to civilians.

I. Introduction

Although the Spanish Constitution does not include an explicit prohibition on the possession of firearms by individuals,[1] the law on firearms is extremely restrictive.[2] There has always been unanimous consent by Spanish society that possession of firearms should be strictly limited and considered an exceptional privilege granted to those who need it because of the nature of their duties, because of extreme circumstances of self-protection, or for the practice of sports, such as hunting or sports shooting.[3]

The Spanish Constitution does not conceive of the right to bear arms as an individual right. In Spain as well as in Europe in general (with the exception of Switzerland), the organization of the state is based on a model of professional armed police forces within the administration of the state, who are the persons in charge of providing security to the population. Individuals are not expected to provide for their own security.[4]

II. Legal Framework on Firearms

The Constitution has reserved to the state the exclusive competence on issues related to the production, trade, possession, and use of firearms and explosives.[5] In furtherance of this

---

[1] CONSTITUCIÓN ESPAÑOLA [C.E.] [SPANISH CONSTITUTION], Dec. 27, 1978, BOLETÍN OFICIAL DEL ESTADO [B.O.E.], Dec. 29, 1978, http://www.boe.es/buscar/act.php?id=BOE-A-1978-31229.

[2] ROSER MARTÍNEZ QUIRANTE, ARMAS: LIBERTAD AMERICANA O PREVENCIÓN EUROPEA? 190 (Ariel Derecho, Barcelona, 2002).

[3] *Id.* at 191.

[4] *Id.*

[5] C.E. art. 149.1.26.

constitutional principle, the Ley Orgánica sobre la Protección de la Seguridad Ciudadana (LOPSC) (Law on the Protection of the Security of the Citizenry)[6] regulates activities related to firearms and explosives, empowering the state to intervene in matters related to the manufacturing, sale, possession, and use of firearms, and includes penalties for violations of the regulations.[7] The LOPSC establishes the restrictive character of the issuance of administrative licenses or permits for the use of firearms, especially when a permit is issued for self-defense, which is limited to instances of extreme necessity.[8] It also empowers the government to regulate the prohibition of specific firearms, ammunition, and explosives that are especially dangerous, as well as their storage.[9]

Reaffirming the principle that public security is provided only by the state,[10] the Ley de Fuerzas y Cuerpos de Seguridad (Law on Security Forces)[11] assigns to the Ministry of Interior through the Guardia Civil (Civil Guard)[12] jurisdiction over matters involving firearms and explosives.[13]

The restrictions on the possession of firearms by individuals and the state's exclusive role with regard to firearms regulation is clearly reflected in the Ley de Seguridad Privada (Law on Private Security),[14] which provides that the security of the population is guaranteed by the public authorities.[15] Not even private security guards may use firearms to perform their duties, except for security guards in charge of the protection of the storage, classification, and transportation of money and other valuables, the protection and surveillance of factories, and storage or transportation of firearms and explosives, or those guarding hazardous facilities or establishments located in isolated areas.[16] The types of firearms to be used while carrying out private security services are determined by the Law on Private Security and may be used exclusively while performing those duties.[17]

---

[6] Ley Orgánica 1/1992 sobre Protección de la Seguridad Ciudadana [Law on the Protection of the Security of the Citizenry] arts. 6 & 7, B.O.E. Feb. 22, 1992, http://www.boe.es/buscar/act.php?id=BOE-A-1992-4252&tn=1&p=20061122#cii.

[7] MARTÍNEZ QUIRANTE, *supra* note 2, at 199.

[8] Ley Orgánica 1/1992, art. 7.1.b.

[9] *Id.* art. 7.1.c.

[10] *Id.* art. 1.1

[11] Ley Orgánica 2/1986, de Fuerzas y Cuerpos de Seguridad [Law on Security Forces] art. 1.1, B.O.E. Mar. 14, 1986, http://www.boe.es/buscar/act.php?id=BOE-A-1986-6859.

[12] The Guardia Civil is a federal police force with quasi-military status.

[13] Ley Orgánica 2/1986, art. 12.1.B.a.

[14] Ley 23/1992 de Seguridad Privada [Law on Private Security], B.O.E Aug. 4, 1992, http://www.boe.es/buscar/act.php?id=BOE-A-1992-18489.

[15] *Id.*, *Exposición de Motivos*, Apartado III.2.

[16] *Id.* art. 14.1.

[17] *Id.* art. 14.2.

However, the backbone of the legal framework on firearms is the 1993 Reglamento de Armas (R.A.) (Regulation on Firearms),[18] which transposed European Union Directive 91/477/CEE on firearms[19] to domestic law and implemented the LOPSC.[20] The R.A. was recently amended by Royal Decree 976/2011[21] to transpose Directive 2008/51/CE of the European Parliament on the control of the acquisition and possession of firearms.[22]

The R.A. provides for the comprehensive and detailed treatment of firearms, and includes requirements for manufacturing, possession, circulation, storage, and trade of firearms by private individuals. It does not apply to firearms used by the armed forces, police, or security forces but does apply to the privately-held weapons of these individuals.[23]

The R.A. classifies firearms as follows:

Table 1: *Firearms Categories*[24]	
Category 1 and 2	Short firearms and long firearms with rifled barrels
Category 3	Long firearms with rifled barrels for sports shooting, shotguns, air guns with muzzle energy in excess of 24.2 joules.
Category 4 and 5	Compressed air rifles and pistols, edged weapons, and knives or machetes
Category 6	Antique or historic firearms
Category 7	Crossbows, bows, blank firing guns, and flare guns.

---

[18] Real Decreto 137/1993 sobre Reglamento de Armas [R.A.] [Regulation on Firearms], B.O.E. Mar. 5, 1993, http://www.boe.es/buscar/act.php?id=BOE-A-1993-6202.

[19] Council Directive 91/477/EEC of 18 June 1991 on the Control of the Acquisition and Possession of Weapons, 1991 O.J. (L 256) 51, http://eur-lex.europa.eu/LexUriServ/LexUriServ.do?uri=CELEX:31991L0477:EN:HTML.

[20] *See* MARTÍNEZ QUIRANTE, *supra* note 2, at 201.

[21] Real Decreto 976/2011 que Modifica el Reglamento de Armas [Royal Decree 976/2011, Amending the Regulation on Firearms], B.O.E. July 9, 2011, http://www.boe.es/buscar/doc.php?id=BOE-A-2011-11778.

[22] Council Directive 2008/51/CE of 21 May 2008 amending Council Directive 91/477/EEC of 18 June 1991 on the Control of the Acquisition and Possession of Weapons, 2008 O.J. (L 179) 5–11, http://eur-lex.europa.eu/LexUriServ/LexUriServ.do?uri=OJ:L:2008:179:0005:0011:EN:PDF.

[23] MARTÍNEZ QUIRANTE, *supra* note 2, at 201.

[24] R.A. art. 3.

III. Licensing Requirements

The minimum age for gun ownership in Spain is eighteen years. However, minors between fourteen and eighteen years old may be granted a special permit to use arms for hunting or sports shooting competitions by (1) submitting criminal background checks of both the minor and his parent or legal representative, (2) holding a permit issued to the parent or legal representative to use the type of firearms to be used by the minor, and (3) submitting a physical and mental aptitude report.[25]

Only licensed gun owners are allowed to lawfully acquire, possess, or transfer a firearm or ammunition,[26] and may only have ammunition that is suitable for the intended firearm.[27] Applicants for a gun owner's license are required to prove that they have a genuine reason to possess a firearm—for example, hunting, target shooting, collection, self-defense, or security.[28]

In order to obtain a firearms license, the applicant must submit to the Guardia Civil firearms section of his domicile an updated criminal background check and certification of good behavior, a photocopy of the applicant's original identity card or residency card, and a report on the applicant's "psychophysical aptitude."[29] The aptitude test is conducted in designated medical facilities, whose physicians send a final report to the competent authorities of the Guardia Civil.[30] The background checks include consideration of domestic violence records,[31] and the applicant must undergo theoretical and practical training and testing to ensure an understanding of firearms safety and applicable legal requirements.[32]

The R.A. identifies nine types of firearms licenses:

---

[25] MARTÍNEZ QUIRANTE, *supra* note 2, at 234.

[26] R.A. art. 96.

[27] Id.

[28] *Id.* arts. 96–99.

[29] *Id.* art. 96.

[30] Royal Decree 2487/1998 provides a detailed regulation on the psychophysical aptitude test requirements and procedures. Real Decreto 2487/1998 Por el que se Regula la Acreditación de la Aptitud Psicofísica Necesaria para Tener y Usar Armas y para Prestar Servicios de Seguridad Privada [Royal Decree 2487/1999 Regulating the Verification of the Psychophysical Aptitude Needed for the Possession and Use of Firearms and for the Rendering of Private Security Services], B.O.E. Dec. 3, 1998, http://www.boe.es/buscar/doc.php?id=BOE-A-1998-27866.

[31] MARTÍNEZ QUIRANTE, *supra* note 2, at 230–36.

[32] Orden del 27 de Marzo de 1998 por la que se Regulan las Pruebas de Capacitación para Obtener Determinadas Licencias de Armas y los Requisitos para la Habilitación de Entidades Dedicadas a la Enseñanza Correspondiente [Order of March 27, 1998, Regulating the Training Tests for Obtaining Certain Firearms Licenses and the Requirements for Training Entities Permits], B.O.E. Mar. 31, 1998, http://www.boe.es/buscar/act.php?id=BOE-A-1998-7416.

Table 2: Firearms Licenses[33]	
License A	For members of the armed forces, police, or civil guard. Valid only during the active service of the holder, allowing him to use all categories of weapons. Equivalent to all other licenses available.[34]
License B	For individuals, for self-protection purposes.[35] Only gives the right to have one category 1 firearm (see *Table 1, Firearms Categories*, above). Valid for three years for holders sixty years of age or younger, two years for holders between sixty and seventy years old, and one year for those above seventy.[36]
License C	For security guards. License valid only during the holder's service; photo ID must be renewed every five years. Firearms from categories 1, 2, and 3 are allowed under this license.
License D	For big game hunting (*caza mayor*). License lasts five years for holders sixty years of age or younger and two years for holders between sixty and seventy years old. Permit allows up to five firearms from category 2.2 (full bore rifles). Weapons must be locked in a safe.[37]
License E	For small game hunting (*caza menor*). Has same expiration terms as License D. Allows up to six category 3.1 firearms (including a) FAC-rated air gun), up to six firearms from category 3.2 (shotguns), up to twelve firearms from category 3.3 (FAC-rated air guns), up to twelve firearms from category 7.2 (crossbows), and up to twelve firearms from category 7.3 (line-launching guns). The total number of weapons under this class may not exceed twelve.[38]
License F	For members of the Federations of Shooting Sports. Valid for three years. Only hunting arms are allowed under this permit. License holder entitled to between one and ten arms depending on the shooter class. Limited to shooting ranges. Firearms must be stored unloaded in the shooters' house or at a shooting club.[39]
License AE	Special permit for individuals to use firearms from category 6 (muzzle loaders) and category 7.4 (Flobert system pistols). Valid for five years. No limit on the number of arms that may be held under this license. Guns must be used exclusively on approved shooting ranges.

---

[33] R.A. arts. 96–97, 103.

[34] *Id.* art. 97.

[35] *Id.* art. 99.

[36] *Id.* art. 104.

[37] *Id.* art. 100.

[38] *Id.* art. 101.

[39] *Id.* art. 96.

License L	Collectors' license for individuals. Firearms from categories 6a and 7a.4 are allowed under this license. No expiration date and no restriction on the number of arms that may be held under this license. These guns may not be fired.
License AEM	Special authorization for the use of firearms by minors between the ages of fourteen and seventeen. Expires when the child turns eighteen years old. Limited to firearms from categories 2 or 3 and requires the supervision of a license holder. Arms may only be used for hunting or competing in junior class competitions or sports events. The minor may use the arms according to the license but not possess or carry them. This license is subject to detailed regulation, especially with regard to qualifications of supervising adult and required training.[40]

IV. Prohibited Firearms

Private individuals are not allowed to possess automatic firearms, firearms disguised as other objects, or armor-piercing, incendiary, or expanding ammunition.[41] The private possession, advertising, sale, and use of semiautomatic assault weapons and handguns, including pistols and revolvers, are permitted only with special authorization.[42]

The R.A. prohibits the acquisition, possession, or use by civilians of firearms designed for war use. These include fully automatic weapons, firearms with a caliber of 20 mm or higher, and all those considered to be firearms for war use by the Ministry of Defense.[43]

V. Record Keeping Requirements

The General Directorate of the Guardia Civil is in charge of maintaining a registry of individual civilians licensed to acquire, possess, sell, or transfer firearms or ammunition, as well as records of the acquisition, possession, and transfer of those weapons.[44]

Licensed firearm dealers are required, on behalf of the regulating authority, to keep a record of each firearm or piece of ammunition purchased, sold, or transferred. It is illegal to deal in firearms as a business without a gun dealer's license.[45]

---

[40] *Id.* art. 109.

[41] *Id.* art. 4.

[42] *Id.* art. 5.

[43] *Id.* art. 6, *as amended by* Real Decreto 1628/2009 por el que se Modifican determinados preceptos del Reglamento de Seguridad Privada y del R.A. [Royal Decree 1628/2009 Modifying Certain Provisions of the Regulation on Private Security and the R.A.], B.O.E. Oct. 31, 2009, http://www.boe.es/buscar/doc.php?id=BOE-A-2009-17245.

[44] R.A. arts. 8.3 & 52–53.

[45] *Id.* art. 10.2.

VI. Safety and Tracking Requirements

Firearms must be kept in safe, locked, and secure storage. The regulations provide for specific measures and requirements for storage while a firearm is in the personal dwelling of its owner or in transit.[46]

Firearm owners must be in control of their weapons at all times.[47] The loss, theft, or destruction of firearms must be reported immediately to the competent authorities.[48] Weapons must be carried from their permanent storage to a shooting range in a secured case and uncocked.[49]

Firearms must also be marked with a unique identifying mark when manufactured, to allow them to be traced and tracked according to the procedures established in the R.A.[50]

VII. Penalties

The R.A. provides for administrative sanctions and fines for violations of its provisions,[51] and the Penal Code[52] establishes a number of crimes related to firearms, including criminal penalties for those who possess or carry illegal weapons or carry weapons without the proper license or authorization.[53]

VIII. Statistics

According to the 2011 annual statistics of the Ministry of Interior,[54] 2,119,942 firearms licenses had been issued in Spain as of December 31, 2011, for a total of 3,516,681 firearms.[55] In 2011, there were 288 deaths caused by firearms. As of July 2011, Spain had a population of 47 million. The rate of deaths by firearms is 0.63 per 100,000 people according to a 2010 report.[56]

---

[46] *Id.* arts. 100.5, 144.a.

[47] *Id.* art. 147.

[48] *Id.* art. 144.c.

[49] *Id.* art. 149.1.

[50] *Id.* arts. 28–30.

[51] *Id.* arts. 155–164.

[52] CÓDIGO PENAL [C.P.] [CRIMINAL CODE], Ley Orgánica 10/1995, Nov. 23, 1995, B.O.E. Nov. 24, 1995, http://www.boe.es/buscar/act.php?id=BOE-A-1995-25444&tn=1&p=20121228#a563.

[53] *Id.* arts. 563–570.

[54] ANUARIO ESTADÍSTICO DEL MINISTERIO DEL INTERIOR 2011 [2011 YEARBOOK OF STATISTICS OF THE MINISTRY OF INTERIOR] 233–37, http://www.interior.gob.es/file/58/58114/58114.pdf.

[55] *Id.* at 234.

[56] For more detailed statistics, *see Spain – Gun Facts, Figures, and the Law*, GUNPOLICY.ORG, http://www.gunpolicy.org/firearms/region/spain (last visited Jan. 24, 2012). Gunpolicy.org, an international bulletin based in Sydney, Australia, includes detailed statistics on gun-related deaths with the latest figures from 2009 and 2010.

The following is a table from the book *Armas: Libertad Americana O Prevención Europea?* (*Arms: American Freedom or European Prevention*) showing the comparative rate per 100,000 persons of death by firearms in the US and Spain for the period 1990–2000:[57]

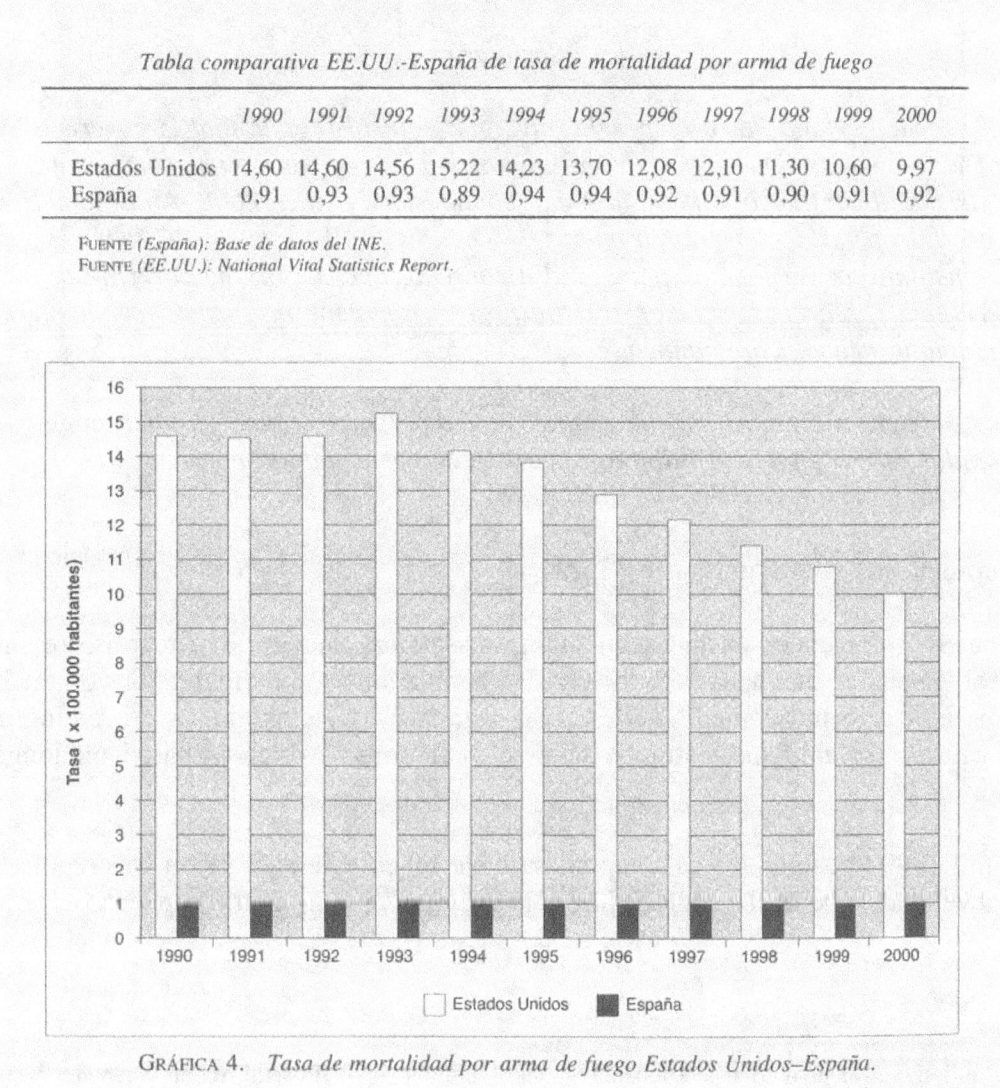

Tabla comparativa EE.UU.-España de tasa de mortalidad por arma de fuego

	1990	1991	1992	1993	1994	1995	1996	1997	1998	1999	2000
Estados Unidos	14,60	14,60	14,56	15,22	14,23	13,70	12,08	12,10	11,30	10,60	9,97
España	0,91	0,93	0,93	0,89	0,94	0,94	0,92	0,91	0,90	0,91	0,92

FUENTE *(España): Base de datos del INE.*
FUENTE *(EE.UU.): National Vital Statistics Report.*

GRÁFICA 4. *Tasa de mortalidad por arma de fuego Estados Unidos–España.*

Prepared by Graciela Rodriguez-Ferrand
Senior Foreign Law Specialist

---

[57] MARTÍNEZ QUIRANTE, *supra* note 2, at 318. Reproduced by permission of the publisher.

SWITZERLAND

FIREARMS CONTROL LEGISLATION AND POLICY

Summary

Switzerland has a comprehensive gun-control regime that is governed by federal law and implemented by the cantons. This regime may be somewhat less restrictive than that of other European countries, yet since 2008 it has complied with European Union requirements. The Swiss Weapons Act requires an acquisition license for handguns and a carrying license for the carrying of any permitted firearm for defensive purposes. Exceptions exist for hunters. Automatic weapons are banned.

Swiss militiamen may keep their issued personal weapon in their home. A popular referendum to prohibit this practice was rejected in February 2011.

I. Development of Swiss Gun-control Law

The Swiss practices on the acquisition, possession, and use of firearms are shaped by gun-control legislation that applies to the civilian population[1] and by regulations on the handling of firearms issued to militiamen.[2] These two regulatory systems aim at preventing abuse of firearms while upholding the statutory right to bear arms,[3] which is based on longstanding Swiss traditions.[4]

Until 1999, the handling of weapons suitable for private possession was regulated at the cantonal level and some of the cantons had very permissive gun-control regimes.[5] The cantonal

---

[1] Bundesgesetz über Waffen, Waffenzubehör und Munition [WG] [Federal Act on Weapons, Weapons Accessories and Ammunition], June 20, 1997, as amended, SYSTEMATISCHE SAMMLUNG DES BUNDESRECHTS [SR] 514.54, http://www.admin.ch/ch/d/sr/c514_54.html.

[2] Verordnung des VBS über die persönliche Ausrüstung der Armeeangehörigen [VPAA-VBS] [Defense Department Regulation on the Personal Equipment of Members of the Army], Dec. 9, 2003, as amended, SR 514.101, http://www.admin.ch/ch/d/sr/c514_101.html. The Swiss militia system is discussed in Part III, below.

[3] WG art. 3 provides that "the right to acquire, possess, and carry weapons is guaranteed within the framework of this Act" (translated by author). The federation has legislative power to prevent the abuse of weapons. Bundesverfassung [BV] [Constitution] art. 107, *translation at* http://www.admin.ch/ch/e/rs/c101.html.

[4] HANS WÜST, SCHWEIZER WAFFENRECHT 16 (1999).

[5] Frank Csaszar, *Waffenrecht und Schusswaffenkriminalität*, ÖSTERREICHISCHE RICHTERZEITUNG 180 (1994).

laws were held together loosely by an intercantonal Weapons Concordat that allowed Switzerland to have the most permissive policy on gun control in all of Europe.[6]

Until the late 1980s, this lack of uniformity in gun control worked well for Switzerland. Crime rates were low and the Swiss were comfortable with private gun ownership because of the militia system. In the early 1990s, however, the crime rate increased, and Swiss guns were frequently implicated in the European terrorist scene and in the wars that ravaged former Yugoslavia. These circumstances led to a climate of domestic and international pressure that persuaded the Swiss to abandon their *laissez faire* attitude toward firearms and start the cumbersome legislative process of enacting a federal weapons law.[7]

The first federal gun-control law (hereinafter the Weapons Act) became effective in Switzerland on January 1, 1999.[8] As originally enacted, the Weapons Act brought a gun-control regime that was similar to the gun-control laws of neighboring countries, albeit less restrictive. Between 2004 and 2010, several amendments made the Weapons Act more stringent.

A significant revision was occasioned by Switzerland's accession to the Schengen Agreement, the common border regime of the European Union (EU).[9] This Revision of the Act[10] became effective on December 12, 2008, the day of Switzerland's accession to the Schengen regime,[11] and its primary purpose was the transposition of the European Union's Weapons Directive[12] into Swiss law.[13] Among these newly enacted measures was the introduction of the European Firearms Pass.[14] Although Switzerland is not an EU Member State, it has close ties with the EU and many of its laws are harmonized with EU law.[15]

---

[6] *Id.*

[7] Bericht der Sicherheitspolitische Kommission des Nationalrats, Oct. 16, 1992, BUNDESBLATT [BBL.] 625 (1993).

[8] Bundesgesetz über Waffen, Waffenzubehör und Munition, June 20, 1997, AMTLICHE SAMMLUNG DES BUNDESRECHTS [AS] 2535 (1998).

[9] Council Decision (1999/435/EC) of 20 May 1999 concerning the definition of the Schengen *acquis* for the purpose of determining, in conformity with the relevant provisions of the Treaty establishing the European Community and the Treaty on European Union, the legal basis for each of the provisions or decisions which constitute the *acquis*, 1999 O.J. (L 176) 1, http://eur-lex.europa.eu/LexUriServ/LexUriServ.do?uri=CELEX:31 999D0435:EN:HTML, valid for Switzerland since Dec. 12, 2008. *See* Eidgenössisches Justizdepartement, Schengen, http://www.bfm.admin.ch/content/bfm/de/home/themen/schengen_dublin/schengen.html (last modified Oct. 27, 2011).

[10] Bundesbeschluss, Dec. 17, 2004, art. 3 no. 6, AS 447 (2008), http://www.admin.ch/ch/d/as/2008/447.pdf.

[11] Verordnung, Nov. 26, 2008, AS 5405.

[12] Council Directive 91/477/EEC of 18 June 1991 on the control of the acquisition and possession of weapons, 1991 O.J. (L 256) 51, http://eur-lex.europa.eu/LexUriServ/LexUriServ.do?uri=CELEX:31991L0477:EN: HTML.

[13] Botschaft, Jan. 11, 2006, no. 1.4.4, BBL. 2713 (2006).

[14] Council Directive 91/477/EEC of 18 June 1991 on the control of the acquisition and possession of weapons, 1991 O.J. (L 256) 51, Annex II, http://eur-lex.europa.eu/LexUriServ/LexUriServ.do?uri=CELEX:31991 L0477:EN:HTML.

[15] CHRISTIAN H. KÄLIN, SWITZERLAND, BUSINESS & INVESTMENT HANDBOOK 65–76 (3rd ed. 2011).

After several incidents in which militiamen killed themselves or others with the issued weapons, reforms were also proposed for a Regulation that allows members of the Swiss militia to keep their assigned personal weapon in their home.[16] In 2010, this Regulation was amended to allow members of the militia to voluntarily deposit their issued firearm in an armory.[17]

On February 13, 2011, a popular referendum was held on a proposal that would have made Swiss gun-control laws stricter in several ways. The proposal called for an end to the practice of letting militiamen keep their weapons at home. In addition, it proposed that gun registration should be carried out by the federation instead of the cantons, and that for a weapons acquisition license, the applicant would have to prove a need for the weapon and the skill and knowledge to handle it.[18]

The Swiss Parliament and the Federal Cabinet advised against the referendum on the grounds that the existing laws were sufficient to protect against gun abuse.[19] The referendum was rejected by 56.3% of those voting, and the voter participation of 49.1% was high as compared to other referenda.[20] It remains to be seen whether the Swiss will change their mind on tougher gun-control laws in the wake of the Daillon massacre of January 3, 2013 in the Canton of Valais, when a thirty-four-year-old militiaman went on a shooting spree, killing three women and wounding two men with his militia weapon.[21] For starters, the incident led to a parliamentary motion urging the Federal Cabinet to create an effective linkage between the cantonal weapons registers.[22]

In September 2012, the Swiss Federal Cabinet recommended a package of measures to the Parliament in response to a parliamentary request for a study on how gun control could be improved.[23] These included the following:

---

[16] Martin Furrer, *Heute wird die Ordonnanz-Waffen Initiative eingereicht*, TAGES-ANZEIGER 1 (Feb. 23, 2009).

[17] Verordnung des VBS über die persönliche Ausrüstung der Armeeangehörigen [VPAA-VBS] [Defense Department Regulation on the Personal Equipment of Members of the Army], Dec. 9, 2003, art. 35a, SR 514.101, as introduced by Verordnung, Dec. 2, 2009, AS 6735 (2009).

[18] Volksinitiative "Für den Schutz vor Waffengewalt", http://www.bj.admin.ch/content/ejpd/de/home/doku mentation/abstimmungen/2011-02-13.html (last modified May 1, 2012).

[19] Press Release, Eidgenössisches Justizdepartement, Bundesrat lehnt Volksinitiative "Für den Schutz vor Waffengewalt" ab (Dec. 16, 2009), http://www.ejpd.admin.ch/content/ejpd/de/home/dokumentation/mi/2009/2009-12-16.html.

[20] *Id.*

[21] *Daillon Tragedy Brings Gun-control into Focus*, SWISSINFO.CH (Jan. 4, 2013), http://www.swissinfo. ch/ger/ politik_schweiz/Bluttat_mit_politischen_Folgen.html?cid=34647320.

[22] *Von der Steinzeit bis zur Eiszeit*, NEUE ZÜRCHER ZEITUNG (Jan. 25, 2013), http://www.nzz.ch/aktuell/ schweiz/von-der-steinzeit-zum-e-formular-1.17959622.

[23] Bericht des Bundesrates, Sept. 5, 2012, http://www.bj.admin.ch/content/dam/data/pressemitteilung/2012/ 2012-09-050/ber-br-d.pdf.

- The military leadership should be informed if, in the course of a pending criminal investigation, it becomes apparent that a member of the militia may endanger himself or others with a weapon.

- The Code of Criminal Procedure should be amended to facilitate such communications.

- The cantonal police should seize weapons as instructed by the courts or prosecutors, or by acting on their own decision in case of an imminent danger.

- The sharing of information from federal databases on denials of weapons licenses and criminal records should be facilitated.

- Cantonal and federal databases with pertinent information for cantonal weapons licenses should be linked.

II. Statistics

On the occasion of the 2011 gun-control referendum, the Swiss Federal Police compiled statistics on gun-related crimes.[24] These showed that during 2009 the police investigated 236 homicides, of which 55 were allegedly committed with a gun.[25] During the same year, 524 aggravated batteries were reported, 11 of which involved gun use, and 3530 robberies were reported, of which 416 were committed with a gun.[26] Switzerland has a population of 7.9 million.[27]

The Swiss Statistical Office prepared a chart that lists the number of deaths caused by guns during the years 1995 through 2010.[28] According to these figures, 70 to 90% of the reported deaths were suicides. The figures also show a gradual decrease of deaths by gun use from an overall number of 444 deaths in 1998 to 241 deaths in 2010. The Statistical Office also stated that 17% of all suicides reported in 2009 were committed with a gun, and that 9% of the suicides committed with a gun were committed with a military weapon.[29]

Until recently, Switzerland had a reputation for combining high levels of gun ownership with a low incidence of mass shootings.[30] This reputation, however, has been marred by the recent shooting rampage in Dainnon.[31]

---

[24] BUNDESAMT FÜR STATISTIC, TATMITTEL SCHUSSWAFFE (Dec. 2010), *available at* http://www.bfs.admin.ch/bfs/portal/de/index/themen/ 19/03/02/dos/03.html.

[25] *Id.* (click on Excel spreadsheet "Tatmittel Schusswaffe 2009").

[26] *Id.*

[27] *Switzerland Population*, INDEX MUNDI, http://www.indexmundi.com/switzerland/population.html (last visited Dec. 21, 2012).

[28] BUNDESAMT FÜR STATISTIC, *supra* note 24 (click on "Schusswaffentodesfälle 1995-2010").

[29] BUNDESAMT FÜR STATISTIC, SCHUSSWAFFENSUIZIDE (Jan. 14, 2011), *available at* http://www.bfs.admin.ch/bfs/portal/de/index/news/03.html (click on "Schusswaffensuizide Stellungnahme BFS").

[30] *In Aftermath of Swiss Shooting, Echoes of U.S. Gun-control Debate*, THE WASHINGTON POST (Feb. 7, 2013), http://www.washingtonpost.com/world/europe/in-aftermath-of-swiss-shooting-echoes-of-us-gun-control-debate/2013/02/07/38457624-6e1d-11e2-ac36-3d8d9dcaa2e2_story.html.

III. The Militia System

In Switzerland, military service is compulsory for all able-bodied men, and alternative civil service is only available for conscientious objectors. Those unwilling to serve must pay a fine.[32] Conscription begins at age nineteen,[33] and the duty to serve ends between the ages of thirty-four and fifty, depending on the rank of the militiaman.[34]

Militiamen are issued personal equipment, which includes a personal weapon and ammunition.[35] The militiaman is authorized to keep the weapon in his home,[36] unless he decides to deposit it in his unit's armory.[37] When the militiaman retires, he may keep the personal weapon,[38] provided it has been properly maintained by the qualified technicians of his military unit.[39]

If there is danger of the abuse or improper handling or maintenance of the weapon, the commandant of the military unit will confiscate the personal weapon.[40] The police, courts, and prosecutors may inform the commandant of circumstances that call for the confiscation of the weapon.[41] The abuse or mishandling of weapons is punishable either by a disciplinary measure or by imprisonment or a fine, depending on the circumstances.[42]

IV. Current Gun-control Law

A. Overview

The Weapons Act contains a comprehensive regime for the licensing of the acquisition and carrying of permitted weapons; the banning of certain weapons, including automatic firearms; and the production and trade in weapons, including the reporting obligations of dealers and a registration system that covers all privately owned guns, including those acquired by inheritance, but not including hunting rifles. The federal Weapons Act is implemented by the cantons and the cantons also keep registers of privately owned guns. The provisions on

---

[31] *See supra* notes 21 and 22, and accompanying text.

[32] BV art. 59.

[33] Militärgesetz, Feb. 3, 1995, as amended, art. 9, SR 510.10, http://www.admin.ch/ch/d/sr/c510_10.html.

[34] *Id.* art. 12.

[35] Verordnung SR 514.101 arts. 1–7.

[36] *Id.* art. 30.

[37] *Id.* art. 26.

[38] *Id.* art. 44.

[39] *Id.* art. 44 in conjunction with art. 12.

[40] *Id.* arts. 7, 35–36.

[41] *Id.*

[42] Militärstrafgesetz art. 72 SR 321.0.

ammunition are in keeping with the principles of the Act, which aims to deter abuse while permitting lawful gun ownership.[43]

B. Acquisition of Guns

An acquisition license is required primarily for handguns. Rifles and semiautomatic long arms that are customarily used by recreational hunters are exempt from the licensing requirement,[44] whereas fully automatic guns are banned.[45] An applicant for a weapons license must be at least eighteen years of age, may not have been placed under guardianship, may not give cause for suspicion that he would endanger himself or others with the weapon, and may not have a criminal record with a conviction for a violent crime or of several convictions for nonviolent crimes.[46] The license is issued by the canton of residence of the applicant but is valid throughout Switzerland. The license is valid for six months, maximally nine months.[47] It is usually valid for the acquisition of one weapon only.[48]

The acquisition license is required only if a weapon is acquired from a dealer. No license is required for transactions between private individuals. Instead, these are permitted as long as the seller verifies the identity and age of the buyer by checking an official identification document and as long as he has no reason to believe that the buyer has been or should be disqualified from gun ownership. The buyer may ascertain these circumstances by requesting information from the cantonal authorities, but only if the buyer consents in writing.[49]

C. Carrying of Guns

The carrying of a gun for defensive purposes requires a carrying license, which will be granted only if the applicant is qualified to acquire guns; demonstrates a need for the weapon to protect himself, others, or property against existing dangers; and has passed an exam to test his required theoretical knowledge and practical skill.[50] The theoretical exam tests knowledge of

- criminal provisions on violent crimes and self-defense, and necessity as a justification or excuse;

- federal and cantonal weapons law provisions;

- types of weapons and ammunition; and

---

[43] BUNDESAMT FÜR POLIZEI FEDPOL, SCHWEIZERISCHES WAFFENRECHT (July 2010), http://www.bj.admin. ch/content/dam/data/sicherheit/waffen/Brosch%c3%bcre/waffenbroschuere-d.pdf.

[44] Weapons Act art. 10.

[45] *Id.* art. 4.

[46] *Id.* art. 8(2).

[47] *Id.* art. 9.

[48] *Id.* art. 9b.

[49] *Id.* art. 10a.

[50] Reglement über die Prüfung für die Waffentragbewilligung [Regulations on the Examination for the Weapons-Carrying License], Sept. 21, 1998, as amended, SR 514.546.1.

- security measures and proper conduct when carrying weapons.[51]

The practical examination tests the applicant's skill in handling the weapon, including loading, unloading, operating the safety device, and shooting.[52]

A carrying license permits the concealed carrying of a handgun.[53] No carrying license is required for the transporting of an unloaded weapon for legitimate purposes, such as travel to and from the shooting range or hunting environment, as long as the ammunition is kept separate from the weapon.[54]

Prepared by Edith Palmer, Chief,
Foreign, Comparative, and
International Law Division II
February 2013

---

[51] *Id.* art. 3.

[52] *Id.* art. 4.

[53] *Id.* art. 27.

[54] *Id.* art. 28.

EUROPEAN UNION

FIREARMS-CONTROL LEGISLATION AND POLICY

Summary

At the European Union level, acquisition and possession of weapons and related matters are regulated by two Directives: (1) Directive 91/477/EEC and (2) Directive 2008/51/EC. These Directives are designed to ensure control of acquisition and possession of weapons, facilitate the flow of firearms in a single market, and transpose into EU law the United Nations Protocol Against the Illicit Manufacturing and Trafficking of Firearms. Both Directives contain minimum requirements; EU Members are free to impose more stringent rules pertaining to firearms and many have done so.

Under Directive 91/477/EEC firearms are classified into four categories based on their level of dangerousness: (1) prohibited, (2) subject to authorization, (3) subject to declaration, and (4) those that are not subject to requirements.

In general, acquisition and possession of firearms is subject to a license and other qualifications that must be met by individuals, such as having a "good cause," being at least eighteen years of age, and not being a danger to themselves or to society. Directive 2008/51/EC requires EU Members to ensure that any firearm or part thereof is marked and registered prior to entering the market. In addition, it requires EU Members, by December 2014, to establish a register of firearms, to which only designated authorities will have access. Dealers are also required to maintain a register of firearms.

The EU has also taken action at the external borders by adopting a Regulation in 2012 to impose controls on export authorizations for firearms. By doing so, the EU transposed into internal law article 10 of the UN Protocol. The Regulation prohibits the export of a firearm to anyone in a third country who is less than eighteen years old.

I. Introduction

The European Union (EU) has not been immune to massacres similar to those that have plagued the United States in recent years. Several EU Member States, as diverse as Norway, Belgium, Finland, and France, have also experienced gun violence and mass shootings.[1] In 2011, more than 5,000 murders (about 20% of all murders) in the EU were committed

---

[1] *Mass Shootings in Europe*, BELGIAN NEWS, EXPATICA.COM (Dec. 13, 2011), http://www.expatica.com/be/news/local_news/mass-shootings-in-europe_195344.html.

with firearms.[2] Two consecutive nightclub shootings in France compelled the French authorities to vow to take steps to deal seriously with gun crime. The Interior Minister of France promised to "make the strict enforcement of gun regulations and the battle against illegal weapons priorities of my ministry."[3]

The unlawful entry and trafficking of illegal firearms coming from neighboring countries, such as the successor states to the former Yugoslav Republic, and from Middle Eastern and North African countries have also been identified as matters of concern for the EU Members individually and for the EU as a whole.[4] In a November 2012 speech Cecilia Malmström, the EU Commissioner for Home Affairs, stated that the number of illicit firearms circulating in the EU today exceeds the number of registered hunters and sports shooters. Hunters and sports shooters number approximately 10 million in the EU.[5]

In November 2011, in response to a questionnaire sent by the European Commission regarding recent trends in crime and offenses, and whether there was an increase in crime involving hunting and sporting guns, the EU Members responded mostly in the negative. A number of EU Members, such as Greece, Poland, Sweden, and Portugal, responded that they had experienced a slight or insignificant rise. Other EU Members, such as Belgium and Ireland, indicated that they had experienced a decline, whereas others, including, Austria Bulgaria, Hungary, Finland, the United Kingdom, and Spain reported stable numbers. The same trends were also discerned with regard to crimes involving other types of firearms, such as military firearms, which are prohibited.[6]

Statistics for homicides committed by firearms in the twenty-seven EU Members can be found in the 2011 *Global Study on Homicide*, prepared by the United Nations Office on Drugs and Crime (UNODC).[7] The Global Study opines that even though it is difficult to establish a link between firearms and homicides, there does seem to be a nexus between firearms availability and homicides.[8] Pursuant to the study, the total number of intentional homicides in

---

[2] Cecilia Malmström, EU Commissioner for Home Affairs, Speech at the Conference on the Fight Against Arms Trafficking: Where Do We Stand? at 2 (Nov. 19, 2012), http://europa.eu/rapid/press-release_SPEECH-12-841_en.htm (click icon for PDF version).

[3] Ben McPartland, *France Vows Crackdown After Nightclub Shootings*, FRANCE 24 (July 10, 2012), http://www.france24.com/en/20120709-france-vows-gun-crackdown-after-nightclub-shootings-lille-bertry-theatro-vamos-balkans-kalashnikov.

[4] Malmström, *supra* note 2, at 3.

[5] *Id.*

[6] *Report from the Commission to the European Parliament and the Council, Possible Advantages and Disadvantages of Reducing the Classification to Two Categories of Firearms (Prohibited or Authorised) with a View to Improving the Functioning of the Internal Market for the Products in Question Through Simplification* at 5, COM (2012) 415 final, http://eur-lex.europa.eu/LexUriServ/LexUriServ.do?uri=COM:2012:0415:FIN:EN:PDF.

[7] Statistics cover the number of homicides by firearms, percentage of homicides by firearms, and homicides by firearms rate per 100,000 population. UNODC, 2011 GLOBAL STUDY ON HOMICIDE: TRENDS, CONTEXT, DATA, http://www.unodc.org/documents/data-and-analysis/statistics/Homicide/Globa_study_on_homicide_2011_web.pdf.

[8] *Id.* at 10.

2010 was estimated at 468,000 worldwide. More than 36% took place in Africa, 31% in the Americas, 27% in Asia, 5% in Europe, and 1% in Oceania.[9]

II. EU Legislation

Neither the Treaty on European Union nor the Treaty on the Functioning of the EU, as amended by the Lisbon Treaty in 2009, contain a right to bear arms for EU citizens.[10] The existence of such a right would be subject to the different legal systems and constitutional traditions of the individual Member States, which are primarily responsible for internal security and public safety. The EU also shares competence to ensure "a high level of security" and to combat crime.[11]

At the EU level, acquisition and possession of weapons and transfers between EU Member States are regulated by two directives: (1) Directive 91/477/EEC of June 1991 on Control of the Acquisition and Possession of Weapons,[12] and (2) Directive 2008/51/EC Amending Directive 91/477/EEC.[13] The impetus behind the first Directive was to facilitate the freedom of movement of firearms within the internal market and, at the same time, to introduce some safeguards concerning acquisition and possession of weapons. Two subsequent factors necessitated the adoption of the 2008 Directive. First, the signing on January 16, 2002, by the European Commission on behalf of the European Community of the United Nations Protocol on the Illicit Manufacturing of and Trafficking in Firearms, Their Parts and Components and Ammunition, annexed to the Convention Against Transnational Organized Crime;[14] and, secondly, the need to address certain issues that arose during the implementation of Directive 91/477/EEC, which were cited by the Commission in its 2000 report.[15] The United Nations Protocol obliged the EU to mark weapons at the time of manufacture and at the time of transfer from government stocks to civilian use, whereas Directive 91/477/EEC did not provide a clear

---

[9] *Id.* at 9.

[10] Consolidated Version of the Treaty on European Union (TEU), 2012 Official Journal of the European Union [O.J.] (C 326) 13, http://eur-lex.europa.eu/LexUriServ/LexUriServ.do?uri=OJ:C:2012:326:0013:0046: EN:PDF; Consolidated Version of the Treaty on the Functioning of the European Union (TFEU), 2012 O.J. (C 327) 47, http://eur-lex.europa.eu/LexUriServ/LexUriServ.do?uri=OJ:C:2012:326:0047:0200:EN:PDF.

[11] TFEU arts. 4.2(j) & 67.

[12] Council Directive 91/477/EEC of 18 June 1991 on Control of the Acquisition and Possession of Weapons, 1991 O.J. (L 256) 51, http://eur-lex.europa.eu/LexUriServ/LexUriServ.do?uri=CELEX:3199 1L0477:en:HTML.

[13] Directive 2008/51/EC of the European Parliament and of the Council of 21 May 2008 Amending Council Directive 91/477/EEC on Control of Acquisition and Possession of Weapons, 2008 O.J. (L 179) 5, http://eur-lex.europa.eu/LexUriServ/LexUriServ.do?uri=OJ:L:2008:179:0005:0011:en:PDF.

[14] Protocol Against the Illicit Manufacturing of and Trafficking in Firearms, Their Parts and Components and Ammunition, supplementing the United Nations Convention Against Transnational Organized Crime, New York, May 31, 2001, 2326 U.N.T.S. 211, http://treaties.un.org/Pages/ViewDetails.aspx?src=TREATY& mtdsg_no=XVIII-12-c&chapter=18&lang=en.

[15] *Report from the Commission to the European Parliament and the Council, the Implementation of Council Directive 91/477/EEC of June 18, 1991, on Control of the Acquisition and Possession of Weapons*, COM (2000) 837 final (Dec. 15, 2000), http://eur-lex.europa.eu/LexUriServ/LexUriServ.do?uri=COM:2000:0837: FIN:en:PDF.

obligation. In addition, the 2008 Directive increased the Protocol's minimum time period for retaining firearms information in registers from ten to twenty years.[16]

A. Directive 91/477/EEC as Amended by Directive 2008/51/EC

Directive 91/477/EEC established minimum requirements, thus giving EU Members the authority to impose stricter controls on the acquisition of weapons. By 2000, all the then-EU Members had transposed the Directive internally.[17] Due to the flexibility granted to EU Members by the Directive no full harmonization has been achieved. For example, a number of EU Members have not adopted the classification of firearms prescribed by Directive 91/477/EEC, since national legislation either requires an authorization of all firearms or imposes a ban on all firearms. Moreover, some EU Members classify as "war weapons" or prohibit firearms considered to be hunting firearms in other Member States.[18] Several Member States, such as France, Belgium, and Austria, had to amend their legislation on long firearms substantially because, prior to Directive 91/477/EEC, they had in place liberal laws and allowed the sale of sporting guns freely.[19] Finally, the Directive does not regulate the carrying of weapons, hunting, or target shooting. As far as implementation of Directive 2008/51/EC, the deadline of July 28, 2010, was established.[20] By July 2015, the Commission is expected to prepare a report on the Directive's implementation, along with further proposals, if needed.[21]

1. Definitions

Whereas Directive 91/477/EEC distinguished between weapons and firearms, Directive 2008/51/EC abandons the distinction and opts for a new and precise definition of firearms. Thus, "firearm" is defined as "any portable barreled weapon that expels, is designed to expel or may be converted to expel a shot, bullet or projectile by the action of a combustible propellant," unless it is excluded for one of the reasons listed in part III of Annex I.[22] In addition, Directive 2008/51/EC, brings within its purview

> an object which is capable of being converted to expel a shot, bullet or projectile by the action of a combustible propellant if:
>
> — it has the appearance of a firearm, and
>
> — as a result of its construction or the material from which it is made, it can be so converted.[23]

---

[16] Directive 2008/51/EC, *supra* note 13, art. 4, para. 4.

[17] *Report from the Commission to the European Parliament and the Council, supra* note 15.

[18] *Id.* at 11.

[19] *Id.* at 12.

[20] Directive 2008/51/EC, *supra* note 13, art. 2.

[21] *Id.* art. 17.

[22] *Id.* art. 1(a).

[23] *Id.*

Directive 2008/51 added new definitions pertaining to "parts," "essential component," "ammunition," and other terms.[24] Annex II of Directive 91/477/EEC provides a number of definitions pertaining to "short firearm," "long firearm," "automatic firearm," "repeating firearm," and others.[25]

Annex I of Directive 91/477/EEC divides firearms into four categories depending on the level of dangerousness. EU Members may opt for stricter division or may move certain firearms from one group to another. The categories are as follows:[26]

Category A –Prohibited
<ul><li>Explosive military missiles and launchers</li><li>Automatic firearms</li><li>Firearms disguised as other objects</li><li>Ammunition with penetrating, explosive, or incendiary projectiles</li><li>Pistol and revolver ammunition with expanding projectiles and the projectiles for such ammunition</li></ul>
Category B – Subject to Authorization
<ul><li>Semiautomatic or repeating short firearms</li><li>Single-shot short firearms with center-fire percussion</li><li>Single-shot firearms with center-fire percussion that are less than 28 cm in length</li><li>Semiautomatic long firearms whose magazines and chambers can together hold more than three rounds</li><li>Repeating and semiautomatic long firearms not longer than 60 cm in length</li><li>Semiautomatic firearms for civilian use that resemble weapons with automatic mechanisms</li></ul>

---

[24] *Id.* art. 1(b).

[25] Directive 91/477/EEC, *supra* note 12, Annex II.

[26] *Id.*, Annex I.

Category C – Subject to Declaration
<ul><li>Repeating long firearms other than those listed in category B, final item</li><li>Long firearms with single-shot rifled barrels</li><li>Semiautomatic long firearms other than those in Category B whose magazine and chamber can hold more than three rounds</li><li>Single-shot short firearms with rimfire percussion and with an overall length of not less than 28 cm</li></ul>
Category D – Other Firearms
<ul><li>Single-shot firearms with smooth-bore barrels[27]</li></ul>

Acquisition or possession of weapons by the armed forces, the police, the public authorities, or by collectors and bodies engaged with the cultural and historical aspects of weapons fall outside the scope of the Directive.[28]

2. Acquisition and Possession of Firearms: Qualifications

Acquisition and possession of firearms is permitted only by those persons who have a license. Acquisition of firearms belonging to categories C and D is subject to a permit in accordance with national law.[29]

Acquisition and possession of firearms is granted to people who have "good cause" and meet the following two additional qualifications:[30]

(a) are at least 18 years of age, except in relation to the acquisition, other than through purchase, and possession of firearms for hunting and target shooting, provided that in that case persons of less than 18 years of age have parental permission, or are under parental guidance or the guidance of an adult with a valid firearms or hunting licence, or are within a licenced or otherwise approved training centre;

(b) are not likely to be a danger to themselves, to public order or to public safety. Having been convicted of a violent intentional crime shall be considered as indicative of such danger.[31]

EU Members have the authority to withdraw authorization for possession if a person no longer meets these criteria.[32]

---

[27] *Id.*

[28] *Id.* art. 2.

[29] Directive 2008/51/EC, *supra* note 13, art. 1(3) (amending Directive 91/477/EEC to add art. 4a).

[30] *Id.* art. 1, para. 4 (amending Directive 91/477/EEC art. 5).

[31] Id.

In addition, EU Members do not have the authority to prevent residents from possessing a firearm that was acquired in another EU Member State unless such a firearm is banned within their territory.[33]

3. Acquisition of Firearms Through Distance Communications

EU Members may authorize the sale of firearms through distance communications, including the Internet. "Distance contracts" are defined by article 2 of Directive 97/7/EC on the Protection of Consumers in Respect of Distance Contracts.[34] Directive 97/7/EC establishes rules regarding the sale of goods or services between a buyer and a seller based on a distance contract for the protection of consumers. In such a case, they are obliged to subject acquisition of firearms to the rules of Directive 91/477/EEC and to control the acquisition of firearms by individuals, with the exception of dealers. Acquisition of firearms through the Internet by individuals who have been convicted by a final court judgment for serious criminal offenses must be prohibited.[35]

4. Marking and Registration

An important requirement introduced by Directive 2008/51/EC is that all Member States must ensure that firearms can be linked to their owners at any time.[36] EU Members must also ensure that any firearm or part that is placed on the market has been marked and registered or that it has been deactivated.[37] In order to identify and trace each firearm, the Directive obliges EU Members, at the time of manufacture of each firearm, to either

- "require a unique marking that includes the name of the manufacturer, the country or place of manufacture, the serial number, and the year of manufacture (if not part of the serial number)"; or

- "maintain any other unique and user-friendly marking with a number or alphanumeric code" that allows easy identification of the country of manufacture by all Members.[38]

EU Members are also required to register every firearm. To this end, by December 2014 they must establish and maintain a computerized data-filing system that allows designated authorities access to registered firearms. Firearms records, such as make, model, serial number,

---

[32] *Id.*

[33] *Id.*

[34] Directive 97/7/EC on the Protection of Consumers in Respect of Distance Contracts, 1997 O.J. (L 144) 19, http://eur-lex.europa.eu/LexUriServ/LexUriServ.do?uri=OJ:L:1997:144:0019:0027:EN:PDF, *as amended by* Directive 2005/29/EC Concerning Unfair Business-to-Consumer Commercial Practices in the Internal Market and Amending [Directives 84/450/EEC, 97/7/EC, 2002/65/EC, and Regulation (EC) No. 2006/2004], http://eur-lex.europa.eu/Result.do?T1=V3&T2=2005&T3=29&RechType=RECH_naturel&Submit=Search.

[35] Directive 2008/51/EC, *supra* note 13, recital 13.

[36] *Id.* art. 1, para. 2 (amending Directive 91/477/EEC art. 4, para. 5).

[37] *Id.* (amending art. 4, para. 1).

[38] *Id.* (amending art. 4, para. 2).

supplier's information, and data on the person who acquires or possesses a firearm, are required to be kept for a minimum of twenty years.[39]

Based on Directive 2008/51/EC, EU Members are required to establish rules regulating the activities of brokers and to include measures such as requiring the registration of brokers and the licensing or authorization of arms brokering activities.[40]

5. European Firearms Pass

A European Firearms Pass, which was initially introduced by Directive 91/477/EEC, is issued by the authorities of a Member State upon request to a person who lawfully possesses and uses a firearm. The pass is nontransferable and is valid for a maximum period of five years, which can be extended. It also contains certain information, such as possession of any firearm by the holder or of any change or characteristic in the firearm and any loss or theft.

Certain Member States have issued large numbers of passes—Austria and France have approximately 38,000 and 39,378 holders of firearms passes, respectively—whereas in other Member States the pass is less widely used; in Italy, for example, there are close to 20,000 holders of firearms passes.[41]

B. Controls on the Possession of Weapons at the External Borders of the EU

Directive 91/477/EEC deals with transfers of firearms for civilian use within the EU territory. A recent Regulation, No. 258/2012, establishes rules for export authorization and import and transit measures for firearms, their parts and components, and ammunition.[42] The Regulation implements article 10 of the United Nations Protocol Against the Illicit Manufacturing of and Trafficking in Firearms.[43] Article 10 requires signatories to adopt or improve administrative procedures designed to exercise control over the manufacturing, marking, import, and export of firearms. The scope of the Regulation covers firearms for civilian use and excludes firearms that are intended for military purposes.[44] Any export of firearms, their parts, and essential components and ammunition is subject to an authorization granted by the competent authorities of the Member States where the exporter is established.[45]

---

[39] *Id.* art. 2, para. 4.

[40] *Id.* (inserting art. 4b).

[41] *Report from the Commission to the European Parliament and the Council, supra* note 6, at 5.

[42] Regulation (EU) No. 258/2012 of the European Parliament and of the Council of 14 March 2012, Implementing Article 10 of the United Nations' Protocol Against the Illicit Manufacturing of and Trafficking in Firearms, Their Parts and Components and Ammunition, Supplementing the United Nations Convention Against Transnational Organized Crime (UN Firearms Protocol) and Establishing Export authorisation, and Import and Transit Measures for Firearms, Their Parts and Components and Ammunition, 2012 O.J. (L 94) 1, http://eur-lex.europa.eu/LexUriServ/LexUriServ.do?uri=OJ:L:2012:094:0001:0015:EN:PDF.

[43] Protocol Against the Illicit Manufacturing of and Trafficking in Firearms, *supra* note 14.

[44] Regulation (EU) No. 258/2012, *supra* note 42, recital 8.

[45] *Id.* art. 4.

Article 11 of Regulation No. 258/2012 requires EU Members to refuse to grant an export authorization if the applicant has a criminal record related to an offense listed in article 2(2) of the Council Framework Decision on the European Arrest Warrant[46] or any other offense punishable by a maximum term of imprisonment of at least four years.[47] EU Members are authorized to annul, suspend, or revoke an export authorization if the conditions for granting it are no longer met.[48]

III. Future Developments

In November 2012, EU Commissioner Malmström called on the European Commission to address the following challenging issues in its 2013 communication on firearms and in its upcoming report on transposition and implementation of Directive 2008/51 by July 2015:

(a) Making more stringent the e-rules of Directives 91/477/ECC and 2008/51/EC. In this context, the Commission should:
- Examine whether certain very dangerous types of firearms not be permitted for civilian use.
- Adopt EU rules on deactivation of firearms, that is firearms which have been declared incapable of being fired.
- Adopt EU rules on technical security features to the effect that only the rightful owner of a firearm can actually use it;

(b) Adopting EU legislation on common minimum rules on criminal sanctions for illicit firearms and trafficking;

(c) Improving cross-border cooperation among law enforcement authorities and examining whether EU agencies, such as Europol and Eurojust, should be more engaged to facilitate coordination and judicial cooperation; and

(d) Reviewing the status of seized and confiscated firearms following investigation and prosecution of crimes by law enforcement authorities.[49]

In a November 2011 questionnaire sent to the EU Member States on possible further mandatory restrictions on categories of firearms under EU legislation (referenced above), a number of EU Members, including Poland, the United Kingdom, Ireland, Denmark, and Latvia, expressed an interest in reducing the classification at the European level to two categories, in order to simplify the issue. Other Members stated their preference for continuing the freedom given to EU Members by the Directive and keeping the current classification to avoid further costs. Supporters of this position included Sweden, Italy, Hungary, and Belgium. Finally, a third group of states, including Slovakia, Netherlands, and Romania, which have already put in

---

[46] *Id.* art. 11, para. 1(a) (citing 2002/584/JHA: Council Framework Decision of 13 June 2002 on the European Arrest Warrant and the Surrender Procedures Between Member States – Statements Made by Certain Member States on the Adoption of the Framework Decision, 2002 O.J. (L 190) 1, http://eur-lex.europa.eu/LexUriServ/LexUriServ.do?uri=CELEX:32002F0584:en:HTML).

[47] *Id.*

[48] *Id.*

[49] Malmström, *supra* note 2, at 4.

place their national systems based on two or three categories, indicated that they welcome the freedom granted by Directive 91/477/EEC.[50]

Prepared by Theresa Papademetriou
Senior Foreign Law Specialist

---

[50] *Report from the Commission to the European Parliament and the Council, supra* note 6, at 7.

FIREARMS-CONTROL LEGISLATION AND POLICY:
BIBLIOGRAPHY OF SELECTED, RECENT ENGLISH-LANGUAGE MATERIALS

CARTER, GREGG LEE. GUN CONTROL IN THE UNITED STATES: A REFERENCE HANDBOOK. 408 pp. Santa Barbara, CA: ABC-CLIO, 2006.   HV7436.C36 2006 FT MEADE
http://lccn.loc.gov/2006010884

FLEMING, ANTHONY K. GUN CONTROL IN THE UNITED STATES AND CANADA: THE IMPACT OF MASS MURDERS AND ASSASSINATIONS ON GUN CONTROL. 159 pp. New York: Continuum, 2012.   HV7436.F58 2012
http://lccn.loc.gov/2011043970

Gould, Chandré & Guy Lamb, eds. HIDE AND SEEK: TAKING ACCOUNT OF SMALL ARMS IN SOUTHERN AFRICA. 334 pp. Pretoria, South Africa: Institute for Security Studies, 2004.
HV7439.A356H53 2004
http://lccn.loc.gov/2005365613

GRUPP, LARRY. THE WORLD-WIDE GUN OWNERS GUIDE: A FIRST-HAND CULTURAL AND COMPARATIVE EXAMINATION OF THE WORLD'S GUN LAWS. 365 pp. Scottsdale, AZ: Bloomfield Press, 2011.   K3661.G78 2011
http://lccn.loc.gov/2011921614

Halbrook, Stephen P. *Symposium on the Legal, Economic, and Human Rights Implications of Civilian Firearms Ownership and Regulation: Citizens in Arms: the Swiss Experience.* 8 TEXAS REVIEW OF LAW AND POLITICS. pp. 141–73. Fall 2003.   K24.E876
http://lccn.loc.gov/98644715

INTER-PARLIAMENTARY UNION. MISSING PIECES: A GUIDE FOR REDUCING GUN VIOLENCE THROUGH PARLIAMENTARY ACTION. 188 pp. Geneva: Centre for Humanitarian Dialogue, 2007.   HV7435.M57 2007
http://lccn.loc.gov/2008384882

Kates, Don B. & Gary A. Mauser. *Would Banning Firearms Reduce Murder and Suicide? A Review of International and Some Domestic Evidence.* 30 HARVARD JOURNAL OF LAW AND PUBLIC POLICY. pp. 649–93. 2007.   K8.A683
http://lccn.loc.gov/79643593

KHAN, SAJAD ANWAR & HASSAN MAHMOOD BUTT. THE MANUAL OF ARMS & EXPLOSIVES LAWS IN PAKISTAN WITH FORENSIC BALLISTICS: ALL RELEVANT LAWS & INCLUDED CASE LAW. 720 pp. Lahore: Khyber Publishers, 2012.   KPL1560A28 2012
http://lccn.loc.gov/2012432183

Kopel, David P., Paul Gallant & Joanne D. Eisen. *Part III Foundations of Constitutionalism: Justice for All: A Better Path to Global Firearms Control.* 2 JINDAL GLOBAL LAW REVIEW. pp. 198-211. Sept. 2010. Forthcoming online.
http://www.jgls.edu.in/JindalGlobalLawReview/JGLS_Review.html
Available currently in LexisNexis (by subscription)

Lovelace, Kacy, ed. CONCEALED WEAPONS. 111 pp. Detroit: Greenhaven Press, 2011.
KF3941.C66 2011
http://lccn.loc.gov/2010042116

MALCOLM, JOYCE LEE. GUNS AND VIOLENCE: THE ENGLISH EXPERIENCE. 340 pp. Cambridge, MA: Harvard University Press, 2002.
HV7439.G72E546 2002
http://lccn.loc.gov/2002020541

Malcolm, Joyce Lee. *Gun Control in England: The Tarnished Gold Standard.* 16 JOURNAL ON FIREARMS AND PUBLIC POLICY. pp. 123–34. 2004.
KF3941.A15J68
http://lccn.loc.gov/2006213290

Masanzu, K. *"Of Guns and Laws": A South African Perspective in Light of United Kingdom and United States Gun Laws.* 39 COMPARATIVE AND INTERNATIONAL LAW JOURNAL OF SOUTHERN AFRICA. pp. 131–51. 2006.
K3.O4
http://lccn.loc.gov/70001086

Masters, Jonathan. U.S. GUN POLICY: GLOBAL COMPARISONS. New York: Council on Foreign Relations, Dec. 21, 2012.
http://www.cfr.org/united-states/us-gun-policy-global-comparisons/p29735

Mauser, Gary A. *The Failed Experiment – Gun Control and Public Safety in Canada, Australia, England, and Wales.* 16 JOURNAL ON FIREARMS AND PUBLIC POLICY. pp. 89–121. 2004.
KF3941.A15J68
http://lccn.loc.gov/2006213290

Miah, Siddiqur Rahman. LAW OF ARMS AND EXPLOSIVES: THE ARMS ACT, 1878, THE EXPLOSIVE SUBSTANCES ACT, 1908, THE EXPLOSIVES ACT, 1884, THE ARMS RULES, 1924, THE EXPLOSIVES RULES, 1940, BISPHORAKA BIDHIMALA, 2004. 444 pp. Dhaka: New Warsi Book Corp., 2006.
KNG1560.A28 2006 GLOBAL
http://lccn.loc.gov/2007340216

Miron, Jeffrey A. *Violence, Guns, and Drugs: A Cross-Country Analysis.* 44 JOURNAL OF LAW AND ECONOMICS. pp. 615–33. Oct. 2001.
K10.O8729
http://lccn.loc.gov/59001643

NATIONAL FORUM AGAINST SMALL ARMS. CHALLENGES TO PEACE AND SECURITY, CONSULTING COMMUNITIES ON SMALL ARMS IN BANGLADESH. Various pages. Dhaka: South Asia Partnership-Bangladesh, 2006.

HV7439.B36N37 2006
http://lccn.loc.gov/2008335629

Roleff, Tamara L., ed. GUN CONTROL. 203 pp. Detroit: Greenhaven Press, 2007.

KF3942.H3G86 2007
http://lccn.loc.gov/2007005374

SABALA, KIZITO. AFRICAN COMMITMENTS TO CONTROLLING SMALL ARMS AND LIGHT WEAPONS. 83 pp. Pretoria: African Human Security Initiative, 2004.   HV7439.A35S33 2004
http://lccn.loc.gov/2005352440

Squires, Peter. *Beyond July 4th?: Critical Reflections on the Self-Defence Debate from a British Perspective.* 2 JOURNAL OF LAW, ECONOMICS AND POLICY. pp. 221–61. Fall 2006.

K10.O873416
http://lccn.loc.gov/2004216037

VERNICK, JON S. et al. *The Ethics of Restrictive Licensing for Handguns: Comparing the United States and Canadian Approaches to Handgun Regulation.* 35 JOURNAL OF LAW, MEDICINE AND ETHICS. pp. 668–78. Dec. 2007.   KF3821.A15L38
http://lccn.loc.gov/93657473

VOICES TO SILENCE GUNS: THE PHILIPPINE PEOPLE'S CONSULTATION REPORT ON THE ARMS TRADE TREATY. 170 pp. Quezon City, Philippines: Philippine Action Network, 2008.

KPM1560 V65 2008
http://lccn.loc.gov/2009316624

Wellford, Charles F., John V. Pepper, & Carol V. Petrie, eds. FIREARMS AND VIOLENCE: A CRITICAL REVIEW. 328 pp. Washington, DC: National Academies Press, 2004.

HV6789.N37 2004
http://lccn.loc.gov/2004024047

Compiled by Constance A. Johnson
Senior Legal Research Analyst